Living Water

Acknowledgments

The compiler would like to thank and acknowledge the help of John A. Tvedtnes, Associate Director of Research at F.A.R.M.S., and Richard R. Hopkins, author of Biblical Mormonism *and* How Greek Philosophy Corrupted the Christian Concept of God, *in the preparation and editing of notes for this work.*

Living Water

A Chronological Reading Of The Four Gospels

Daniel R. Hopkins

COPYRIGHTS

Cornerstone Publishing & Distribution, Inc.
Salt Lake City & Phoenix

© 1999 Cornerstone Publishing & Distribution, Inc.

All Rights Reserved

04 02 00   5 4 3 2 1

Printed in the United States of America

International Standard Book Number 1-929281-02-1

Cover art: *The New Testament*, © 1991 Susan Bangerter
Used by Permission

Cover design by Adam R. Hopkins

CONTENTS

EVENTS	PRIMARY TEXT	PG
PREFACE		xi
HOW TO USE THE VOLUME		xii

THE PRE-MORTAL MISSIONS

THE PROLOGUE	John 1:1-14	1

THE BIRTHS

THE ANNOUNCEMENT OF JOHN'S BIRTH	Luke 1:5-25	2
THE ANNOUNCEMENT OF JESUS' BIRTH	Luke 1:26-38	3
MARY VISITS ELISABETH	Luke 1:39-56	3
JOSEPH'S DREAM	Matt. 1:18-25	4
THE BIRTH OF JOHN THE BAPTIST	Luke 1:57-80	4
THE BIRTH OF JESUS CHRIST	Luke 2:1-7	5
THE ANGELS AND THE SHEPHERDS	Luke 2:8-20	6
THE PRESENTATION OF JESUS AT THE TEMPLE	Luke 2:21-38	6
THE WISE MEN VISIT	Matt. 2:1-12	7
HAROD SLAYS THE CHILDREN OF BETHLEHEM	Matt. 2:13-23	8
CHRIST'S YOUTH	Luke 2:40-52	9

JOHN'S MINISTRY AND JESUS' PREPARATIONS

THE PREACHINGS OF JOHN THE BAPTIST	Luke 3:1-17	10
THE BAPTISM OF JESUS	Matt. 3:13-17	11
JOHN'S TESTIMONY OF JESUS	John 1:28-34	13
THE TEMPTATIONS OF JESUS	Luke 4:1-13	13
THE FIRST DISCIPLES	John 1:35-51	14
THE WEDDING AT CANA	John 2:1-12	15

FIRST YEAR: THE EARLY JUDEAN MINISTRY

JESUS CLEANSES THE TEMPLE	John 2:13-25	16
JESUS AND NICODEMUS	John 3:1-21	16
THE LAST TESTIMONY OF JOHN THE BAPTIST	John 3:22-36	17

FIRST YEAR: THE GALILEAN MINISTRY

JESUS AND THE SAMARIAN WOMAN	John 4:1-42	19
THE HEALING OF A NOBLEMAN'S SON	John 4:43-54	20
JESUS IN NAZARETH	Luke 4:16-30	21
A DEVIL IN CAPERNAUM	Mark 1:22-28	22
FISHERS OF MEN	Matt. 4:18-24	22
A GREAT MULTITUDE OF FISHES	Luke 5:1-12	23
JESUS HEALS A LEPER	Mark 1:41-45	24
THE CALLING OF THE TWELVE APOSTLES	Mark 3:14-19	24
INSTRUCTING AND SENDING THE TWELVE	Matt. 10:5-42	24
JESUS HEALS A MULTITUDE	Luke 6:17-19	26
THE SERMON ON THE MOUNT	Matt. 4:25; 5 – 7	26
THE CENTURION'S SERVANT	Luke 7:1-10	32
THE WIDOW'S SON	Luke 7:11-17	33

CONTENTS

EVENTS	PRIMARY TEXT	PG
PETER'S MOTHER-IN-LAW	Matt. 8:14-15	33
HE TOOK OUR INFIRMITIES	Matt. 8:16-17	33
DISCIPLES TESTED	Matt. 8:18-22	33
JESUS CALMS THE TEMPEST	Mark 4:35-41	34
A LEGION OF DEMONS CAST OUT	Mark 5:1-20	34
A PARALYTIC MAN HEALED	Mark 2:1-17	35
THE CALLING OF LEVI (MATTHEW)	Luke 5:27-31	36
A CONFLICT OVER FASTING	Luke 5:33-35	36
PARABLE OF THE CLOTH AND THE WINESKINS	Luke 5:36-39	36
HEALING THE WOMAN ON THE WAY WITH JAIRUS	Mark 5:21-34	36
THE DAUGHTER OF JAIRUS	Mark 5:35-43	37
TWO BLIND MEN AND A MUTE	Matt. 9:27-34	38
MESSENGERS FROM JOHN THE BAPTIST	Matt. 11:2-19	38
JESUS' FEET WASHED; THE TWO DEBTORS	Luke 7:36-50	39

SECOND YEAR: THE GALILEAN MINISTRY

THE INVALID OF BETHESDA	John 5:1-13	40
IDENTITY, MISSION AND WITNESSES OF CHRIST	John 5:14-47	40
THE HARVEST IS PLENTEOUS	Matt. 9:35-38	42
MARY CALLED MAGDALENE	Luke 8:1-3	42
THE SABBATH MADE FOR MAN	Mark 2:23-28	42
THE MAN WITH THE WITHERED HAND	Luke 6:6-11	43
A MULTITUDE ON THE SEA SHORE	Mark 3:7-12	43
BLASPHEMY AGAINST THE HOLY GHOST	Matt. 12:22-37	44
WE WOULD SEE A SIGN FROM THEE	Matt. 12:38-42	44
WHEN THE UNCLEAN SPIRIT IS GONE OUT	Matt. 12:43-45	45
BROTHER, AND SISTER, AND MOTHER	Matt. 12:46-50	45
PARABLE OF THE SOWER	Mark 4:1-20	45
PARABLE OF THE CANDLE	Mark 4:21-25	47
PARABLE OF WHEAT AND TARES	Matt. 13:24-30	47
PARABLE OF THE MUSTARD SEED	Matt. 13:31-32	47
PARABLE OF THE LEAVEN	Matt. 13:33	48
WITHOUT A PARABLE SPAKE HE NOT	Matt. 13:34-35	48
PARABLE OF WHEAT AND TARES EXPLAINED	Matt. 13:36-43	48
THE KINGDOM OF HEAVEN IS LIKE UNTO . . .	Matt. 13:44-53	49
JESUS IN NAZARETH AGAIN	Mark 6:1-6	49
THE DEATH OF JOHN THE BAPTIST	Mark 6:14-29	50

THIRD YEAR: THE GALILEAN MINISTRY

FEEDING THE FIVE THOUSAND	John 6:1-15	51
WALKING UPON THE SEA	Mark 6:45-52	52
HEALING AT GENNESARET	Mark 6:53-56	52
THE BREAD OF LIFE	John 6:22-59	53
DISCIPLES TESTED BY JESUS' TEACHINGS	John 6:60-71	54

CONTENTS

EVENTS	PRIMARY TEXT	PG
WHAT DEFILES A MAN	Mark 7:1-23	55
THIRD YEAR: THE NORTH GALILEAN MINISTRY		
THE WOMAN OF CANAAN	Matt. 15:21-28	57
A HEALING; FEEDING THE FOUR THOUSAND	Matt. 15:29-39	57
A SIGN FROM HEAVEN	Matt. 16:1-4	58
BEWARE THE LEAVEN OF THE PHARISEES	Matt. 16:5-12	58
THE BLIND MAN IN BETHSAIDA	Mark 8:22-26	59
UPON THIS ROCK	Matt. 16:13-20	59
CHRIST REVEALS HIS DEATH	Matt. 16:21-28	59
THE TRANSFIGURATION	Matt. 17:1-13	60
THOU DUMB AND DEAF SPIRIT	Mark 9:14-29	61
TAXES PAID WITH MONEY FROM A FISH	Matt. 17:24-27	61
WHO IS THE GREATEST	Matt. 18:1-6	62
PARABLE OF THE LOST SHEEP	Matt. 18:10-14	62
HE THAT IS NOT AGAINST US	Mark 9:38-41	63
IF THY RIGHT HAND OFFEND THEE	Mark 9:43-50	63
UNTIL SEVENTY TIMES SEVEN	Matt. 18:15-22	64
PARABLE OF THE TWO DEBTORS	Matt. 18:23-35	64
PARABLE OF THE LOST COIN	Luke 15:8-10	65
PARABLE OF THE PRODIGAL SON	Luke 15:11-32	65
THE WORLD HATETH ME	John 7:2-9	66
THIRD YEAR: THE LATER JUDEAN MINISTRY		
AN EXAMPLE OF NON-VIOLENCE	Luke 9:51-56	67
THE MISSION OF THE SEVENTY	Luke 10:1-12	67
CHRIST UPBRAIDS CERTAIN CITIES	Matt. 11:20-24	67
THE SEVENTY RETURN	Luke 10:17-20	68
JESUS REJOICES	Luke 10:21-24	68
PARABLE OF THE GOOD SAMARITAN	Luke 10:25-37	68
A VISIT WITH MARTHA AND MARY	Luke 10:38-42	69
INSTRUCTION ABOUT PRAYER	Luke 11:1-13	69
BLESSINGS	Luke 11:27-28	70
PARABLE OF THE FOOLISH RICH MAN	Luke 12:13-21	70
EXCEPT YE REPENT	Luke 13:1-5	71
A WOMAN HEALED ON THE SABBATH	Luke 13:10-17	71
O JERUSALEM, JERUSALEM	Luke 13:31-35	71
HEALING A MAN WITH DROPSY	Luke 14:1-6	72
PARABLE OF THE CHIEF WEDDING ROOMS	Luke 14:7-14	72
PARABLE OF THE GREAT SUPPER	Luke 14:15-24	73
THE COST OF FOLLOWING JESUS	Luke 14:25-33	73
SALT WHICH IS GOOD	Luke 14:34-35	74

CONTENTS

EVENTS	PRIMARY TEXT	PG
PARABLE OF THE UNJUST STEWARD	Luke 16:1-15	74
THE LAW AND THE PROPHETS	Luke 16:16-23	75
PARABLE OF THE RICH MAN AND LAZARUS	Luke 16:19-31	76
TEN LEPERS ARE CLEANSED	Luke 17:11-19	76
PARABLE OF THE UNJUST JUDGE	Luke 18:1-8	77
PARABLE OF THE PHARISEE AND THE PUBLICAN	Luke 18:9-14	77
JESUS AT THE FEAST OF TABERNACLES	John 7:10-24	77
I AM NOT COME OF MYSELF	John 7:25-31	78
YE SHALL SEEK ME, AND NOT FIND ME	John 7:32-36	78
RIVERS OF LIVING WATER	John 7:37-39	79
A DIVISION AMONG THE PEOPLE	John 7:40-44	79
NEVER MAN SPAKE LIKE THIS MAN	John 7:45-53	79
THE ADULTEROUS WOMAN	John 8:1-11	80
THE LIGHT OF THE WORLD	John 8:12-20	80
WHITHER I GO, YE CANNOT COME	John 8:21-30	81
THE TRUTH SHALL MAKE YOU FREE	John 8:31-38	81
YE ARE OF YOUR FATHER THE DEVIL	John 8:39-47	81
BEFORE ABRAHAM WAS I AM	John 8:48-59	82
SABBATH HEALING OF A MAN BORN BLIND	John 9:1-12	82
WHEREAS I WAS BLIND, NOW I SEE	John 9:13-34	83
THE BLINDNESS OF THE PHARISEES	John 9:35-41	84
PARABLE OF THE SHEEPFOLD	John 10:1-6	84
THE GOOD SHEPHERD	John 10:7-21	85
ABOUT MARRIAGE AND DIVORCE	Matt. 19:3-12	85
BLESSING THE LITTLE CHILDREN	Mark 10:13-16	86
THE RICH YOUNG MAN	Mark 10:17-31	86
PARABLE OF THE LABORERS IN THE VINEYARD	Matt. 20:1-16	87
DECLARATION AT THE FEAST OF THE DEDICATION	John 10:22-42	88
THIRD YEAR: THE PEREAN MINISTRY		
THE DEATH OF LAZARUS	John 11:1-16	89
JESUS' COMING DEATH AND RESURRECTION	Mark 10:32-34	89
THE PETITION OF THE SONS OF ZEBEDEE	Matt. 20:20-28	90
HE THAT IS GREATEST AMONG YOU	Luke 22:24-30	90
THE HEALING OF BARTIMAEUS	Mark 10:46-52	91
THE HOUSE OF ZACCHAEUS	Luke 19:1-10	91
PARABLE OF THE POUNDS	Luke 19:11-28	91
I AM THE RESURRECTION, AND THE LIFE	John 11:17-27	92
JESUS WEEPS	John 11:28-37	93
LAZARUS, COME FORTH	John 11:38-44	93
PLOTTING TO KILL JESUS	John 11:45-57	94
ANOINTING JESUS' FEET	John 12:1-8	94
A PLOT AGAINST LAZARUS	John 12:9-11	95

CONTENTS

EVENTS	PRIMARY TEXT	PG
WEEK OF THE ATONING SACRIFICE: SUNDAY		
THY KING COMETH	Mark 11:1-11	96
HE THAT LOVETH HIS LIFE SHALL LOSE IT	John 12:20-26	97
A VOICE FROM HEAVEN	John 12:27-36	97
BLINDED THEIR EYES, HARDENED THEIR HEART	John 12:37-43	97
HE THAT SEETH ME SEETH HIM THAT SENT ME	John 12:44-50	98
WEEK OF THE ATONING SACRIFICE: MONDAY		
CURSING THE FIG TREE	Mark 11:12-14	98
DEN OF THIEVES	Mark 11:15-19	98
WEEK OF THE ATONING SACRIFICE: TUESDAY		
FAITH TO MOVE MOUNTAINS	Mark 11:20-26	99
PARABLE OF THE BARREN FIG TREE	Luke 13:6-9	99
BY WHAT AUTHORITY?	Mark 11:27-33	99
PARABLE OF THE TWO SONS	Matt. 21:28-32	100
PARABLE OF THE WICKED HUSBANDMEN	Matt. 21:33-46	100
PARABLE OF THE MARRIAGE FEAST	Matt. 22:1-14	101
THE QUESTION OF TRIBUTE	Matt. 22:15-22	102
THE SADDUCEES' QUESTION	Luke 20:27-40	102
THE GREAT COMMANDMENT	Mark 12:28-34	103
WHOSE SON IS HE?	Matt. 22:41-46	103
THE WIDOW'S OFFERING	Mark 12:41-44	104
WOE UNTO YOU PHARISEES	Matt. 23:1-36	104
JESUS LAMENTS OVER JERUSALEM	Matt. 23:37-39	106
NOT ONE STONE UPON ANOTHER	Matt. 24:1-2	106
WHAT IS THE SIGN OF THY COMING?	Matt. 24:3-6,9-13,15-28	106
THE SECOND COMING OF THE SON OF MAN	Matt. 24:7,12-14,29-51	107
PARABLE OF THE TEN VIRGINS	Matt. 25:1-13	109
PARABLE OF THE TALENTS	Matt. 25:14-30	109
PARABLE OF THE SHEEP AND THE GOATS	Matt. 25:31-46	110
BETRAYAL BY CRAFT	Matt. 26:1-5	111
ANOINTING JESUS' HEAD	Mark 14: 3-9	111
SATAN INFLUENCES JUDAS	Luke 22:1-6	112
WEEK OF THE ATONING SACRIFICE: THURSDAY		
THE UPPER ROOM—THE SACRAMENT	Luke 22:7-25	112
THE UPPER ROOM—WASHING THE FEET	John 13:2-20	113
THE UPPER ROOM—JUDAS REVEALED, DEPARTS	John 13:21-30	114
THE UPPER ROOM—A NEW COMMANDMENT	John 13:31-35	114
THE UPPER ROOM—THE WAY, THE TRUTH, THE LIFE	John 14:1-14	115
THE UPPER ROOM—THE COMFORTER	John 14:15-31	115
THE UPPER ROOM—I AM THE TRUE VINE	John 15:1-17	116

CONTENTS

EVENTS	PRIMARY TEXT	PG
THE UPPER ROOM—NOT OF THE WORLD	John 15:18-16:4	117
THE UPPER ROOM—A GUIDE TO ALL TRUTH	John 16:4-15	117
THE UPPER ROOM—SORROW SHALL TURN TO JOY	John 16:16-24	118
THE UPPER ROOM—I HAVE OVERCOME THE WORLD	John 16:25-33	118
THE UPPER ROOM—THE GREAT INTERCESSORY PRAYER	John 17:1-26	119
THE UPPER ROOM—PURSE AND SCRIPT	Luke 22:35-38	120
PETER TO DENY CHRIST	Luke 22:31-34	120
THE GARDEN OF GETHSEMANE	Matt. 26:36-46	121
WHOMSOEVER I SHALL KISS IS HE	John 18:2-11	122
WEEK OF THE ATONING SACRIFICE: FRIDAY		
TAKEN BEFORE ANNAS, THE HIGH PRIEST	John 18:12-14	123
QUESTIONED BY ANNAS	John 18:19-24	123
BEFORE THE COUNSEL	Matt. 26:58-67	123
BEFORE THE COCK CREW	Mark 14:66-72	124
THE TRIAL BEFORE PILATE	John 18:28-38	124
BEFORE HAROD	Luke 23:8-12	125
THE SENTENCING	John 18:38-19:16	126
THE DEATH OF JUDAS	Matt. 27:3-10	127
THE CRUCIFIXION	Luke 23:26-49	128
HE WAS DEAD ALREADY	John 19:31-37	130
ENTOMBED	Luke 23:50-56	130
WEEK OF THE ATONING SACRIFICE: SATURDAY		
SEALING THE STONE, SETTING A WATCH	Matt. 27:62-66	131
MISSION TO THE SPIRIT WORLD	1 Pet. 3:18-20	131
THE GLORIFIED PALESTINIAN MINISTRY		
HE IS RISEN	Mark 16:1-8	133
JESUS APPEARS TO MARY	John 20:11-18	134
RESURRECTION OF THE SAINTS	Matt. 27:52-53	134
REPORT OF THE WATCH	Matt. 28:11-15	134
THE WAY TO EMMAUS	Luke 24:13-35	135
JESUS APPEARS TO HIS DISCIPLES	Luke 24:36-49	136
EXCEPT I SHALL SEE, I WILL NOT BELIEVE	John 20:24-31	136
APPEARANCE AT THE SEA OF TIBERIAS	John 21:1-14	137
FEED MY SHEEP	John 21:15-19	138
THOU SHALT TARRY	John 21:20-24	138
THE GREAT COMMISSION	Matt. 28:16-20	139
THE PROMISE OF THE HOLY GHOST	Acts 1:2-5	139
THE ASCENSION	Acts 1:6-11	140
APPENDIX: HARMONIZED PASSAGES		141

PREFACE

The concept for this book came to me while serving in the Dominican Republic East Mission. I had more time to study the scriptures than most missionaries, due to the custom of Siesta. From about noon to three o'clock every day I would have lunch and study. When I began studying the four gospels, I found myself flipping back and forth from verse to verse, chapter to chapter, and book to book. I enjoyed following Christ's life in chronological order, but I did not like all the flipping around I had to do. Then the idea came to me to merge the four gospels and arrange them in chronological order. I could then read Christ's life all together as one story from beginning to end.

Using the typewriter in the branch office, I began the project. Except to eat, I worked on it with every free moment I had for the next two months. After it was completed I titled it "The Mortal Ministry of the Son of God" and packed it away. It wasn't until we began studying the New Testament again this year that I re-read my work. It was originally intended for personal use, but after re-formatting and adding notations, I was excited to see it in print for others to enjoy.

It is such a wonderful experience to read the life of our Savior in the flow of one story, and at the same time be able to compare the different writings of those magnificent disciples, Mathew, Mark, Luke and John. Before this work I practically ignored the writings of Mark. But in compiling this book I learned that, though his writings are shorter, he offers valuable details when describing some events we would otherwise not have. Luke also adds marvelous details, not just of the birth of our Savior, but also insights into the compassion of Christ. We would never have known that the Lord healed the ear of the soldier whom Peter struck if it were not for Luke. Nor would we have the invaluable information about the visit of the resurrected Christ to His disciples and how He ate with them. Matthew carefully points out fulfilled prophecy from the Old Testament, ever working to convert Jews and non-believers to Christ. And John's writings are so tender, so personal. We read the uttering of prayers we would never enjoy without his inspired writings. One could not know the life of Christ missing any one of the four gospels. Together they reveal the history of the most important life ever lived on this earth.

This book is not an attempt to alter or distort the story of Jesus Christ in any way. Nor do I claim any special authority in compiling this work. If scholarship or revelation shows that I have made some error in this arrangement, I defer to that higher authority. However, nothing has been added to this account. The words are those found in the King James Version of the New Testament, the Joseph Smith Translation and a few excerpts from the Doctrine & Covenants. I believe all those words are sacred and true. My only intention is to present a tool for enjoying the four Gospels, not a replacement for them. I encourage everyone to read each Gospel individually and comprehensively, and most of all, to come to know the Savior Jesus Christ and become like him.

I chose the title because of the many meanings it carries. *Living Water* could represent Christ himself, the scriptures or eternal salvation. It is to never thirst, to have everlasting life. So I felt it a fitting title for the life of Jesus of Nazareth, our Lord and Savior, the same who said, "But unto him that keepeth my commandments I will give the mysteries of my kingdom, and the same shall be in him a well of living water, springing up unto everlasting life." (D&C 63:23)

— Daniel R. Hopkins

HOW TO USE THIS VOLUME

This volume was arranged to provide an account of Christ's life that could be read in a single, chronological flow. Some minor punctuation changes have been made to allow a smooth narrative, and the verses have been rearranged into more modern paragraphs. Where the JST appears, the corresponding language of the KJV is shown in the notes (unless the JST has added to the text).

The bars at the top of each page identify the period in Christ's life. (An asterisk (*) there identifies the first event of the day during The Week of the Atoning Sacrifice.) This harmony was prepared by using a primary text selected from the King James Version (KJV) to describe each event in Christ's life. That text is cited to the right and above the line identifying the event (see the sample below). Additional information in other passages was inserted in logical order. The verse numbers are indicated by plain subscripts (except for insertions of one verse or less). Bold text indicates an insertion from one of the four Standard Works. Underlined plain text indicates an insertion from the Joseph Smith Translation (JST). (Dashed underlining indicates text omitted from the JST.) Italics are used to indicate words added to the text by the King James translators. Small caps indicate languages (GR is Greek; HEB is Hebrew; AR is Aramaic), and segments or versions of the Bible (OT is the Old Testament). Large and small caps indicate quotations from the Old Testament. Comments about the text are indicated by letters of the alphabet; textual insertions are indicated by numbered notes. IE indicates a more modern wording.

THE PREACHINGS OF JOHN THE BAPTIST — Luke 3:1-17

₁Now in the fifteenth year of the reign of Tiberius Caesar, Pontius Pilate being governor of Judaea, and Herod being tetrarch of Galilee, and his brother Philip tetrarch of Ituraea and of the region of Trachonitis, and Lysanias the tetrarch of Abilene, ₂Annas and Caiaphas being the high priests, the word of God came unto John the son of Zacharias in the wilderness. ¹And the same John had his ᵃraiment of camel's hair, and a leathern girdle about his loins; and his meat was locusts and wild honey.

. . .

₄₁₉And this is the record of John, when the Jews sent priests and Levites from Jerusalem to ask him, Who art thou? ₂₀And he confessed, and denied not ⁵that he was Elias; but confessed, ⁵saying; I am not the Christ.
₂₁And they asked him, ⁶saying; How then art thou Elias? And he saith, I am not ⁶that Elias who was to restore all things. And they asked him, saying, Art thou ᶜthat prophet? And he answered, No.
₂₂Then said they unto him, Who art thou? that we may give an answer to them that sent us. What sayest thou of thyself?
₂₃He said, I am the voice of one crying in the wilderness, ₄As it is written in the book of the ⁷prophet ᵈEsaias; and these are the words, saying, ᵉTHE VOICE OF ONE CRYING IN THE WILDERNESS, PREPARE YE THE WAY OF THE LORD, MAKE HIS PATHS STRAIGHT.

1	Matt. 3:4
a	GR: clothing
	. . .
4	John 1:19-23
5	JST John 1:21
6	JST John 1:22
c	a reference to the Messiah
7	JST Luke 3:4
d	GR: Isaiah
e	Isa. 40:3

xii

THE PRE-MORTAL MISSIONS

THE PROLOGUE   **John 1:1-14**

₁In the beginning ¹was the gospel preached through the Son. And the gospel was the Word, and the Word ¹was with the Son, and the Son was with God, and the ²Son was ¹of God. ₂The same was in the beginning with God. ₃All things were made by him; and without him was not any thing made that was made. ₄In him ³was the gospel, and the gospel was ³the life; and the life was the light of men. ₅And the light shineth in ⁴the world; and the ⁴world ªcomprehended it not.

₆There was a man sent from God, whose name *was* John. ₇The same came ⁵into the world for a witness, to bear witness of the Light, ⁶to bear record of the gospel through the Son, unto all, that through him men might believe. ₈He was not that Light, but ⁷came to bear witness of that Light.

₉*That* was the true Light, which lighteth every man that cometh into the world. ⁸Even the Son of God. ₁₀He ⁸who was in the world, and the world was made by him, and the world knew him not. ₁₁He came unto his own, and his own received him not.

₁₂But as many as received him, to them gave he ᵇpower to become the sons of God, ⁹only to them that believe on his name: ¹⁰He was ₁₃born, not of blood, nor of the will of the flesh, nor of the will of man, but of God. ₁₄And the ¹¹same Word was made flesh, and dwelt among us, (and we beheld his glory, the glory as of the only begotten of the Father,) full of grace and truth.

---

1 JST John 1:1
(The JST has never been accepted by the Church as part of its canon of scripture. It's value cannot be denied, but one must not assume that it is without error. Joseph was not fully satisfied with it, and frequently made corrections.)

2 JST John 1:1; KJV: Word

3 JST John 1:4

4 JST John 1:5; KJV: darkness

a IE: perceived (used in the JST)

5 JST John 1:7

6 JST John 1:7; KJV: that all *men* through him

7 JST John 1:8; KJV: *was sent*

8 JST John 1:10

b IE: authority, right, privilege

9 JST John 1:12; KJV: *even*

10 JST John 1:13; KJV: Which were

11 JST John 1:14
(This verse implies that Christ is the Word. "The gospel" is the good news of Christ, hence a deeper meaning is intended, in light of verses 1-7 in the JST.)

THE BIRTHS

THE ANNOUNCEMENT OF JOHN'S BIRTH — Luke 1:5-25

5 There was in the days of Herod, the king of Judaea, a certain priest named ªZacharias, of the ᵇcourse of Abia: and his wife *was* of the daughters of Aaron, and her name *was* Elisabeth. 6 And they were both righteous before God, walking in all the commandments and ordinances of the Lord blameless. 7 And they had no child, because that Elisabeth was barren, and they both were *now* well ᶜstricken in years.

8 And it came to pass, that while he executed the priest's office before God in the order of his ¹priesthood, 9 According to the custom of the priest's office, his lot was to ᵈburn incense when he went into the temple of the Lord. 10 And the whole multitude of the people were praying without at the time of incense.

11 And there appeared unto him an angel of the Lord standing on the right side of the altar of incense. 12 And when Zacharias saw *him*, he was troubled, and fear fell upon him.

13 But the angel said unto him, Fear not, Zacharias: for thy prayer is heard; and thy wife Elisabeth shall bear thee a son, and thou shalt call his name John. 14 And thou shalt have joy and gladness; and many shall rejoice at his birth. 15 For he shall be great in the sight of the Lord, and ᵉshall drink neither wine nor strong drink; and he shall be filled with the Holy Ghost, even from his mother's womb. 16 And many of the children of Israel shall he turn to the Lord their God. 17 ᶠAnd he shall go before him in the spirit and power of ᵍElias, ʰTO TURN THE HEARTS OF THE FATHERS TO THE CHILDREN, and the disobedient to the wisdom of the just; to make ready a people prepared for the Lord.

18 And Zacharias said unto the angel, Whereby shall I know this? for I am an old man, and my wife well ᶜstricken in years. 19 And the angel answering said unto him, I am ⁱGabriel, that stand in the presence of God; and am sent to speak unto thee, and to shew thee these glad tidings. 20 And, behold, thou shalt be dumb, and not able to speak, until the day that these things shall be performed, because thou believest not my words, which shall be fulfilled in their season.

21 And the people waited for Zacharias, and marvelled that he tarried so long in the temple. 22 And when he came out, he could not speak unto them: and they perceived that he had seen a ʲvision in the temple: for he beckoned unto them, and remained speechless.

23 And it came to pass, that, as soon as the days of his ministration were accomplished, he departed to his own house. 24 And after those days his wife Elisabeth conceived, and hid herself five months, saying, 25 Thus hath the Lord dealt with me in the days wherein he looked on *me*, to take away my reproach among men.

---

a GR form of HEB name Zachariah

b OT: Abijah, listed in 1 Chron. 24:10 with priestly courses. See 1 Chron. 28:13, 21; 2 Chron. 5:11; 8:14; 31:2, 15, 17; Ezra 6:18

c GR: advanced

1 JST Luke 1:8; KJV: course

d 1 Chron. 23:13

e Lev. 10:9; Num. 6:3

f See Mal. 3:1; 4:5-6

g GR form of HEB name Elijah

h Mal. 4:6

i See Dan. 8:16; 9:21

j See Isa. 6:1; Amos 9:1

THE BIRTHS

THE ANNOUNCEMENT OF JESUS' BIRTH   Luke 1:26-38

₂₆And in the sixth month the angel Gabriel was sent from God unto a city of Galilee, named Nazareth, ₂₇To a virgin espoused to a man whose name was Joseph, of the house of David; and the virgin's name *was* Mary. ₂₈And the angel came in unto her, and said, Hail, *thou that art highly favoured,* the Lord *is* with thee: blessed *art* thou among women.

₂₉And when she saw *him,* she was troubled at his saying, and cast in her mind what manner of salutation this should be.

₃₀And the angel said unto her, Fear not, Mary: for thou hast found favour with God. ₃₁And, behold, thou shalt conceive in thy womb, and bring forth a son, and shalt call his name JESUS. ₃₂He shall be great, and shall be called the Son of the Highest: and the Lord God shall give unto him the throne of his father David: ₃₃And he shall reign over the house of Jacob for ever; and ªof his kingdom there shall be no end.

₃₄Then said Mary unto the angel, How shall this be, seeing I know not a man?

₃₅And the angel answered and said unto her, The Holy Ghost shall come upon thee, and the power of the Highest shall overshadow thee: therefore also that holy thing which shall be born of thee shall be called the Son of God. ₃₆And, behold, thy ᵇcousin Elisabeth, she hath also conceived a son in her old age: and this is the sixth month with her, who was called barren. ₃₇For with God ᶜnothing shall be impossible.

₃₈And Mary said, Behold the handmaid of the Lord; be it unto me according to thy word. And the angel departed from her.

a See Ps. 145:13; Dan. 4:3, 34; 7:14, 27; 2 Pet. 1:11

b GR: a relative (not necessarily a cousin)

c Related here to conceiving children. See Gen. 18:14.

MARY VISITS ELISABETH   Luke 1:39-56

₃₉And Mary arose in those days, and went into the hill country with haste, into a city of Juda; ₄₀And entered into the house of Zacharias, and ªsaluted Elisabeth.

₄₁And it came to pass, that, when Elisabeth heard the salutation of Mary, the babe leaped in her womb; and Elisabeth was filled with the Holy Ghost: ₄₂And she spake out with a loud voice, and said, Blessed *art* thou among women, and blessed *is* the fruit of thy womb. ₄₃And ᵇwhence *is* this to me, that the mother of my Lord should come to me? ₄₄For, lo, as soon as the voice of thy salutation sounded in mine ears, the babe leaped in my womb for joy. ₄₅And blessed *is* she that believed: for there shall be a performance of those things which were told her from the Lord.

₄₆ᶜAnd Mary said, My soul doth magnify the Lord, ₄₇And my spirit hath rejoiced in God my Saviour. ₄₈For he hath regarded the low estate

a IE: greeted

b GR: how

c Verse 46-55 is called "The Magnificat." Compare with the praise of Hannah when she learned she would bear Samuel. 1 Sam. 2:1-10.

THE BIRTHS

MARY VISITS ELISABETH (cont.) — Luke 1:39-56

of his handmaiden: for, behold, from henceforth all generations shall call me blessed. 49For he that is mighty hath done to me great things; and holy *is* his name. 50And his mercy *is* on them that fear him from generation to generation. 51He hath shewed strength with his arm; he hath scattered the proud in the imagination of their hearts. 52He hath put down the mighty from *their* seats, and exalted them of low degree. 53He hath filled the hungry with good things; and the rich he hath sent empty away. 54He hath ᵈholpen his servant Israel, in remembrance of *his* mercy; 55As he spake to our fathers, to Abraham, and to his seed for ever.

56And Mary abode with her about three months, and returned to her own house.

d IE: helped

JOSEPH'S DREAM — Matt. 1:18-25

18Now, ¹as it is written, the birth of Jesus Christ was ᵃon this wise: After his mother, Mary, was espoused to Joseph, before they came together, she was found with child of the Holy Ghost. 19Then Joseph her husband, being a just *man*, and not willing to make her a publick example, was minded to put her away privily.

20But while he thought on these things, behold, the angel of the Lord appeared unto him in a dream, saying, Joseph, thou son of David, fear not to take unto thee Mary thy wife: for that which is conceived in her is of the Holy Ghost. 21And she shall bring forth a son, and thou shalt call his name ᵇJESUS: for he shall save his people from their sins.

22Now all this was done, that it might be fulfilled which was spoken of the Lord by the prophet, saying, 23ᶜBEHOLD, A VIRGIN SHALL BE WITH CHILD, AND SHALL BRING FORTH A SON, AND THEY SHALL CALL HIS NAME EMMANUEL, which being interpreted is, ᵈGod WITH US.

24Then Joseph being raised from sleep did as the angel of the Lord had bidden him, and took unto him his wife: 25And knew her not till she had brought forth her firstborn son: and he called his name JESUS.

1 JST Matt. 2:1; this addition suggests Matthew may have been using an earlier text when he wrote his Gospel.

a IE: in this way

b HEB: Joshua or Jehoshua, means "Jehovah saves"

c Isa. 7:14

d Isa. 8:10

THE BIRTH OF JOHN THE BAPTIST — Luke 1:57-80

57Now Elisabeth's full time came that she should be delivered; and she brought forth a son. 58And her neighbours and her ᵃcousins heard how the Lord had shewed great mercy upon her; and they rejoiced with her. 59And it came to pass, that on the eighth day they came to circumcise the child; and they called him Zacharias, after the name of his father.

60And his mother answered and said, Not *so*; but he shall be called John.

61And they said unto her, There is none of thy kindred that is called by this name. 62And they made signs to his father, how he would have

a GR: relatives

4

THE BIRTHS

THE BIRTH OF JOHN THE BAPTIST (cont.)   Luke 1:57-80

him called. ₆₃And he asked for a writing table, and wrote, saying, His name is John. And they marvelled all. ₆₄And his mouth was opened immediately, and his tongue *loosed*, and he spake, and praised God.

₆₅And fear came on all that dwelt round about them: and all these sayings were ᵇnoised abroad throughout all the hill country of Judaea. ₆₆And all they that heard *them* laid *them* up in their hearts, saying, What manner of child shall this be! And the hand of the Lord was with him.

₆₇And his father Zacharias was filled with the Holy Ghost, and prophesied, saying, ₆₈Blessed *be* the Lord God of Israel; for he hath visited and redeemed his people, ₆₉And hath raised up an ᶜHORN OF SALVATION for us in the house of his servant David; ₇₀As he spake by the mouth of his holy prophets, which have been since the world began: ₇₁That we should be ᵈSAVED FROM OUR ENEMIES, AND FROM THE HAND OF ALL THAT HATE US; ₇₂To perform the mercy *promised* to our fathers, and to remember his holy covenant; ₇₃The oath which he sware to our father Abraham, ₇₄That he would grant unto us, that we being delivered out of the hand of our enemies might serve him without fear, ₇₅In holiness and righteousness before him, all the days of our life.

₇₆And thou, child, shalt be called the prophet of the Highest: for thou shalt ᵉGO BEFORE THE FACE OF THE LORD TO PREPARE HIS WAYS; ₇₇To give knowledge of salvation unto his people by the remission of their sins, ₇₈Through the tender mercy of our God; whereby the ᶠdayspring from on high hath visited us, ᵍTO GIVE LIGHT TO THEM THAT SIT IN DARKNESS AND IN THE SHADOW OF DEATH, to guide our feet into the way of peace.

₈₀And the child grew, and waxed strong in spirit, and was in the deserts till the day of his shewing unto Israel.

b GR: discussed

c 1 Sam. 2:1

d Ps. 106:10

e Mal. 3:1

f GR: dawn

g Isa. 9:2

THE BIRTH OF JESUS CHRIST   Luke 2:1-7

₁And it came to pass in those days, that there went out a decree from Caesar Augustus, that ¹his empire should be ᵃtaxed. ₂(*And* this ᵇtaxing was first made when Cyrenius was governor of Syria.) ₃And all went to be taxed, every one into his own city.

₄And Joseph also went up from Galilee, out of the city of Nazareth, into Judaea, unto the city of David, which is called Bethlehem; (because he was of the house and lineage of David:) ₅To be taxed with Mary his espoused wife, being great with child. ₆And so it was, that, while they were there, the days were accomplished that she should be delivered.

₇And she brought forth her firstborn son, and wrapped him in swaddling clothes, and laid him in a manger; because there was no room for them in the ²inns.

1 JST Luke 2:1; KJV: all the world

a GR: enrolled, registered

b GR: enrollment

2 JST Luke 2:7; KJV: inn

THE BIRTHS

THE ANGELS AND THE SHEPHERDS — Luke 2:8-20

₈And there were in the same country shepherds abiding in the field, keeping watch over their flock by night. ₉And, lo, the angel of the Lord came upon them, and the glory of the Lord shone round about them: and they were sore afraid. ₁₀And the angel said unto them, Fear not: for, behold, I bring you good tidings of great joy, which shall be to all people. ₁₁For unto you is born this day in the city of David a Saviour, which is Christ the Lord. ₁₂And this *shall be* a sign unto you; Ye shall find the babe wrapped in swaddling clothes, lying in a manger. ₁₃And suddenly there was with the angel a multitude of the heavenly host praising God, and saying, ₁₄Glory to God in the highest, and on earth peace, good will toward men.

₁₅And it came to pass, as the angels were gone away from them into heaven, the shepherds said one to another, Let us now go even unto Bethlehem, and see this thing which is come to pass, which the Lord hath made known unto us. ₁₆And they came with haste, and found Mary, and Joseph, and the babe lying in a manger.

₁₇And when they had seen *it*, they made known abroad the saying which was told them concerning this child. ₁₈And all they that heard *it* ªwondered at those things which were told them by the shepherds. ₁₉But Mary kept all these things, and pondered *them* in her heart.

₂₀And the shepherds returned, glorifying and praising God for all the things that they had heard and seen, as it was told unto them.

a IE: marveled

THE PRESENTATION OF JESUS AT THE TEMPLE — Luke 2:21-38

₂₁And when eight days were accomplished for the circumcising of the child, his name was called JESUS, which was so named of the angel before he was conceived in the womb.

₂₂And when the days of her purification according to the law of Moses were accomplished, they brought him to Jerusalem, to present *him* to the Lord; ₂₃(As it is written in the law of the Lord, ªEVERY MALE THAT OPENETH THE WOMB SHALL BE CALLED HOLY TO THE LORD;) ₂₄And to offer a sacrifice according to that which is said in the law of the Lord, ᵇA PAIR OF TURTLEDOVES, OR TWO YOUNG PIGEONS.

₂₅And, behold, there was a man in Jerusalem, whose name *was* Simeon; and the same man *was* just and devout, waiting for the consolation of Israel: and the Holy Ghost was upon him. ₂₆And it was revealed unto him by the Holy Ghost, that he should not see death, before he had seen the Lord's Christ. ₂₇And he came by the Spirit into the temple: and when the parents brought in the child Jesus, to do for him

a Exod. 13:2, 12; 22:29.

b Lev. 5:11; 12:8

THE BIRTHS

THE PRESENTATION OF JESUS AT THE TEMPLE (cont.) — Luke 2:21-38

after the custom of the law, 28Then took he him up in his arms, and blessed God, and said, 29cLord, now lettest thou thy servant depart in peace, according to thy word: 30For mine eyes have seen thy salvation, 31Which thou hast prepared before the face of all people; 32dA LIGHT eTO LIGHTEN THE GENTILES, and the glory of thy people Israel.
   33And Joseph and his mother marvelled at those things which were spoken of him.
   34And Simeon blessed them, and said unto Mary his mother, Behold, this *child* is fset for the fall and rising again of many in Israel; and for a sign which shall be spoken against; 35(Yea, a sword shall pierce through thy own soul also,) that the thoughts of many hearts may be revealed.
   36And there was one Anna, a prophetess, the daughter of Phanuel, of the tribe of Aser: she was of a great age, and had lived with an husband seven years from her virginity; 37And she *was* a widow of about fourscore and four years, which departed not from the temple, but served *God* with fastings and prayers night and day. 38And she coming in that instant gave thanks likewise unto the Lord, and spake of him to all them that looked for redemption in Jerusalem.

c cf. Gen 46:30

d Isa. 42:6; 49:6

e GR: for revelation to

f IE: appointed

THE WISE MEN VISIT — Matt. 2:1-12

   1Now when Jesus was born in Bethlehem of Judaea in the days of Herod the king, behold, there came wise men from the east to Jerusalem, 2Saying, Where is 1the child that is born 2the Messiah of the Jews? for we have seen his star in the east, and are come to worship him.
   3When Herod the king had heard *these things*, he was troubled, and all Jerusalem with him. 4And when he had gathered all the chief priests, and scribes of the people together, he ademanded of them, 3saying, Where 3is the place that is written of by the prophets, in which Christ should be born? 3For he greatly feared, yet he believed not the prophets.
   5And they said unto him, 4It is written by the prophets, that he should be born in Bethlehem of Judaea, for thus 5have they said, 6The word of the Lord came unto us, saying, 6bAND THOU BETHLEHEM, 6WHICH LIETH *IN* THE LAND OF 7JUDEA, 6IN THEE SHALL BE BORN A PRINCE, WHICH ART NOT THE LEAST AMONG THE PRINCES OF 7JUDEA: FOR OUT OF THEE SHALL COME 8THE MESSIAH, THAT SHALL 9SAVE MY PEOPLE ISRAEL.
   7Then Herod, when he had privily called the wise men, cenquired of them diligently what time the star appeared. 8And he sent them to Bethlehem, and said, Go and search diligently for the young child; and when ye have found *him*, bring me word again, that I may come and worship him also.

1 JST Matt. 3:2; KJV: he

2 JST Matt. 3:2; KJV: King

a GR: inquired

3 JST Matt. 3:4

4 JST Matt. 3:5

5 JST Matt. 3:5; KJV: it is written by the prophet,

6 JST Matt. 3:6

b Micah 5:2

7 JST Matt. 3:6; KJV: Juda

8 JST Matt. 3:6; KJV: a Governor

9 JST Matt. 3:6; KJV: rule (GR: nurture, protect)

THE BIRTHS

THE WISE MEN VISIT (cont.) — Matt. 2:1-12

₉When they had heard the king, they departed; and, lo, the star, which they saw in the east, went before them, till it came and stood over where the young child was. ₁₀When they saw the star, they rejoiced with exceeding great joy.

₁₁And when they were come into the house, they saw the young child with Mary his mother, and fell down, and worshipped him: and when they had opened their treasures, they presented unto him gifts; gold, and frankincense, and myrrh.

₁₂And being warned of God in a dream that they should not return to Herod, they departed into their own country another way.

c See Matt. 2:16

HEROD SLAYS THE CHILDREN OF BETHLEHEM — Matt. 2:13-23

₁₃And when they were departed, behold, the angel of the Lord appeareth to Joseph in a dream, saying, Arise, and take the young child and his mother, and flee into Egypt, and be thou there until I bring thee word: for Herod will seek the young child to destroy him.

₁₄When he arose, he took the young child and his mother by night, and departed into Egypt: ₁₅And was there until the death of Herod: that it might be fulfilled which was spoken of the Lord by the prophet, saying, ᵃOUT OF EGYPT HAVE I CALLED MY SON.

₁₆Then Herod, when he saw that he was ᵇmocked of the wise men, was ᶜexceeding wroth, and sent forth, and slew all the children that were in Bethlehem, and in all the ᵈcoasts thereof, from two years old and under, according to the time which he had diligently enquired of the wise men. ₁₇Then was fulfilled that which was spoken by ᵉJeremy the prophet, saying, ₁₈ᶠIN RAMA WAS THERE A VOICE HEARD, LAMENTATION, AND WEEPING, AND GREAT MOURNING, RACHEL WEEPING *FOR* HER CHILDREN, AND WOULD NOT BE COMFORTED, BECAUSE THEY ARE NOT.

₁₉But when Herod was dead, behold, an angel of the Lord appeareth in a dream to Joseph in Egypt, ₂₀Saying, Arise, and take the young child and his mother, and go into the land of Israel: for they are dead which sought the young child's life. ₂₁And he arose, and took the young child and his mother, and came into the land of Israel.

₂₂But when he heard that Archelaus did reign in Judaea in the ᵍroom of his father Herod, he was afraid to go thither: notwithstanding, being warned of God in a dream, he turned aside into the parts of Galilee: ₂₃And he came and dwelt in a city called Nazareth: that it might be fulfilled which was spoken by the prophets, ʰHE SHALL BE CALLED A NAZARENE.

a Hosea 11:1; Num. 24:8

b GR: deceived by

c GR: greatly enraged

d GR: surrounding regions

e IE: Jeremiah

f Jer. 31:15

g GR: place

h The source of this quote was long unidentified. Some cited Isa. 11:1. New information indicates the text is found in the Dead Sea Scrolls.

THE BIRTHS

CHRIST'S YOUTH   **Luke 2:40-52**

40 And ¹it came to pass that Jesus grew ²up with his brethren, and waxed strong in spirit, filled with wisdom: ²and waited upon the Lord for the time of his ministry to come, and the grace of God was upon him. ³And he served under his father, and he spake not as other men, neither could he be taught; for he needed not that any man should teach him.

41 Now his parents went to Jerusalem every year at the feast of the passover. 42 And when he was twelve years old, they went up to Jerusalem after the custom of the feast. 43 And when they had fulfilled the days, as they returned, the child Jesus tarried behind in Jerusalem; and Joseph and his mother knew not *of it*. 44 But they, supposing him to have been in the company, went a day's journey; and they sought him among *their* kinsfolk and acquaintance. 45 And when they found him not, they turned back again to Jerusalem, seeking him.

46 And it came to pass, that after three days they found him in the temple, sitting in the midst of the ᵃdoctors, ⁴and they were hearing him, and asking him questions. 47 And all that heard him were astonished at his understanding and answers.

48 And when they saw him, they were amazed: and his mother said unto him, Son, why hast thou thus dealt with us? behold, thy father and I have sought thee sorrowing.

49 And he said unto them, How is it that ye sought me? ᵇwist ye not that I must be about my Father's business?

50 And they understood not the saying which he spake unto them. 51 And he went down with them, and came to Nazareth, and was subject unto them: but his mother kept all these sayings in her heart.

52 And Jesus increased in wisdom and stature, ᶜAND IN FAVOUR WITH GOD AND MAN. ⁵And after many years, the hour of his ministry drew nigh.

---

1 JST Matt. 3:24;
KJV: the child

2 JST Matt. 3:24

3 JST Matt. 3:25

a GR: teachers

4 JST Luke 2:46;
KJV: both hearing them and asking them

b IE: knew

5 JST Matt. 3:26

c 1 Sam. 2:26

JOHN'S MINISTRY AND JESUS' PREPARATIONS

THE PREACHINGS OF JOHN THE BAPTIST — Luke 3:1-17

₁Now in the fifteenth year of the reign of Tiberius Caesar, Pontius Pilate being governor of Judaea, and Herod being tetrarch of Galilee, and his brother Philip tetrarch of Ituraea and of the region of Trachonitis, and Lysanias the tetrarch of Abilene, ₂Annas and Caiaphas being the high priests, the word of God came unto John the son of Zacharias in the wilderness. ¹And the same John had his ªraiment of camel's hair, and a leathern girdle about his loins; and his meat was locusts and wild honey.

₃And he came into all the country about Jordan, preaching the baptism of repentance for the remission of sins; ²And saying, ᵇRepent ye: for the kingdom of heaven is at hand. ³₅Then went out to him Jerusalem, and all Judaea, and all the region round about Jordan, ₆And were baptized of him in Jordan, confessing their sins.

⁴₁₉And this is the record of John, when the Jews sent priests and Levites from Jerusalem to ask him, Who art thou?

₂₀And he confessed, and denied not ⁵that he was ᶜElias; but confessed, ⁵saying; I am not the Christ.

₂₁And they asked him, ⁶saying; How then art thou ᶜElias? And he saith, I am not ⁷that Elias who was to restore all things. And they asked him, saying, Art thou ᵈthat prophet? And he answered, No.

₂₂Then said they unto him, Who art thou? that we may give an answer to them that sent us. What sayest thou of thyself?

₂₃He said, I am the voice of one crying in the wilderness, ₄As it is written in the book of the ⁸prophet ᵉEsaias; and these are the words, saying, ᶠTHE VOICE OF ONE CRYING IN THE WILDERNESS, PREPARE YE THE WAY OF THE LORD, MAKE HIS PATHS STRAIGHT. ⁹₅For behold, and lo, he shall come, as it is written in the book of the prophets, to take away the sins of the world, and to bring salvation unto the heathen nations, to gather together those who are lost, who are of the sheepfold of Israel; ₆Yea, even the dispersed and afflicted; and also to prepare the way, and make possible the preaching of the gospel unto the Gentiles; ₇And to be a light unto all who sit in darkness, unto the uttermost parts of the earth; to bring to pass the resurrection from the dead, and to ascend up on high, to dwell on the right hand of the Father, ₈Until the fullness of time, and the law and the testimony shall be sealed, and the keys of the kingdom shall be delivered up again unto the Father; ₉To administer justice unto all; to come down in judgment upon all, and to convince all the ungodly of their ungodly deeds, which they have committed; and all this in the day that he shall come; ₁₀For it is a day of power; yea, ⁵⁹EVERY VALLEY SHALL BE FILLED, AND EVERY MOUNTAIN AND HILL SHALL BE BROUGHT LOW; THE CROOKED SHALL BE MADE STRAIGHT, AND THE ROUGH

---

1 Matt. 3:4
a GR: clothing
2 Matt. 3:2
b GR: a change of heart or mind, i.e., a conversion
3 Matt. 3:5-6
4 John 1:19-23
5 JST John 1:21
6 JST John 1:22; KJV: What then? Art
7 JST John 1:22
c GR: Elijah
d Refers to the Messiah, the Prophet of Deut. 18:15-19.
8 JST Luke 3:4; KJV: words of Esaias the prophet,
e GR: Isaiah
f Isa. 40:3
9 JST Luke 3:5-10
g Isa. 40:4

JOHN'S MINISTRY AND JESUS' PREPARATIONS

THE PREACHINGS OF JOHN THE BAPTIST (cont.) **Luke 3:1-17**

WAYS [h]SHALL BE MADE SMOOTH; 6[i]AND ALL FLESH SHALL SEE [j]THE SALVATION OF GOD.

[10]But when he saw many of the Pharisees and Sadducees come to his baptism, 7Then said he to the multitude that came forth to be baptized of him, O [k]generation of vipers, who hath warned you to flee from the wrath to come? [11]Why is it that ye receive not the preaching of him whom God hath sent? If ye receive not this in your hearts, ye receive not me; and if ye receive not me, ye receive not him of whom I am sent to bear record; and for your sins ye have no cloak.

8Bring forth therefore fruits worthy of repentance, and begin not to say within yourselves, [12]Abraham is our father; we have kept the commandments of God, and none can inherit the promises but the children of Abraham; [13]and we only have power to bring seed unto our father Abraham; for I say unto you, That God is able of these stones to raise up children unto Abraham. 9And now also the axe is laid unto the root of the trees: every tree therefore which bringeth not forth good fruit is hewn down, and cast into the fire.

10And the people asked him, saying, What shall we do then?

11He answereth and saith unto them, He that hath two coats, let him impart to him that hath none; and he that hath meat, let him do likewise.

12Then came also publicans to be baptized, and said unto him, Master, what shall we do?

13 And he said unto them, Exact no more than that which is appointed you. [14]19For it is well known unto you, [l]Theophilus, that after the manner of the Jews, and according to the custom of their law in receiving money into the treasury, that out of the abundance which was received, was appointed unto the poor, every man his portion;

20And after this manner did the publicans also, wherefore John said unto them, Exact no more than that which is appointed you.

14And the soldiers likewise demanded of him, saying, And what shall we do?

And he said unto them, Do violence to no man, neither accuse *any* [m]falsely; and be content with your wages.

15And as the people were in expectation, and all men mused in their hearts of John, whether he were the Christ, or not;

[15]24And they who were sent were of the Pharisees. 25And they asked him, and said unto him, Why baptizest thou then, if thou be not [16]the Christ, nor [n]Elias [17]who was to restore all things, neither that prophet?

16John answered, saying unto *them* all, I indeed baptize you with water; [18]upon your [19]11repentance; [20]and when he of whom I bear record cometh, who is mightier than I, whose shoes I am not worthy

h	omitted from JST Luke 3:10
i	Isa. 40:5
j	Isa. 52:10
10	Matt. 3:7
k	GR: offspring
11	JST Matt. 3:34
12	JST Luke 3:13; KJV: We have Abraham to *our* father
13	JST Matt. 3:36
14	JST Luke 3:19-20
l	Acts and the Gospel of Luke were written to Theophilus (Luke 1:3 and Acts 1:1).
m	In Greek, this refers to extortion
15	John 1:24-25
16	JST John 1:26; KJV (V. 25): that
n	GR: Elijah
17	JST John 1:26
18	JST Matt. 3:38; KJV (3:11): unto
19	Matt. 3:11-12
20	JST Matt. 3:38; KJV (3:11): but he that cometh after me

JOHN'S MINISTRY AND JESUS' PREPARATIONS

THE PREACHINGS OF JOHN THE BAPTIST (cont.) — Luke 3:1-17

to bear, ²¹(or whose place I am not able to fill,) as I said, I indeed baptize you before he cometh, that when he cometh he may **baptize you with the Holy Ghost and** *with* **fire.** ²²And it is he of whom I shall bear record, ₁₂Whose ᵒfan ²³shall be in his hand, and he will thoroughly purge his floor, and gather his wheat into the ᵖgarner; but ²⁴in the fullness of his own time he will burn up the chaff with unquenchable fire.

²⁵₁₅John bare witness of him, and cried, saying, This was he of whom I spake, He that cometh after me, is preferred before me; for he was before me. ²⁶For in the beginning was the Word, even the Son, who is made flesh, and sent unto us by the will of the Father. And as many as believe on his name shall receive of his fullness. ₁₆**And of his fullness have all we received,** ²⁷even immortality and eternal life, through his **grace.** ₁₇**For the law was given** ²⁸through **Moses, but** ²⁹life **and truth came** ²⁸through **Jesus Christ.** ³⁰For the law was after a carnal commandment, to the administration of death; but the gospel was after the power of an endless life, through Jesus Christ, the Only Begotten Son, who is in the bosom of the Father. ₁₈**No man hath seen God at any time;** ³¹except he hath borne record of the Son; for except it is through him no man can be saved.

21	JST Matt. 3:38 (KJV: Matt. 3:11)
22	JST Matt. 3:39 (KJV: Matt. 3:12)
o	GR: winnowing fork
23	JST Matt. 3:39; KJV (3:12): *is*
p	GR: storehouse
24	JST Matt. 3:39
25	John 1:15-18
26	JST John 1:16
27	JST John 1:16; KJV: and grace for
28	JST John 1:17; KJV: by
29	JST John 1:17; KJV: grace
30	JST John 1:18
31	JST John 1:19; KJV: the only begotten Son, which is in the bosom of the Father, he hath declared *him*

THE BAPTISM OF JESUS — Matt. 3:13-17

₁₃Then cometh Jesus from Galilee to Jordan unto John, to be baptized of him. ₁₄But John forbade him, saying, I have need to be baptized of thee, and comest thou to me?

₁₅And Jesus, answering, said unto him, ᵃSuffer ¹me to be baptized of thee now: for thus it ᵇbecometh us to fulfill all righteousness.

Then he ᵃsuffered him. ²And John went down into the water and baptized him. ₁₆And Jesus, when he was baptized, went up ᶜstraightway out of the water: ³and John saw, and, lo, the heavens were opened unto him, and he saw the Spirit of God descending like a dove, and lighting upon ⁴Jesus. ₁₇And lo ⁵he heard a voice from heaven, saying, This is my beloved Son, in whom I am well pleased. ⁵Hear ye him.

a	IE: permit, allow
1	JST Matt. 3:43; KJV: *it to be so*
b	IE: is fitting for
2	JST Matt. 3:44
c	IE: immediately
3	JST Matt. 3:45
4	JST Matt. 3:45; KJV: him
5	JST Matt. 3:46

JOHN'S MINISTRY AND JESUS' PREPARATIONS

JOHN'S TESTIMONY OF JESUS — John 1:28-34

₂₉The next day John seeth Jesus coming unto him, and saith, Behold the Lamb of God, which taketh away the sin of the world. ¹And John bare record of him unto the people, saying, ₃₀This is he of whom I said, After me cometh a man which is preferred before me: for he was before me. ₃₁And ²I knew him, and that he should be made manifest to Israel, therefore am I come baptizing with water. ₃₂And John bare record, saying, ³When he was baptized of me, I saw the Spirit descending from heaven like a dove, and it abode upon him. ₃₃And ⁴I knew him; he that sent me to baptize with water, the same said unto me, Upon whom thou shalt see the Spirit descending, and remaining on him, the same is he which baptizeth with the Holy Ghost. ₃₄And I saw, and bare record that this is the Son of God.

₂₈ᵃThese things were done in Bethabara beyond Jordan, where John was baptizing. **⁵₁₈And many other things in his exhortation preached he unto the people. ₁₉But Herod the tetrarch, being reproved by him for Herodias his brother Philip's wife, and for all the evils which Herod had done, ₂₀Added yet this above all, that he shut up John in prison.**

1 JST John 1:29

2 JST John 1:30; KJV: I knew him not: but

3 JST John 1:31

4 JST John 1:32; KJV: I knew him not: but

a This verse appears here to improve the flow of the narrative with the supplemental passage.

5 Luke 3:18-20

THE TEMPTATIONS OF JESUS — Luke 4:1-13

¹And Jesus himself began to be about thirty years of age, ₁And Jesus being full of the Holy Ghost returned from Jordan, and was led by the Spirit into the wilderness, **²And after forty days, the devil came unto him, to tempt him.** ₂And in those days he did eat nothing: and when they were ended, he afterward hungered. ₃And the devil said unto him, If thou be the Son of God, command this stone that it be made bread. ₄And Jesus answered him, saying, It is written, That ᵃMAN SHALL NOT LIVE BY BREAD ALONE, BUT BY EVERY WORD OF GOD. ₅And the ³Spirit taketh him up into an high mountain, ⁴and he beheld all the kingdoms of the world in a moment of time. ₆And the devil said unto him, All this power will I give thee, and the glory of them: for that is delivered unto me; and to whomsoever I will I give it. ₇If thou therefore wilt worship me, all shall be thine. ₈And Jesus answered and said unto him, Get thee behind me, Satan: for it is written, ᵇTHOU SHALT WORSHIP THE LORD THY GOD, AND HIM ONLY SHALT THOU SERVE. ₉And ⁵the Spirit brought him to Jerusalem, and set him on a pinnacle of the temple, ⁶and the devil came unto him, and said unto him, If thou be the Son of God, cast thyself down from hence: ₁₀For it is written, ᶜHE SHALL GIVE HIS ANGELS CHARGE OVER THEE, TO KEEP THEE: ₁₁And ᵈIN THEIR HANDS THEY SHALL BEAR THEE UP, LEST AT ANY TIME THOU DASH THY FOOT AGAINST A STONE.

1 Luke 3:23 (Genealogies omitted; See Luke 3:23-38 and Matt. 1:1-17)

2 JST Luke 4:2 ; KJV: Being forty days tempted of the devil.

a Deut. 8:3

3 JST Luke 4:5; KJV: devil, taking

4 JST Luke 4:5; KJV: shewed unto him

b Deut. 6:13

5 JST Luke 4:9; KJV: he

6 JST Luke 4:9

c Ps. 91:11

d Ps. 91:12

JOHN'S MINISTRY AND JESUS' PREPARATIONS

THE TEMPTATIONS OF JESUS — Luke 4:1-13

₁₂And Jesus answering said unto him, It is said, ᵉTHOU SHALT NOT TEMPT THE LORD THY GOD.

₁₃And when the devil had ended all the temptation, he departed from him for a season.

e Deut. 6:16

THE FIRST DISCIPLES — John 1:35-51

₃₅Again the next day after John stood, and two of his disciples; ₃₆And looking upon Jesus as he walked, he saith, Behold the Lamb of God!

₃₇And the two disciples heard him speak, and they followed Jesus.

₃₈Then Jesus turned, and saw them following, and saith unto them, What seek ye? They said unto him, Rabbi, (which is to say, being interpreted, Master,) where dwellest thou?

₃₉He saith unto them, Come and see. They came and saw where he dwelt, and abode with him that day: for it was about the tenth hour.

₄₀One of the two which heard John *speak*, and followed him, was Andrew, Simon Peter's brother. ₄₁He first findeth his own brother Simon, and saith unto him, We have found the Messias, which is, being interpreted, the Christ. ₄₂And he brought him to Jesus.

And when Jesus beheld him, he said, Thou art Simon the son of Jona: thou shalt be called Cephas, which is by interpretation, ¹a seer, or A stone. ¹And they were fishermen. And they straightway left all, and followed Jesus.

₄₃The day following Jesus would go forth into Galilee, and findeth Philip, and saith unto him, Follow me. ₄₄Now Philip was of Bethsaida, the city of Andrew and Peter.

₄₅Philip findeth Nathanael, and saith unto him, We have found him, of whom Moses in the law, and the prophets, did write, Jesus of Nazareth, the son of Joseph.

₄₆And Nathanael said unto him, Can there any good thing come out of Nazareth?

Philip saith unto him, Come and see.

₄₇Jesus saw Nathanael coming to him, and saith of him, Behold an Israelite indeed, in whom is no ᵃguile!

₄₈Nathanael saith unto him, Whence knowest thou me?

Jesus answered and said unto him, Before that Philip called thee, when thou wast under the fig tree, I saw thee.

₄₉Nathanael answered and saith unto him, Rabbi, thou art the Son of God; thou art the King of Israel.

₅₀Jesus answered and said unto him, Because I said unto thee, I saw thee under the fig tree, believest thou? thou shalt see greater things than these. ₅₁And he saith unto him, Verily, verily, I say unto you,

1 JST John 1:42

a GR: deceit, fraud

JOHN'S MINISTRY AND JESUS' PREPARATIONS

THE FIRST DISCIPLES — John 1:35-51

Hereafter ye shall see heaven open, and the angels of God ascending and descending upon the Son of man.

THE WEDDING AT CANA — John 2:1-12

₁And the third day ¹of the week, there was a marriage in Cana of Galilee; and the mother of Jesus was there: ₂And both Jesus was called, and his disciples, to the marriage.

₃And when they wanted wine, the mother of Jesus saith unto him, They have no wine.

₄Jesus saith unto her, Woman, what ²wilt thou have me to do for thee? That will I do; for mine hour is not yet come.

₅His mother saith unto the servants, Whatsoever he saith unto you, do *it*.

₆And there were set there six waterpots of stone, after the manner of the purifying of the Jews, containing two or three ᵃfirkins apiece.

₇Jesus saith unto them, Fill the waterpots with water. And they filled them up to the brim. ₈And he saith unto them, Draw out now, and bear unto the governor of the feast. And they bare *it*.

₉When the ruler of the feast had tasted the water that was made wine, and knew not whence it was: (but the servants which drew the water knew;) the governor of the feast called the bridegroom, ₁₀And saith unto him, Every man at the beginning doth set forth good wine; and when men have well drunk, then that which is worse: *but* thou hast kept the good wine until now.

₁₁This beginning of miracles did Jesus in Cana of Galilee, and manifested forth his glory; and his disciples believed on him.

₁₂After this he went down to Capernaum, he, and his mother, and his brethren, and his disciples: and they continued there not many days.

---

1 JST John 2:1

2 JST John 2:4; KJV: have I to do with thee?

a A measure equivalent to about 8⁷⁄₈ gallons.

JESUS CLEANSES THE TEMPLE *   John 2:13-25

₁₃And the Jews' passover was at hand, and Jesus went up to Jerusalem, ₁₄And found in the temple those that sold oxen and sheep and doves, and the changers of money sitting: ₁₅And when he had made a ᵃscourge of small cords, he drove them all out of the temple, and the sheep, and the oxen; and poured out the changers' money, and overthrew the tables;

₁₆And said unto them that sold doves, Take these things hence; make not my Father's house an house of merchandise.

₁₇And his disciples remembered that it was written, ᵇTHE ZEAL OF THINE HOUSE HATH ᶜEATEN ME UP.

₁₈Then answered the Jews and said unto him, What sign shewest thou unto us, seeing that thou doest these things?

₁₉Jesus answered and said unto them, Destroy this temple, and in three days I will raise it up.

₂₀Then said the Jews, Forty and six years was this temple in building, and wilt thou rear it up in three days?

₂₁But he spake of the temple of his body. ₂₂When therefore he was risen from the dead, his disciples remembered that he had said this unto them; and they believed the scripture, and the word which Jesus had said.

₂₃Now when he was in Jerusalem at the passover, in the feast *day*, many believed in his name, when they saw the miracles which he did. ₂₄But Jesus did not ᵈcommit himself unto them, because he knew all ¹things, ₂₅And needed not that any should testify of man: for he knew what was in man.

* John places this event at the beginning of Christ's ministry. Matthew, Mark and Luke place it at the end. None of the writers mention more than one cleansing, but John often added material without repeating the full account given in the other Gospels, so both cleansings are included in this harmony.

a IE: whip

b Ps. 69:9

c GR: consumed

d GR: entrust

1 JST John 2:24; KJV: *men*

JESUS AND NICODEMUS   John 3:1-21

₁There was a man of the Pharisees, named Nicodemus, a ruler of the Jews: ₂The same came to Jesus by night, and said unto him, Rabbi, we know that thou art a teacher come from God: for no man can do these miracles that thou doest, except God be with him.

₃Jesus answered and said unto him, Verily, verily, I say unto thee, Except a man be born ᵃagain, he cannot see the kingdom of God.

₄Nicodemus saith unto him, How can a man be born when he is old? can he enter the second time into his mother's womb, and be born?

₅Jesus answered, Verily, verily, I say unto thee, Except a man be born of water and *of* the Spirit, he cannot enter into the kingdom of God. ₆That which is born of the flesh is flesh; and that which is born of the Spirit is spirit. ₇Marvel not that I said unto thee, Ye must be born again. ₈The ᵇwind bloweth where it listeth, and thou hearest the sound thereof, but canst not tell whence it cometh, and whither it goeth: so is every

a - GR from above, anew

b - GR wind, spirit

16

FIRST YEAR — **THE EARLY JUDEAN MINISTRY**

JESUS AND NICODEMUS (cont.) — John 3:1-21

one that is born of the Spirit. ₉Nicodemus answered and said unto him, How can these things be? ₁₀Jesus answered and said unto him, Art thou a master of Israel, and knowest not these things? ₁₁Verily, verily, I say unto thee, We speak that we do know, and testify that we have seen; and ye receive not our ᶜwitness. ₁₂If I have told you earthly things, and ye believe not, how shall ye believe, if I tell you *of* heavenly things? ₁₃And no man hath ascended up to heaven, but he that came down from heaven, *even* the Son of man which is in heaven. ₁₄And as Moses lifted up the serpent in the wilderness, even so must the Son of man be lifted up: ₁₅That whosoever believeth in him should not perish, but have eternal life.

₁₆For God so loved the world, that he gave his only begotten Son, that whosoever believeth in him should not perish, but have everlasting life. ₁₇For God sent not his Son into the world to condemn the world; but that the world through him might be saved.

₁₈He that believeth on him is not condemned: but he that believeth not is condemned already, because he hath not believed in the name of the only begotten Son of God ¹which before was preached by the mouth of the holy prophets; for they testified of me. ₁₉And this is the condemnation, that light is come into the world, and men loved darkness rather than light, because their deeds were evil. ₂₀For every one that doeth evil hateth the light, neither cometh to the light, lest his deeds should be reproved. ₂₁But he that doeth truth cometh to the light, that his deeds may be made manifest, that they are wrought in God.

c The Greek construction suggests that verses 11-21 contain a direct quotation.

1 JST John 3:18

THE LAST TESTIMONY OF JOHN THE BAPTIST — John 3:22-36

₂₂After these things came Jesus and his disciples into the land of Judaea; and there he tarried with them, and baptized.

₂₃And John also was baptizing in AEnon near to Salim, because there was much water there: and they came, and were baptized. ₂₄For John was not yet cast into prison.

₂₅Then there arose a question between *some* of John's disciples and the Jews about purifying. ₂₆And they came unto John, and said unto him, Rabbi, he that was with thee beyond Jordan, to whom thou barest witness, behold, the same baptizeth, and ¹he receiveth of all people who come to him.

₂₇John answered and said, A man can receive nothing, except it be given him from heaven. ₂₈Ye yourselves bear me witness, that I said, I am not the Christ, but that I am sent before him. ₂₉He that hath the bride is the bridegroom: but the friend of the bridegroom, which standeth and heareth him, rejoiceth greatly because of the bridegroom's voice: this my joy therefore is fulfilled. ₃₀He must increase, but I *must* decrease.

1 JST John 3:27; KJV: all *men*

THE LAST TESTIMONY OF JOHN THE BAPTIST (cont.) — John 3:22-36

₃₁He that cometh from above is above all: he that is of the earth is earthly, and speaketh of the earth: he that cometh from heaven is above all. ₃₂And what he hath seen and heard, that he testifieth; and no man receiveth his testimony. ₃₃He that hath received his testimony hath ᵃset to his seal that God is true. ₃₄For he whom God hath sent speaketh the words of God: for God giveth ²him not the Spirit by measure, for he dwelleth in him, even the fulness.
₃₅The Father loveth the Son, and hath given all things into his hand. ₃₆He that believeth on the Son hath everlasting life: and ³shall receive of his fullness. But he that ᵇbelieveth not the Son, shall not ⁴receive of his fullness; for the wrath of God abideth on him.

a IE: declared that, certified that

2 JST John 3:34; KJV: not the Spirit by measure *unto him*.

3 JST John 3:36

b GR: disbelieves, disobeys, is uncompliant to

4 JST John 3:36; kjv: see life; but

FIRST YEAR

THE GALILEAN MINISTRY

JESUS AND THE SAMARIAN WOMAN John 4:1-42

₁When therefore ᵃthe Lord knew how the Pharisees had heard that Jesus made and baptized more disciples than John, ¹They sought more diligently some means that they might put him to death; for many received John as a prophet, but they believed not on Jesus. ²Now the Lord knew this, ₂ though ³he himself baptized not ⁴so many as his disciples; ⁵For he suffered them for an example, preferring one another. ₃And he left Judea, and departed again into Galilee, ₄And said unto his disciples, I must needs go through Samaria.

₅Then cometh he to a city of Samaria, which is called ᵇSychar, near to ᶜthe parcel of ground that Jacob gave to his son Joseph. ₆Now Jacob's well was there. Jesus therefore, being wearied with *his* journey, sat thus on the well: *and* it was about the sixth hour. ₇There cometh a woman of Samaria to draw water:

Jesus saith unto her, Give me to drink. ₈(For his disciples were gone away unto the city to buy meat.)

₉Then saith the woman of Samaria unto him, How is it that thou, being a Jew, askest drink of me, which am a woman of Samaria? for the Jews have no dealings with the Samaritans.

₁₀Jesus answered and said unto her, If thou knewest the gift of God, and who it is that saith to thee, Give me to drink; thou wouldest have asked of him, and he would have given thee ᵈliving water.

₁₁The woman saith unto him, Sir, thou hast nothing to draw with, and the well is deep: from whence then hast thou that living water? ₁₂Art thou greater than our father Jacob, which gave us the well, and drank thereof himself, and his children, and his cattle?

₁₃Jesus answered and said unto her, Whosoever drinketh of this water shall thirst again: ₁₄But whosoever drinketh of the water that I shall give him shall never thirst; but the water that I shall give him shall be in him a well of water springing up into everlasting life.

₁₅The woman saith unto him, Sir, give me this water, that I thirst not, neither come hither to draw.

₁₆Jesus saith unto her, Go, call thy husband, and come hither.

₁₇The woman answered and said, I have no husband.

Jesus said unto her, Thou hast well said, I have no husband: ₁₈For thou hast had five husbands; and he whom thou now hast is not thy husband: in that saidst thou truly.

₁₉The woman saith unto him, Sir, I perceive that thou art a prophet. ₂₀Our fathers worshipped in ᵉthis mountain; and ye say, that in Jerusalem is the place where men ought to worship.

₂₁Jesus saith unto her, Woman, believe me, the hour cometh, when ye shall neither in this mountain, nor yet at Jerusalem, worship the Father. ₂₂Ye worship ye know not what: we know what we worship: for sal-

a omitted from JST John 4:1

1 JST John 4:2

2 JST John 4:3

3 JST John 4:3; KJV: Jesus

4 JST John 4:3; KJV: . . ., but

5 JST John 4:4

b OT: Shechem

c See Josh. 24:32

d See Jer. 2:13. This is a Hebrew idiom referring to running water (as in a stream) rather than well water.

e Mount Gerizim, beside Shechem.

JESUS AND THE SAMARIAN WOMAN (cont.)   John 4:1-42

vation is of the Jews. ₂₃But the hour cometh, and now is, when the true worshippers shall worship the Father in spirit and in truth: for the Father seeketh such to worship him. ⁶For unto such hath ₂₄ᶠGod ⁷promised his Spirit: and they that worship him must worship ᵍ*him* in spirit and in truth.

₂₅The woman saith unto him, I know that Messias cometh, which is called Christ: when he is come, he will tell us all things.

₂₆Jesus saith unto her, ʰI that speak unto thee am *he*.

₂₇And upon this came his disciples, and marvelled that he talked with the woman: yet no man said, What seekest thou? or, Why talkest thou with her?

₂₈The woman then left her waterpot, and went her way into the city, and saith to the men, ₂₉Come, see a man, which told me all things that ever I did: is not this the Christ? ₃₀Then they went out of the city, and came unto him.

₃₁In the mean while his disciples prayed him, saying, Master, eat. ₃₂But he said unto them, I have meat to eat that ye know not of. ₃₃Therefore said the disciples one to another, Hath any man brought him *ought* to eat?

₃₄Jesus saith unto them, My meat is to do the will of him that sent me, and to finish his work. ₃₅Say not ye, There are yet four months, and *then* cometh harvest? behold, I say unto you, Lift up your eyes, and look on the fields; for they are white already to harvest. ₃₆And he that reapeth receiveth wages, and gathereth fruit unto life eternal: that both he that soweth and he that reapeth may rejoice together. ₃₇And herein is that saying true, One soweth, and another reapeth. ₃₈I sent you to reap that whereon ye bestowed no labour: ⁸the prophets have laboured, and ye are entered into their labours.

₃₉And many of the Samaritans of that city believed on him for the saying of the woman, which testified, He told me all that ever I did. ₄₀So when the Samaritans were come unto him, they besought him that he would tarry with them: and he abode there two days. ₄₁And many more believed because of his own word; ₄₂And said unto the woman, Now we believe, not because of thy saying: for we have heard *him* ourselves, and know that this is indeed the Christ, the Saviour of the world.

6 JST John 4:26

f The text of this phrase in the KJV reads literally in the Greek: "Spirit [a spirit] the God"

7 JST John 4:26; KJV: *is* a

g omitted from JST John 4:26

h GR: I AM (These words are identical to the Septuagint version of Exod. 3:14 which identifies Jehovah. The literal translation of this declaration is: "I AM He speaking to you." In Greek, this identifies the speaker as "I AM," whom the Jews knew as Jehovah.)

8 JST John 4:40; KJV: other men

THE HEALING OF A NOBLEMAN'S SON   John 4:43-54

₄₃Now after two days he departed thence, and went into Galilee, ¹₁₄**preaching the gospel of the kingdom of God,** ₁₅**And saying, The time is fulfilled, and the kingdom of God** ᵃ**is at hand: repent ye, and believe the gospel.** ₄₄For Jesus himself testified, that a prophet hath no honour in his own country. ₄₅Then when he was come into Galilee, the Galilaeans received him, having seen all the things that he did at

1 Mark 1:14-15

a GR: has arrived

FIRST YEAR — THE GALILEAN MINISTRY

THE HEALING OF A NOBLEMAN'S SON (cont.) — John 4:43-54

Jerusalem at the feast: for they also went unto the feast. ₄₆So Jesus came again into Cana of Galilee, where he made the water wine. And there was a certain nobleman, whose son was sick at Capernaum. ₄₇When he heard that Jesus was come out of Judaea into Galilee, he went unto him, and besought him that he would come down, and heal his son: for he was at the point of death. ₄₈Then said Jesus unto him, Except ye see signs and wonders, ye will not believe. ₄₉The nobleman saith unto him, Sir, come down ere my child die. ₅₀Jesus saith unto him, Go thy way; thy son liveth. And the man believed the word that Jesus had spoken unto him, and he went his way. ₅₁And as he was now going down, his servants met him, and told *him*, saying, Thy son liveth. ₅₂Then enquired he of them the hour when he began to amend. And they said unto him, Yesterday at the seventh hour the fever left him. ₅₃So the father knew that *it was* at the same hour, in the which Jesus said unto him, Thy son liveth: and ᵇhimself believed, and his whole house. ₅₄This *is* again the second miracle *that* Jesus did, when he was come out of Judaea into Galilee.

b GR: he himself

JESUS IN NAZARETH — Luke 4:16-30

₁₆And he came to Nazareth, where he had been brought up: and, as his custom was, he went into the synagogue on the sabbath day, and stood up for to read. ₁₇And there was delivered unto him the book of the prophet ᵃEsaias. And when he had opened the book, he found the place where it was written, ₁₈ᵇTHE SPIRIT OF THE LORD *IS* UPON ME, BECAUSE HE HATH ANOINTED ME TO PREACH THE GOSPEL TO THE POOR; HE HATH SENT ME TO HEAL THE BROKENHEARTED, TO PREACH DELIVERANCE TO THE CAPTIVES, AND RECOVERING OF SIGHT TO THE BLIND, TO ᶜSET AT LIBERTY THEM THAT ARE BRUISED, ₁₉ ᵈTO PREACH THE ACCEPTABLE YEAR OF THE LORD. ₂₀And he closed the book, and he gave *it* again to the minister, and sat down. And the eyes of all them that were in the synagogue were fastened on him. ₂₁And he began to say unto them, This day is this scripture fulfilled in your ears. ₂₂And all bare him witness, and ᵉwondered at the gracious words which proceeded out of his mouth. And they said, Is not this Joseph's son? ₂₃And he said unto them, Ye will surely say unto me this proverb, Physician, heal thyself: whatsoever we have heard done in Capernaum, do also here in thy country. ₂₄And he said, Verily I say unto you, No

a GR: Isaiah
b Isa. 61:1
c Dan. 9:24
d Isa. 61:2
e IE: marveled

21

FIRST YEAR — THE GALILEAN MINISTRY

JESUS IN NAZARETH (cont.) — Luke 4:16-30

prophet is accepted in his own country. ₂₅But I tell you of a truth, many widows were in Israel in the days of ᶠElias, when the heaven was shut up three years and six months, when great famine was throughout all the land; ₂₆ᵍBut unto none of them was ᶠElias sent, save unto ʰSarepta, *a city* of Sidon, unto a woman *that was* a widow. ₂₇ⁱAnd many lepers were in Israel in the time of ʲEliseus the prophet; and none of them was cleansed, saving Naaman the Syrian.

₂₈And all they in the synagogue, when they heard these things, were filled with wrath, ₂₉And rose up, and thrust him out of the city, and led him unto the brow of the hill whereon their city was built, that they might cast him down headlong. ₃₀But he passing through the midst of them went his way,

f	GR: Elijah
g	See 1 Kings 17:9-10
h	OT: Zarephath
i	See 2 Kings 5:1-14
j	GR: Elisha

A DEVIL IN CAPERNAUM — Mark 1:22-28

¹And came down to Capernaum, a city of Galilee, and taught them on the sabbath days. ₂₂And they were astonished at his doctrine: ²**for his word was with power.** He taught them as one that had authority, and not as the scribes.

₂₃And there was in their synagogue a man with an unclean spirit; and he cried out ³**with a loud voice,** ₂₄Saying, Let *us* alone; ᵃwhat have we to do with thee, thou Jesus of Nazareth? art thou come to destroy us? I know thee who thou art, the Holy One of God.

₂₅And Jesus rebuked him, saying, Hold thy peace, and come out of him.

₂₆And when the unclean spirit had torn him, and cried with a loud voice, he came out of him.

₂₇And they were all amazed, insomuch that they questioned among themselves, saying, What thing is this? what new doctrine *is* this? for with authority commandeth he even the unclean spirits, and they do obey him.

₂₈And immediately his fame spread abroad throughout all the region round about Galilee.

1	Luke 4:31
2	Luke 4:32
3	Luke 4:33
a	GR: what business do you have with us

FISHERS OF MEN — Matt. 4:18-24

₁₈And Jesus, walking by the sea of Galilee, saw two brethren, Simon called Peter, and Andrew his brother, casting a net into the sea: for they were fishers. ₁₉And he saith unto them, ¹I am he of whom it is written by the prophets; follow me, and I will make you fishers of men. ₂₀And they straightway left *their* nets, and followed him.

₂₁And going on from thence, he saw other two brethren, James *the son* of Zebedee, and John his brother, in a ship with Zebedee their father, mending their nets; and he called them. ₂₂And they immediately

1	JST Matt. 4:18

FIRST YEAR — **THE GALILEAN MINISTRY**

FISHERS OF MEN (cont.) — Matt. 4:18-24

left the ship and their father, and followed him.

²₃₅And in the morning, rising up a great while before day, he went out, and departed into a solitary place, and there prayed. ₃₆And Simon and they that were with him followed after him. ₃₇And when they had found him, they said unto him, All *men* seek for thee. ₃₈And he said unto them, Let us go into the next towns, that I may preach there also: for therefore came I forth.

₂₃And Jesus went about all Galilee, teaching in their synagogues, and preaching the gospel of the kingdom, and healing all manner of sickness and all manner of disease among the people ³which believed on his name. ₂₄And his fame went throughout all Syria: and they brought unto him all sick people that were taken with divers diseases and torments, and those which were possessed with devils, and those which were lunatick, and those that had the ªpalsy; and he healed them.

2 Mark 1:35-38
3 JST Matt. 4:22
a GR: paralysis

A GREAT MULTITUDE OF FISHES — Luke 5:1-12

₁And it came to pass, that, as the people pressed upon him to hear the word of God, he stood by the lake of ªGennesaret, ₂And saw two ships standing by the lake: but the fishermen were gone out of them, and were washing *their* nets. ₃And he entered into one of the ships, which was Simon's, and prayed him that he would thrust out a little from the land. And he sat down, and taught the people out of the ship.

₄Now when he had left speaking, he said unto Simon, Launch out into the deep, and let down your nets for a ᵇdraught.

₅And Simon answering said unto him, Master, we have toiled all the night, and have taken nothing: nevertheless at thy word I will let down the net.

₆And when they had this done, they inclosed a great multitude of fishes: and their net ᶜbrake. ₇And they beckoned unto *their* partners, which were in the other ship, that they should come and help them. And they came, and filled both the ships, so that they began to sink.

₈When Simon Peter saw *it*, he fell down at Jesus' knees, saying, Depart from me; for I am a sinful man, O Lord. ₉For he was astonished, and all that were with him, at the draught of the fishes which they had taken: ₁₀And so *was* also James, and John, the sons of Zebedee, which were partners with Simon.

And Jesus said unto Simon, Fear not; from henceforth thou shalt ᵈcatch men.

₁₁And when they had brought their ships to land, they forsook all, and followed him.

a gr: Chinnoreth (Num. 34:11; Deut. 3:17; Josh. 13:27). In the New Testament, this lake is usually called the Sea of Galilee or the Sea of Tiberias.
b IE: catch, haul
c GR: was breaking
d IE: capture, take alive

FIRST YEAR — **THE GALILEAN MINISTRY**

JESUS HEALS A LEPER — Mark 1:41-45

¹And it came to pass, when he was in a certain city, behold a man full of leprosy: who seeing Jesus fell on *his* face, and besought him, saying, Lord, if thou wilt, thou canst make me clean. ₄₁And Jesus, moved with compassion, put forth *his* hand, and touched him, and saith unto him, I will; be thou clean.
₄₂And as soon as he had spoken, immediately the leprosy departed from him, and he was cleansed. ₄₃And he ᵃstraitly charged him, and forthwith sent him away; ₄₄And saith unto him, See thou say nothing to any man: but go thy way, ᶜshew thyself to the priest, and offer for thy cleansing those things which Moses commanded, for a testimony unto them.
₄₅But he went out, and began to publish *it* much, and to ᵇblaze abroad the matter, insomuch that Jesus could no more openly enter into the city, but was without in desert places: and they came to him from every quarter.

1 Luke 5:12
a IE: warned him sternly
b IE: spread widely
c See Lev. 14:2-32

THE CALLING OF THE TWELVE APOSTLES — Mark 3:14-19

¹₁₂And it came to pass in those days, that he went out into a mountain to pray, and continued all night in prayer to God. ₁₃And when it was day, he called *unto him* his disciples: and of them he chose twelve, whom also he named apostles;
²And when he had called unto *him* his twelve disciples, he gave them ᵃpower *against* unclean spirits, to cast them out, and to heal all manner of sickness and all manner of disease.
₁₄And he ordained twelve, that they should be with him, and that he might send them forth to preach, ₁₅And to have ᵃpower to heal sicknesses, and to cast out devils:
₁₆And Simon he surnamed Peter; ₁₇And James the *son* of Zebedee, and John the brother of James; and he surnamed them Boanerges, which is, The sons of thunder: ₁₈And Andrew, and Philip, and Bartholomew, and Matthew, and Thomas, and James the *son* of Alphaeus, and Thaddaeus, and Simon the ᵇCanaanite, ₁₉And Judas Iscariot, which also betrayed him: and they ᶜwent into an house.

1 Luke 6:12-13
2 Matt. 10:1
a GR: authority over
b This is an error in the Greek text. The Aramaic for "Zealot" is *kanai* (Luke 6:15; Acts 1:13); *kena'ani* is "Canaanite." All Christ's apostles were Jews.
c IE: went home

INSTRUCTING AND SENDING THE TWELVE — Matt. 10:5-42

₅These twelve Jesus sent forth, and commanded them, saying, Go not into the way of the Gentiles, and into *any* city of the Samaritans enter ye not: ₆But go rather to the lost sheep of the house of Israel.
₇And as ye go, preach, saying, The kingdom of heaven is ᵃat hand. ₈Heal the sick, cleanse the lepers, raise the dead, cast out devils: ᵇfreely ye have received, freely give. ₉Provide neither gold, nor silver, nor brass in your purses, ₁₀Nor ᶜscrip for *your* journey, neither two coats, neither shoes, nor yet staves: for the workman is worthy of his

a GR: has come
b GR: without payment
c GR: traveling bag, or beggar's bag

FIRST YEAR — THE GALILEAN MINISTRY

INSTRUCTING AND SENDING THE TWELVE (cont.) **Matt. 10:5-42**

meat. 11And into whatsoever city or town ye shall enter, enquire who in it is worthy; and there abide till ye go thence. 12And when ye come into an house, salute it. 13And if the house be worthy, let your peace come upon it: but if it be not worthy, let your peace return to you.

14And whosoever shall not receive you, nor hear your words, when ye depart out of that house or city, shake off the dust of your feet. 15Verily I say unto you, It shall be more tolerable for the land of Sodom and Gomorrha in the day of judgment, than for that city.

16Behold, I send you forth as sheep in the midst of wolves: be ye therefore wise as serpents, and ᵈharmless as doves. 17But beware of men: for they will deliver you up to the councils, and they will scourge you in their synagogues; 18And ye shall be brought before governors and kings ᵉfor my sake, for a ᶠtestimony against them and the Gentiles.

19But when they deliver you up, ᵍtake no thought how or what ye shall speak: for it shall be given you in that same hour what ye shall speak. 20For it is not ye that speak, but the Spirit of your Father which speaketh in you.

21And the brother shall deliver up the brother to death, and the father the child: and the children shall rise up against *their* parents, and cause them to be put to death. 22And ye shall be hated of all *men* ʰfor my name's sake: but he that endureth to the end shall be saved.

23But when they persecute you in this city, flee ye into another: for verily I say unto you, Ye shall not have gone over the cities of Israel, till the Son of man be come. 24The disciple is not above *his* master, nor the servant above his lord. 25It is enough for the disciple ⁱthat he be as his master, and the servant as his lord. If they have called the master of the house Beelzebub, how much more *shall they call* them of his household?

26Fear them not therefore: for there is nothing covered, that shall not be revealed; and hid, that shall not be known. 27What I tell you in darkness, *that* speak ye in light: and what ye hear in the ear, *that* preach ye upon the housetops. 28And fear not them which kill the body, but are not able to kill the soul: but rather fear him which is able to destroy both soul and body in hell.

29Are not two sparrows sold for a farthing? and one of them shall not fall on the ground without your Father. 30But the very hairs of your head are all numbered. 31Fear ye not therefore, ye are of more value than many sparrows.

32Whosoever therefore shall ʲconfess me before men, him will I confess also before my Father which is in heaven. 33But whosoever shall deny me before men, him will I also deny before my Father which is in heaven.

d GR: guileless

e IE: on account of me

f GR: witness to

g GR: do not be anxiously concerned

h IE: because of my name

i GR: that he become

j GR: solemnly covenant with, promise me

FIRST YEAR — **THE GALILEAN MINISTRY**

INSTRUCTING AND SENDING THE TWELVE (cont.) — Matt. 10:5-42

₃₄Think not that I am come to send peace on earth: I came not to send peace, but a sword. ₃₅For I am come to set a man at variance against his father, and the daughter against her mother, and the daughter in law against her mother in law. ₃₆And a man's foes *shall be* they of his own household. ₃₇He that loveth father or mother more than me is not worthy of me: and he that loveth son or daughter more than me is not worthy of me. ₃₈And he that taketh not his cross, and followeth after me, is not worthy of me. ₃₉He that ¹<u>seeketh to save</u> his life shall ᵏlose it: and he that loseth his life for my sake shall find it.

₄₀He that receiveth you receiveth me, and he that receiveth me receiveth him that sent me. ₄₁He that receiveth a prophet in the name of a prophet shall receive a prophet's reward; and he that receiveth a righteous man in the name of a righteous man shall receive a righteous man's reward.

₄₂And whosoever shall give to drink unto one of these little ones a cup of cold *water* only in the name of a disciple, verily I say unto you, he shall in no wise lose his reward.

1 JST Matt. 10:34; KJV: findeth

k GR: sacrifice

JESUS HEALS A MULTITUDE — Luke 6:17-19

¹And it came to pass, when Jesus had made an end of commanding his twelve disciples, he departed thence to teach and to preach in their cities. ₁₇And he came down with them, and stood in the plain, and the company of his disciples, and a great multitude of people out of all Judaea and Jerusalem, and from the sea coast of Tyre and Sidon, which came to hear him, and to be healed of their diseases; ₁₈And they that were vexed with unclean spirits: and they were healed. ₁₉And the whole multitude sought to touch him: for there went ᵃvirtue out of him, and healed *them* all.

1 Matt. 11:1

a GR: power

THE SERMON ON THE MOUNT — Matt. 4:25; 5-7

₂₅And there followed him great multitudes of people from Galilee, and *from* Decapolis, and *from* Jerusalem, and *from* Judaea, and *from* beyond Jordan. **¹And he lifted up his eyes** ₅:₁And seeing the multitudes, he went up into a mountain: and when he was set, his disciples came unto him: ₂And he opened his mouth, and taught them, saying, ²₃<u>Blessed are they who shall believe on me; and again, more blessed are they who shall believe on your words, when ye shall testify that ye have seen me and that I am.</u> ₄<u>Yea, blessed are they who shall believe on your words, and come down into the depth of humility, and be baptized in my name; for they shall be visited with fire and the Holy Ghost, and shall receive a remission of their sins.</u>

₃ᵃBlessed *are* the ᵇpoor in spirit, ³<u>who come unto me</u>: for theirs is the

1 Luke 6:20

2 JST Matt. 5:3-4

a "Beatitudes" is from Latin, *beatus*, meaning "to be fortunate, or blessed."

b GR: lacking worldly wealth or influence

3 JST Matt. 5:5

26

THE SERMON ON THE MOUNT (cont.)   Matt. 5

kingdom of heaven. ₄Blessed *are* they that mourn: for they shall be comforted. ₅Blessed *are* the ᶜmeek: for they shall inherit the earth. ₆Blessed *are* they which do hunger and thirst after righteousness: for they shall be filled ⁴with the Holy Ghost. ₇Blessed *are* the merciful: for they shall obtain mercy. ₈Blessed *are* the pure in heart: for they shall see God. ₉Blessed *are* the peacemakers: for they shall be called the children of God. ₁₀Blessed *are* they which are persecuted for ⁵my name's sake: for theirs is the kingdom of heaven. ₁₁Blessed are ye, when *men* shall revile you, and persecute *you*, and shall say all manner of evil against you falsely, ᵈfor my sake. ₁₂Rejoice, and be exceeding glad: for great *is* your reward in heaven: for so persecuted they the prophets which were before you.

₁₃Ye are the ᵉsalt of the earth: but if the salt have lost his savour, wherewith shall it be salted? it is thenceforth good for nothing, but to be cast out, and to be trodden under foot of men. ₁₄Ye are the light of the world. A city that is set on an hill cannot be hid. ₁₅Neither do men light a candle, and put it under a bushel, but on a candlestick; and it giveth light unto all that are in the house. ₁₆Let your light so shine before ⁶this world, that they may see your good works, and glorify your Father which is in heaven.

₁₇Think not that I am come to destroy the law, or the prophets: I am not come to destroy, but to fulfil. ₁₈For verily I say unto you, Till heaven and earth pass, one jot or one tittle shall in no wise pass from the law, till all be fulfilled. ₁₉Whosoever, therefore, shall break one of these least commandments, and shall teach men so ⁷to do, he shall ⁷in no wise be ⁸saved in the kingdom of heaven: but whosoever shall do and teach ⁹these commandments of the law until it be fulfilled, the same shall be called great, ⁷and shall be saved in the kingdom of heaven. ₂₀For I say unto you, That except your righteousness shall exceed *the righteousness* of the scribes and Pharisees, ye shall in no case enter into the kingdom of heaven.

₂₁Ye have heard that it was said by them of old time, ᶠTHOU SHALT NOT KILL; and whosoever shall kill shall be ᵍin danger of the judgment: ₂₂But I say unto you, That whosoever is angry with his brother ʰwithout a cause shall be ᵍin danger of the judgment: and whosoever shall say to his brother, ⁱRaca, shall be in danger of the ʲcouncil: but whosoever shall say, Thou fool, shall be in danger of hell fire. ₂₃Therefore if thou bring thy gift to the altar, and there rememberest that thy brother hath ought against thee; ₂₄Leave there thy gift before the altar, and go thy way; first be reconciled to thy brother, and then come and offer thy gift.

₂₅ᵏAgree with thine adversary quickly, whiles thou art in the way with him; lest at any time the adversary deliver thee to the judge, and the judge deliver thee to the officer, and thou be cast into prison. ₂₆Verily I

---

c GR: gentle, forgiving

4 JST Matt. 5:8

5 JST Matt. 5:12; KJV: righteousness'

d IE: on account of me

e Salt is a token of the covenant, part of the sacrifice. See Lev. 2:13 and Num. 18:19.

6 JST Matt. 5:18; KJV: men

7 JST Matt. 5:21

8 JST Matt. 5:21; KJV: called the least

9 JST Matt. 5:21; KJV: them

f Exod. 20:13

g GR: subject to condemnation

h omitted in JST Matt. 5:22, 3 Ne. 12:22, and many early mss.

i GR: emptyheaded. A word suggesting contempt and derision, in both Aramaic and Greek

j Refers to the Sanhedrin

k GR: be well-disposed toward

FIRST YEAR — THE GALILEAN MINISTRY

THE SERMON ON THE MOUNT (cont.) — Matt. 5

say unto thee, Thou shalt by no means come out thence, till thou hast paid ˡthe uttermost farthing.

₂₇Ye have heard that it was said by them of old time, ᵐTHOU SHALT NOT COMMIT ADULTERY: ₂₈But I say unto you, That whosoever looketh on a woman to lust after her hath committed adultery with her already in his heart.

₂₉And if thy right eye ⁿoffend thee, pluck it out, and cast it from thee: for it is profitable for thee that one of thy members should perish, and not that thy whole body should be cast into hell. ₃₀And if thy right hand offend thee, cut it off, and cast it from thee: for it is profitable for thee that one of thy members should perish, and not that thy whole body should be cast into hell. ¹⁰And now this I speak, a parable concerning your sins; wherefore, cast them from you, that ye may not be hewn down and cast into the fire.

₃₁It hath been said, Whosoever shall put away his wife, ᵒLET HIM GIVE HER A WRITING OF DIVORCEMENT: ₃₂But I say unto you, That whosoever shall put away his wife, saving for the cause of fornication, causeth her to commit adultery: and whosoever shall marry her that is divorced committeth adultery.

₃₃Again, ye have heard that it hath been said by them of old time, ᵖThou shalt not ᑫforswear thyself, but shalt perform unto the Lord thine oaths: ₃₄But I say unto you, Swear not at all; neither by heaven; for it is God's throne: ₃₅Nor by the earth; for it is his footstool: neither by Jerusalem; for it is the city of the great King. ₃₆Neither shalt thou swear by thy head, because thou canst not make one hair white or black. ₃₇But let your communication be, Yea, yea; Nay, nay: for whatsoever is more than these cometh ʳof evil.

₃₈Ye have heard that it hath been said, ˢAN EYE FOR AN EYE, AND A TOOTH FOR A TOOTH: ₃₉But I say unto you, That ye resist not evil: but whosoever shall smite thee on thy right cheek, turn to him the other also. ₄₀And if any man will sue thee at the law, and take away thy coat, let him have thy cloke also. ₄₁And whosoever shall compel thee to go a mile, go with him twain. ₄₂Give to him that asketh thee, and from him that would borrow of thee turn not thou away.

₄₃Ye have heard that it hath been said, ᵗTHOU SHALT LOVE THY NEIGHBOUR, and hate thine enemy. ₄₄But I say unto you, Love your enemies, bless them that curse you, do good to them that hate you, and pray for them which despitefully use you, and persecute you; ₄₅That ye ᵘmay be the children of your Father which is in heaven: for he maketh his sun to rise on the evil and on the good, and sendeth rain on the just and on the unjust. ₄₆For if ye love them which love you, what reward have ye? do not even the publicans the same? ₄₇And if ye salute your brethren only, what do ye more than others? do not even the publicans so? ¹¹Ye are

---

l GR: the last kodrantes (from a Latin word, *quadrans*), one-fourth of an *as* or two mites.

m Exod. 20:14

n GR: cause to stumble

10 JST Matt. 5:34

o Deut. 24:1

p Num. 30:2; Deut. 6:13; 10:20

q IE: break your oath, perjure yourself

r GR: from the evil one

s Exod. 21:24; Lev. 24:20; Deut. 19:21

t Lev. 19:18

u GR: may become

11 JST Matt. 5:50

28

FIRST YEAR — **THE GALILEAN MINISTRY**

THE SERMON ON THE MOUNT (cont.) — Matt. 5 - 6

therefore commanded to be ₄₈ᵛperfect, even as your Father which is in heaven is perfect.

₁₂And it came to pass that, as Jesus taught his disciples, he said unto them, ₆:₁Take heed that ye do not your ʷalms before men, to be seen of them: otherwise ye have no reward of your Father which is in heaven. ₂Therefore when thou doest *thine* alms, do not sound a trumpet before thee, as the ˣhypocrites do in the synagogues and in the streets, that they may have glory of men. Verily I say unto you, They have their reward. ₃But when thou doest alms, let not thy left hand know what thy right hand doeth: ₄That thine alms may be in secret: and thy Father which seeth in secret himself shall reward thee openly.

₅And when thou prayest, thou shalt not be as the hypocrites *are*: for they love to pray standing in the synagogues and in the corners of the streets, that they may be seen of men. Verily I say unto you, They have their reward. ₆But thou, when thou prayest, enter into thy closet, and when thou hast shut thy door, pray to thy Father which is in secret; and thy Father which seeth in secret shall reward thee openly. ₇But when ye pray, use not vain repetitions, as the heathen *do*: for they think that they shall be heard for their much speaking. ₈Be not ye therefore like unto them: for your Father knoweth what things ye have need of, before ye ask him.

₉After this manner therefore pray ye: Our Father which art in heaven, ʸHallowed be thy name. ₁₀Thy kingdom come. Thy will be done ᶻin earth, as *it is* in heaven. ₁₁Give us this day our daily bread. ₁₂And forgive us our debts, as we forgive our ᵃᵃdebtors. ₁₃And ¹³suffer us not to be led into temptation, but ᵇᵇdeliver us from evil: ᶜᶜFOR THINE IS THE KINGDOM, AND THE POWER, AND THE GLORY, ᵈᵈFOR EVER. Amen.

₁₄For if ye forgive men their trespasses, your heavenly Father will also forgive you: ₁₅But if ye forgive not men their trespasses, neither will your Father forgive your trespasses.

₁₆Moreover when ye fast, be not, as the hypocrites, of a sad countenance: for they disfigure their faces, that they may appear unto men to fast. Verily I say unto you, They ᵉᵉhave their reward. ₁₇But thou, when thou fastest, anoint thine head, and wash thy face; ₁₈That thou appear not unto men to fast, but unto thy Father which is in secret: and thy Father, which seeth in secret, shall reward thee openly.

₁₉Lay not up for yourselves treasures upon earth, where moth and rust doth corrupt, and where thieves ᶠᶠbreak through and steal: ₂₀But lay up for yourselves treasures in heaven, where neither moth nor rust doth corrupt, and where thieves do not break through nor steal: ₂₁For where your treasure is, there will your heart be also. ₂₂The light of the body is the eye: if therefore thine eye be ᵍᵍsingle ¹⁴to the glory of God, thy whole

---

v GR: complete, finished, fully developed

12 JST Matt. 6:1

w GR: merciful deeds, acts of religious devotion

x GR: pretenders, actors (who wore masks on stage to play their parts)

y GR: Let thy name be sanctified

z GR: on

aa GR: one who has not made amends for an offense or paid a debt

13 JST Matt. 6:14; KJV: lead us not

bb GR: protect us from the evil one

cc 1 Chron. 29:11

dd Ps. 145:11

ee GR: receive

ff GR: dig through (as an earthen wall)

gg GR: healthy, sincere, without guile

14 JST Matt. 6:22

FIRST YEAR — THE GALILEAN MINISTRY

THE SERMON ON THE MOUNT (cont.) — Matt. 6 - 7

body shall be full of light. ₂₃But if thine eye be evil, thy whole body shall be full of darkness. If therefore the light that is in thee be darkness, how great *is* that darkness!

₂₄No man can serve two masters: for either he will hate the one, and love the other; or else he will hold to the one, and despise the other. Ye cannot serve God and ʰʰmammon.

¹⁵₂₅And, again, I say unto you, Go ye into the world, and care not for the world; for the world will hate you, and will persecute you, and will ⁱⁱturn you out of their synagogues. ₂₆Nevertheless, ye shall go forth from house to house, teaching the people; and I will go before you. ₂₇And your heavenly Father will provide for you, whatsoever things ye need for food, what ye shall eat; and for raiment, what ye shall wear or put on. ₂₅Therefore I say unto you, Take no ʲʲthought for your life, what ye shall eat, or what ye shall drink; nor yet for your body, what ye shall put on. Is not the life more than meat, and the body than raiment? ₂₆Behold the fowls of the air: for they sow not, neither do they reap, nor gather into barns; yet your heavenly Father feedeth them. Are ye not much better than they? ₂₇Which of you by taking thought can add one cubit unto his stature? ₂₈And why take ye thought for raiment? Consider the lilies of the field, how they grow; they toil not, neither do they spin: ₂₉And yet I say unto you, That even Solomon in all his glory was not arrayed like one of these. ₃₀Wherefore, if God so clothe the grass of the field, which to day is, and to morrow is cast into the oven, **¹⁶**how much more will he not provide for you, if ye are not of little faith.

₃₁Therefore ᵏᵏtake no thought, saying, What shall we eat? or, What shall we drink? or, Wherewithal shall we be clothed? ₃₂(For after all these things do the Gentiles seek:) for your heavenly Father knoweth that ye have need of all these things. **¹⁷**Wherefore, seek not the things of this world, ₃₃But seek ye first **¹⁷**to build up the kingdom of God, and **¹⁷**to establish his righteousness, and all these things shall be added unto you. ₃₄Take therefore no thought for the morrow: for the morrow shall take thought for the things of itself. Sufficient unto the day *is* the evil thereof.

¹⁸Now these are the words which Jesus taught his disciples that they should say unto the people. 7:1Judge not **¹⁹**unrighteously, that ye be not judged; **¹⁹**but judge righteous judgment. ₂For with what judgment ye judge, ye shall be judged: and with what measure ye mete, it shall be measured to you again.

₃And **²⁰**again, ye shall say unto them, Why **²⁰**is it that thou beholdest the ˡˡmote that is in thy brother's eye, but considerest not the ᵐᵐbeam that is in thine own eye? ₄Or how wilt thou say to thy brother, Let me pull out the mote out of thine eye; and **²¹**canst not behold a beamⁿⁿ in thine own eye?

---

hh IE: riches

15 JST Matt. 6:25-27

ii IE: excommunicate you

jj GR: anxious concern

16 JST Matt. 6:34; KJV: *shall he* not much more *clothe* you, O ye

kk GR: do not be anxious

17 JST Matt. 6:38

18 JST Matt. 7:1

19 JST Matt. 7:2

20 JST Matt. 7:4

ll GR: speck, chip, or splinter

mm GR: the beam used to hold up the roof of a house

21 JST Matt. 7:5

nn The KJV translators added *is* to the text at this point.

THE GALILEAN MINISTRY

THE SERMON ON THE MOUNT (cont.) — Matt. 7

22₆And Jesus said unto his disciples, Beholdest thou the scribes, and the Pharisees, and the priests, and the Levites? They teach in their synagogues, but do not observe the law, nor the commandments; and all have gone out of the way, and are under sin. ₇Go thou and say unto them, Why teach ye men the law and the commandments, when ye yourselves are the children of corruption? **23**₈Say unto them, Ye hypocrites, ₅first cast out the beam out of thine own eye; and then shalt thou see clearly to cast out the mote out of thy brother's eye.

24₉Go ye into the world, saying unto all, Repent, for the kingdom of heaven has come nigh unto you. **25**₁₀And the mysteries of the kingdom ye shall keep within yourselves; for it is not meet to give ₆that which is holy unto the dogs, neither cast ye your pearls unto swine, lest they trample them under their feet. **26**For the world cannot receive that which ye, yourselves, are not able to bear; wherefore ye shall not give your pearls unto them, lest they turn again and rend you.

27Say unto them, Ask of God; ₇ask, and it shall be given you; seek, and ye shall find; knock, and it shall be opened unto you. ₈For every one that asketh, receiveth; and he that seeketh, findeth; and unto him that knocketh, it shall be opened.

28₁₄And then said his disciples unto him, They will say unto us, We ourselves are righteous, and need not that any man should teach us. God, we know, heard Moses and some of the prophets; but us he will not hear. ₁₅And they will say, We have the law for our salvation, and that is sufficient for us.

₁₆Then Jesus answered, and said unto his disciples, ₁₇Thus shall ye say unto them, What man among you, having a son, and he shall be standing out, and shall say, Father, open thy house that I may come in and sup with thee, will not say, Come in, my son; for mine is thine, and thine is mine? ₉Or what man is there of you, whom if his son ask bread, will he give him a stone? ₁₀Or if he ask a fish, will he give him a serpent? ₁₁If ᵒᵒye then, being evil, know how to give good gifts unto your children, how much more shall your Father which is in heaven give good things to them that ask him?

₁₂Therefore all things whatsoever ye would that men should do to you, do ye even so to them: for this is the law and the prophets.

₁₃Enter ye in at the ᵖᵖstrait gate: for wide *is* the gate, and broad *is* the way, that leadeth to destruction, and many there be which go in thereat: ₁₄Because strait *is* the gate, and narrow *is* the way, which leadeth unto life, and few there be that find it.

₁₅Beware of false prophets, which come to you in sheep's clothing, but inwardly they are ravening wolves. ₁₆Ye shall ᵠᵠknow them by their fruits. Do men gather grapes of thorns, or figs of thistles? ₁₇Even so every good tree bringeth forth ʳʳgood fruit; but a ˢˢcorrupt tree bringeth

---

22 JST Matt. 7:6-7
23 JST Matt. 7:8; KJV: Thou hypocrite
24 JST Matt. 7:9
25 JST Matt. 7:10; KJV: Give not
26 JST Matt. 7:11; KJV: and
27 JST Matt. 7:12
28 JST Matt. 7:14-17

oo GR: although you are wicked
pp IE: narrow
qq GR: recognize
rr GR: beautiful, precious, without blemish
ss GR: decayed, rotten, stale

THE GALILEAN MINISTRY

THE SERMON ON THE MOUNT (cont.) Matt. 7

forth ᵗᵗevil fruit. ₁₈A good tree cannot bring forth evil fruit, neither *can* a corrupt tree bring forth good fruit. ₁₉Every tree that bringeth not forth good fruit is hewn down, and cast into the fire. ₂₀Wherefore by their fruits ye shall know them.

₂₁Not every one that saith unto me, Lord, Lord, shall enter into the kingdom of heaven; but he that doeth the will of my Father which is in heaven. ²⁹For the day soon cometh, that men shall come before me to judgment, to be judged according to their works. ₂₂Many will say to me in that day, Lord, Lord, have we not prophesied in thy name? and in thy name have cast out devils? and in thy name done many wonderful works? ₂₃And then will I profess unto them, I never knew you: depart from me, ye that work ᵘᵘiniquity.

₂₄Therefore whosoever heareth these sayings of mine, and doeth them, I will liken him unto a wise man, which built his house upon ᵛᵛa rock: ₂₅And the rain descended, and the floods came, and the winds blew, and beat upon that house; and it fell not: for it was founded upon a rock. ₂₆And every one that heareth these sayings of mine, and doeth them not, shall be likened unto a foolish man, which built his house upon the sand: ₂₇And the rain descended, and the floods came, and the winds blew, and beat upon that house; and it fell: and great was the fall of it. ₂₈And it came to pass, when Jesus had ended these sayings ³⁰with his disciples, the people were astonished at his doctrine: ₂₉For he taught them as *one* having authority ³¹from God, and not as ³¹having authority from the scribes.

tt GR: corrupt, spoiled, degenerate

29 JST Matt. 7:31

uu GR: lawlessness

vv GR: the rock

30 JST Matt. 7:36

31 JST Matt. 7:37

THE CENTURION'S SERVANT Luke 7:1-10

₁Now when he had ended all his sayings in the audience of the people, he entered into Capernaum.

₂And a certain centurion's servant, who was dear unto him, was sick, and ready to die. ₃And when he heard of Jesus, he sent unto him the elders of the Jews, beseeching him that he would come and heal his servant.

₄And when they came to Jesus, they besought him ᵃinstantly, saying, That he was worthy for whom he should do this: ₅For he loveth our nation, and he hath built us a synagogue.

₆Then Jesus went with them.

And when he was now not far from the house, the centurion sent friends to him, saying unto him, Lord, trouble not thyself: for I am not worthy that thou shouldest enter under my roof: ₇Wherefore neither thought I myself worthy to come unto thee: but say in a word, and my servant shall be healed. ₈For I also am a man set under authority, having under me soldiers, and I say unto one, Go, and he goeth; and to another, Come, and he cometh; and to my servant, Do this, and he

a GR: earnestly

THE GALILEAN MINISTRY

THE CENTURION'S SERVANT (cont.) — Luke 7:1-10

doeth it.

₉When Jesus heard these things, he marvelled at him, and turned him about, and said unto the people that followed him, I say unto you, I have not found so great faith, no, not in Israel. ₁₀And they that were sent, returning to the house, found the servant whole that had been sick.

THE WIDOW'S SON — Luke 7:11-17

₁₁And it came to pass the day after, that he went into a city called Nain; and many of his disciples went with him, and much people. ₁₂Now when he came nigh to the gate of the city, behold, there was a dead man carried out, the only son of his mother, and she was a widow: and much people of the city was with her. ₁₃And when the Lord saw her, he had compassion on her, and said unto her, Weep not. ₁₄And he came and touched the bier: and they that bare *him* stood still. And he said, Young man, I say unto thee, Arise. ₁₅And he that was dead sat up, and began to speak. And he delivered him to his mother. ₁₆And there came a fear on all: and they glorified God, saying, That a great prophet is risen up among us; and, That God hath visited his people. ₁₇And this rumour of him went forth throughout all Judaea, and throughout all the region round about.

PETER'S MOTHER-IN-LAW — Matt. 8:14-15

₁₄And when Jesus was come into Peter's house, he saw his wife's mother ᵃlaid, and sick of a fever. ₁₅And he ᵇtouched her hand, and the fever left her: and she arose, and ministered unto them.

a GR: lying sick and feverish
b GR: took hold of

HE TOOK OUR INFIRMITIES — Matt. 8:16-17

₁₆When the even was come, they brought unto him many that were possessed with devils: and he cast out the spirits with *his* word, and healed all that were sick: ₁₇That it might be fulfilled which was spoken by ᵃEsaias the prophet, saying, ᵇHIMSELFᶜ TOOK OUR INFIRMITIES, AND ᵈBARE OUR SICKNESSES.

a GR: Isaiah
b Isa. 53:4
c GR: he himself
d GR: carried away

DISCIPLES TESTED — Matt. 8:18-22

₁₈Now when Jesus saw great multitudes about him, he gave commandment to depart unto the other side.

₁₉And a certain scribe came, and said unto him, Master, I will follow thee whithersoever thou goest.

₂₀And Jesus saith unto him, The foxes have holes, and the birds of the air *have* nests; but the Son of man hath not where to lay *his* head.

₂₁And another of his disciples said unto him, Lord, ᵃsuffer me first to go and bury my father.

₂₂But Jesus said unto him, Follow me; and let the dead bury their

a GR: allow

FIRST YEAR	THE GALILEAN MINISTRY	
DISCIPLES TESTED (cont.)		**Matt. 8:18-22**

dead: $_{60}$but go thou and preach the kingdom of God. $_{61}$And another also said, Lord, I will follow thee; but let me first go bid them farewell, which are at home at my house. $_{62}$And Jesus said unto him, No man, having put his hand to the plough, and looking back, is fit for the kingdom of God.

1 Luke 9:60-62

JESUS CALMS THE TEMPEST	**Mark 4:35-41**

$_{35}$And the same day, when the even was come, he saith unto them, Let us pass over unto the other side. $_{36}$And when they had sent away the multitude, they took him even as he was in the ship. And there were also with him other little ships. $_{37}$And there arose a great storm of wind, and the waves beat into the ship, so that it was now full. $_{38}$And he was in the hinder part of the ship, asleep on a pillow: and they awake him, and say unto him, Master, carest thou not that we perish? $_{39}$And he arose, and rebuked the wind, and said unto the sea, Peace, be still. And the wind ceased, and there was a great calm. $_{40}$And he said unto them, Why are ye so fearful? how is it that ye have no faith? $_{41}$And they feared exceedingly, and said one to another, What manner of man is this, that even the wind and the sea obey him?

A LEGION OF DEMONS CAST OUT	**Mark 5:1-20**

$_{1}$And they came over unto the other side of the sea, into the country of the ^{1}**Gergesenes**. $_{2}$And when he was come out of the ship, immediately there met him out of the tombs ^{a}a man with an unclean spirit, $_{3}$Who had *his* dwelling among the tombs; and no man could bind him, no, not with chains: $_{4}$Because that he had been often bound with fetters and chains, and the chains had been ^{b}plucked asunder by him, and the fetters broken in pieces: neither could any *man* tame him. $_{5}$And always, night and day, he was in the mountains, and in the tombs, crying, and cutting himself with stones.

$_{6}$But when he saw Jesus afar off, he ran and worshipped him, $_{7}$And cried with a loud voice, and said, What have I to do with thee, Jesus, *thou* Son of the most high God? I adjure thee by God, that thou torment me not. $_{8}$For he said unto him, Come out of the man, *thou* unclean spirit. $_{9}$And he asked him, What *is* thy name? And he answered, saying, My name *is* Legion: for we are many. $_{10}$And he besought him much that he would not send them away out of the country. $_{11}$Now there was there nigh unto the mountains a great herd of swine feeding. $_{12}$And all the devils besought him, saying, Send us into the swine, that we may enter into them. $_{13}$And forthwith Jesus gave them leave. And the unclean spirits went out, and entered into the swine: and the herd ran violently down a steep place into the sea, (they were about two thousand;) and were

1 Matt. 8:28

a Matthew says there were two men. That does not imply a conflict. Mark (and Luke) may have felt that only one was noteworthy.

b IE: broken, taken apart

A LEGION OF DEMONS CAST OUT (cont.)   Mark 5:1-20

ᶜchoked in the sea.   **c** IE: drowned
₁₄And they that fed the swine fled, and told *it* in the city, and in the country. And they went out to see what it was that was done. ₁₅And they come to Jesus, and see him that was possessed with the devil, and had the legion, sitting, and clothed, and in his right mind: and they were afraid.

₁₆And they that saw *it* told them how it befell to him that was possessed with the devil, and *also* concerning the swine. ₁₇And they began to pray him to depart out of their coasts. ₁₈And when he was come into the ship, he that had been possessed with the devil prayed him that he might be with him.

₁₉Howbeit Jesus suffered him not, but saith unto him, Go home to thy friends, and tell them how great things the Lord hath done for thee, and hath had compassion on thee.

₂₀And he departed, and began to publish in Decapolis how great things Jesus had done for him: and all *men* did marvel.

A PARALYTIC MAN HEALED   Mark 2:1-12

₁And again he entered into Capernaum after *some* days; and it was noised that he was ᵃin the house. ₂And straightway many were gathered together, insomuch that there was no room to receive *them*, no, not so much as about the door: and he preached the word unto them.

₃And they come unto him, bringing one sick of the palsy, which was borne of four. ₄And when they could not come nigh unto him for the press, they uncovered the roof where he was: and when they had broken *it* up, they let down the bed wherein the sick of the palsy lay.

₅When Jesus saw their faith, he said unto the sick of the palsy, Son, thy sins be forgiven thee.

₆But there were certain of the scribes sitting there, and reasoning in their hearts, ₇Why doth this *man* thus speak blasphemies? who can forgive sins but God only?

₈And immediately when Jesus perceived in his spirit that they so reasoned within themselves, he said unto them, Why reason ye these things in your hearts? ₉ᵇWhether is it easier to say to the sick of the palsy, *Thy* sins be forgiven thee; or to say, Arise, and take up thy bed, and walk? ₁₀But that ye may know that the Son of man hath power on earth to forgive sins, (he saith to the sick of the palsy,) ₁₁I say unto thee, Arise, and take up thy bed, and go thy way into thine house.

₁₂And immediately he arose, took up the bed, and went forth before them all; insomuch that they were all amazed, and glorified God, saying, We never saw it on this fashion.

a IE: at home

b JST Luke 5:23 reads: "Does it require more power to forgive sins than to make the sick rise up and walk?"

FIRST YEAR — **THE GALILEAN MINISTRY**

THE CALLING OF LEVI (MATTHEW) — Luke 5:27-31

¹₁₃And he went forth again by the sea side; and all the multitude resorted unto him, and he taught them. ₁₄And as he passed by, he ₂₇saw a ᵃpublican, named ᵇLevi, sitting at the ᶜreceipt of custom: and he said unto him, Follow me. ₂₈And he left all, rose up, and followed him.

₂₉And Levi made him a great feast in his own house: and there was a great company of publicans and ²sinners that sat ²also together with Jesus and his disciples. **And when the scribes and Pharisees saw him eat with publicans and sinners, they** ₃₀murmured against his disciples, saying, Why do ye eat and drink with publicans and sinners? ³**When Jesus heard it, he saith** ₃₁unto them, They that are whole ³**have no need of the** physician; but they that are sick. ₃₂I came not to call the righteous, but sinners to repentance.

1 Mark 2:13-14
a a collector of Roman taxes for profit
b This was Matthew.
c GR: tax office
2 Mark 2:16
3 Mark 2:17

A CONFLICT OVER FASTING — Luke 5:33-35

₃₃And they said unto him, Why do the disciples of John fast often, and make prayers, and likewise *the disciples* of the Pharisees; but thine eat and drink? ₃₄And he said unto them, Can ye make the children of the bridechamber fast, while the bridegroom is with them? ₃₅But the days will come, when the bridegroom shall be taken away from them, and then shall they fast in those days.

PARABLE OF THE CLOTH AND THE WINESKINS — Luke 5:36-39

₃₆And he spake also a parable unto them; No man putteth a piece of a new garment upon an old; if otherwise, then both the new maketh a rent, and the piece that was *taken* out of the new ᵃagreeth not with the old. ₃₇And no man putteth new wine into old ᵇbottles; else the new wine will burst the bottles, and be spilled, and the bottles shall perish. ₃₈But new wine must be put into new bottles; and both are preserved. ₃₉No man also having drunk old *wine* straightway desireth new: for he saith, The old is better.

a gr: correspond, i.e., be of a congruous nature
b gr: leather bags or wineskins

HEALING THE WOMAN ON THE WAY WITH JAIRUS — Mark 5:21-34

₂₁And when Jesus was passed over again by ship unto the other side, much people gathered unto him: and he was nigh unto the sea. ₂₂And, behold, there cometh one of the rulers of the synagogue, Jairus by name; and when he saw him, he fell at his feet, ₂₃And besought him greatly, saying, My little daughter lieth at the point of death: *I pray thee,* come and lay thy hands on her, that she may be healed; and she shall live. ₂₄And *Jesus* went with him; and much people followed him, and thronged him.

₂₅And a certain woman, which had an ᵃissue of blood twelve

a GR: hemorrhage

36

FIRST YEAR — THE GALILEAN MINISTRY

HEALING THE WOMAN ON THE WAY WITH JAIRUS (cont.) Mark 5:21-34

years, ₂₆And had suffered many things of many physicians, and had spent all that she had, and was nothing bettered, but rather grew worse, ₂₇When she had heard of Jesus, came in the press behind, and touched his garment. ₂₈For she said, If I may touch but his clothes, I shall be whole. ₂₉And straightway the fountain of her blood was dried up; and she felt in *her* body that she was healed of that plague.

₃₀And Jesus, immediately knowing in himself that ᵇvirtue had gone out of him, turned him about in the press, and said, Who touched my clothes? ₃₁And his disciples said unto him, Thou seest the multitude thronging thee, and sayest thou, Who touched me? ₃₂And he looked round about to see her that had done this thing.

₃₃But the woman fearing and trembling, knowing what was done in her, came and fell down before him, and told him all the truth.

₃₄And he said unto her, Daughter, thy faith hath made thee whole; go in peace, and be whole of thy plague.

b GR: power, strength

THE DAUGHTER OF JAIRUS Mark 5:35-43

₃₅While he yet spake, there came from the ruler of the synagogue's *house certain* which said, Thy daughter is dead: why troublest thou the Master any further? ₃₆As soon as Jesus heard the word that was spoken, he saith unto the ruler of the synagogue, Be not afraid, only believe. ₃₇And he suffered no man to follow him, save Peter, and James, and John the brother of James. ₃₈And he cometh to the house of the ruler of the synagogue, and seeth the tumult, and them that wept and wailed greatly. ₃₉And when he was come in, he saith unto them, Why make ye this ᵃado, and weep? the ᵇdamsel is not dead, but sleepeth. ₄₀And they laughed him to scorn. But when he had put them all out, he taketh the father and the mother of the damsel, and them that were with him, and entereth in where the damsel was lying.

₄₁And he took the damsel by the hand, and said unto her, ᶜTalitha cumi; which is, being interpreted, Damsel, I say unto thee, arise. ₄₂And straightway the damsel arose, and walked; for she was [of the age] of twelve years. And they were astonished with a great astonishment. ₄₃And he charged them straitly that no man should know it; and commanded that something should be given her to eat. ¹**And the fame hereof went abroad into all that land.**

a GR: uproar, tumult

b IE: girl

c AR: Girl arise!

1 Matt. 9:26

TWO BLIND MEN AND A MUTE — Matt. 9:27-34

₂₇And when Jesus departed thence, two blind men followed him, crying, and saying, *Thou* Son of David, have mercy on us. ₂₈And when he was come into the house, the blind men came to him: and Jesus saith unto them, Believe ye that I am able to do this? They said unto him, Yea, Lord. ₂₉Then touched he their eyes, saying, According to your faith be it unto you. ₃₀And their eyes were opened; and Jesus ᵃstraitly charged them, saying, See *that* no man know *it*. ₃₁But they, when they were departed, spread abroad his fame in all that country.

₃₂As they went out, behold, they brought to him a dumb man possessed with a devil. ₃₃And when the devil was cast out, the dumb spake: and the multitudes marvelled, saying, It was never so seen in Israel. ₃₄But the Pharisees said, He casteth out devils through the prince of the devils.

a IE: warned them sternly

MESSENGERS FROM JOHN THE BAPTIST — Matt. 11:2-19

₂Now when John had heard in the prison the works of Christ, he sent two of his disciples, ₃And said unto him, Art thou he that should come, or do we look for another? ₄Jesus answered and said unto them, Go and shew John again those things which ye do hear and see: ₅The blind receive their sight, and the lame walk, the lepers are cleansed, and the deaf hear, the dead are raised up, and the poor have the gospel preached to them. ₆And blessed is [he], whosoever shall not be offended in me.

₇And as they departed, Jesus began to say unto the multitudes concerning John, What went ye out into the wilderness to see? A reed shaken with the wind? ₈But what went ye out for to see? A man clothed in soft raiment? behold, they that wear soft *clothing* are in kings' houses. ₉But what went ye out for to see? A prophet? yea, I say unto you, and more than a prophet. ₁₀For this is [he], of whom it is written, ᵃBEHOLD, I SEND MY MESSENGER BEFORE THY FACE, WHICH SHALL PREPARE THY WAY BEFORE THEE. ₁₁Verily I say unto you, Among them that are born of women there hath not risen a greater than John the Baptist: ᵇnotwithstanding he that is least in the kingdom of heaven is greater than he. ₁₂And from the days of John the Baptist until now the kingdom of heaven suffereth violence, and ᶜthe violent take it by force. ¹But the days will come, when the violent shall have no power; ₁₃For all the prophets and the law prophesied ¹that it should be thus until John. ²Yea, as many as have prophesied have foretold of these days. ₁₄And if ye will receive *it*, ³verily, he was the Elias, which was for to come ⁴and prepare all things. ₁₅He that hath ears to hear, let him hear.

₁₆But whereunto shall I liken this generation? It is like unto children sitting in the markets, and calling unto their fellows, ₁₇And saying, We

a Isa. 40:3; Mal. 3:1

b IE: but he who is less important

c IE: violent men are seizing control of it, or plundering it

1 JST Matt. 11:13

2 JST Matt. 11:14

3 JST Matt. 11:15; KJV: this is

4 JST Matt. 11:15

FIRST YEAR — THE GALILEAN MINISTRY

MESSENGERS FROM JOHN THE BAPTIST (cont.)   Matt. 11:2-19

have piped unto you, and ye have not danced; we have mourned unto you, and ye have not lamented. ₁₈For John came neither eating nor drinking, and they say, He hath a devil. ₁₉The Son of man came eating and drinking, and they say, Behold a man gluttonous, and a ᵈwinebibber, a friend of publicans and sinners. But wisdom is justified of her ᵉchildren.

d GR: drunkard

e GR: deeds, works

JESUS' FEET WASHED; THE TWO DEBTORS *   Luke 7:36-50

₃₆And one of the Pharisees desired him that he would eat with him. And he went into the Pharisee's house, and sat down to meat.

₃₇And, behold, a woman in the city, which was a sinner, when she knew that *Jesus* sat at meat in the Pharisee's house, brought an alabaster box of ointment, ₃₈And stood at his feet behind *him* weeping, and began to wash his feet with tears, and did wipe *them* with the hairs of her head, and kissed his feet, and anointed *them* with the ointment.

₃₉Now when the Pharisee which had bidden him saw *it*, he spake within himself, saying, This man, if he were a prophet, would have known who and what manner of woman *this is* that toucheth him: for she is a sinner.

₄₀And Jesus answering said unto him, Simon, I have somewhat to say unto thee.

And he saith, Master, say on.

₄₁ᵃThere was a certain creditor which had two debtors: the one owed five hundred ᵇpence, and the other fifty. ₄₂And when they had nothing to pay, he frankly forgave them both. Tell me therefore, which of them will love him most?

₄₃Simon answered and said, I suppose that *he*, to whom he forgave most.

And he said unto him, Thou hast rightly judged. ₄₄And he turned to the woman, and said unto Simon, Seest thou this woman? I entered into thine house, thou gavest me no water for my feet: but she hath washed my feet with tears, and wiped *them* with the hairs of her head. ₄₅Thou gavest me no kiss: but this woman since the time I came in hath not ceased to kiss my feet. ₄₆My head with oil thou didst not anoint: but this woman hath anointed my feet with ointment. ₄₇Wherefore I say unto thee, Her sins, which are many, are forgiven; for she loved much: but to whom little is forgiven, *the same* loveth little.

₄₈And he said unto her, Thy sins are forgiven.

₄₉And they that sat at meat with him began to say within themselves, Who is this that forgiveth sins also?

₅₀And he said to the woman, Thy faith hath saved thee; go in peace.

* cf. John 12:1-8 (John's account is not assumed to contradict that of Luke, who places this event much earlier in Jesus' ministry. Again, both have been included.)

a cf. Matt. 18:23-35

b GR: *denarii*; one *denarius* was a poor workman's daily wage

SECOND YEAR — THE GALILEAN MINISTRY

THE INVALID OF BETHESDA — John 5:1-13

₁After this there was ᵃa feast of the Jews; and Jesus went up to Jerusalem. ₂Now there is at Jerusalem by the sheep *market* a pool, which is called in the Hebrew tongue Bethesda, having five porches. ₃In these lay a great multitude of impotent folk, of blind, halt, withered, waiting for the moving of the water. ₄For an angel went down at a certain season into the pool, and troubled the water: whosoever then first after the troubling of the water stepped in was made whole of whatsoever disease he had.

₅And a certain man was there, which had an infirmity thirty and eight years. ₆When Jesus saw him lie, and knew that he had been now a long time *in that case*, he saith unto him, Wilt thou be made whole?

₇The impotent man answered him, Sir, I have no man, when the water is troubled, to put me into the pool: but while I am coming, another steppeth down before me.

₈Jesus saith unto him, Rise, take up thy bed, and walk. ₉And immediately the man was made whole, and took up his bed, and walked: and on the same day was the sabbath.

₁₀The Jews therefore said unto him that was cured, It is the sabbath day: it is not lawful for thee to carry *thy* bed.

₁₁He answered them, He that made me whole, the same said unto me, Take up thy bed, and walk.

₁₂Then asked they him, What man is that which said unto thee, Take up thy bed, and walk? ₁₃And he that was healed wist not who it was: for Jesus had conveyed himself away, a multitude being in *that* place.

ᵃ "the feast" in many mss., implying the Passover

IDENTITY, MISSION AND WITNESSES OF CHRIST — John 5:14-47

₁₄Afterward Jesus findeth him in the temple, and said unto him, Behold, thou art made whole: sin no more, lest a worse thing come unto thee.

₁₅The man departed, and told the Jews that it was Jesus, which had made him whole. ₁₆And therefore did the Jews persecute Jesus, and sought to slay him, because he had done these things on the sabbath day.

₁₇But Jesus answered them, My Father worketh hitherto, and I work. ₁₈Therefore the Jews sought the more to kill him, because he not only had broken the sabbath, but said also that God was his Father, making himself equal with God.

₁₉Then answered Jesus and said unto them, Verily, verily, I say unto you, The Son can do nothing of himself, but what he seeth the Father do: for what things soever he doeth, these also doeth the Son likewise.

40

THE GALILEAN MINISTRY

SECOND YEAR

IDENTITY, MISSION AND WITNESSES OF CHRIST (cont.)   John 5:14-47

₂₀For the Father loveth the Son, and sheweth him all things that himself doeth: and he will shew him greater works than these, that ye may marvel. ₂₁For as the Father raiseth up the dead, and quickeneth *them*; even so the Son quickeneth whom he will. ₂₂For the Father judgeth no man, but hath committed all judgment unto the Son: ₂₃That all *men* should honour the Son, even as they honour the Father. He that honoureth not the Son honoureth not the Father which hath sent him.

   ₂₄Verily, verily, I say unto you, He that heareth my word, and believeth on him that sent me, hath everlasting life, and shall not come into condemnation; but is passed from death unto life. ₂₅Verily, verily, I say unto you, The hour is coming, and now is, when the dead shall hear the voice of the Son of God: and they that hear shall live. ₂₆For as the Father hath life in himself; so hath he given to the Son to have life in himself; ₂₇And hath given him authority to execute judgment also, because he is the Son of man. ₂₈Marvel not at this: for the hour is coming, in the which all that are in the graves shall hear his voice, ₂₉And shall come forth; they that have done good, unto the resurrection of life; and they that have done evil, unto the resurrection of damnation.

   ₃₀I can of mine own self do nothing: as I hear, I judge: and my judgment is just; because I seek not mine own will, but the will of the Father which hath sent me. ₃₁If I bear witness of myself, my witness is not true.

   ₃₂There is another that beareth witness of me; and I know that the witness which he witnesseth of me is true. ₃₃Ye sent unto John, and he bare witness unto the truth. **¹**<u>And he received not his</u> ₃₄testimony from man: but **²**<u>of God, and ye yourselves say that he is a prophet, therefore ye ought to receive his testimony.</u> These things I say, that ye might be saved. ₃₅He was a burning and a shining light: and ye were willing for a season to rejoice in his light.

   ₃₆But I have **³**<u>a</u> greater witness than **⁴**<u>the testimony</u> of John: for the works which the Father hath given me to finish, the same works that I do, bear witness of me, that the Father hath sent me. ₃₇And the Father himself, which hath sent me, hath borne witness of me. Ye have neither heard his voice at any time, nor seen his shape. ₃₈And ye have not his word abiding in you: for whom he hath sent, him ye believe not.

   ₃₉Search the scriptures; for in them ye think ye have eternal life: and they are they which testify of me. ₄₀And ye will not come to me, that ye might have life. ₄₁I receive not honour from men. ₄₂But I know you, that ye have not the love of God in you.

   ₄₃I am come in my Father's name, and ye receive me not: if another shall come in his own name, him ye will receive. ₄₄How can ye believe, which receive honour one of another, and seek not the honour that *cometh* from God only?

---

1 JST John 5:35; KJV: But I receive not

2 JST John 5:35

3 JST John 5:37

4 JST John 5:37; kjv: *that*

| SECOND YEAR | THE GALILEAN MINISTRY | |

IDENTITY, MISSION AND WITNESSES OF CHRIST (cont.) — John 5:14-47

₄₅Do not think that I will accuse you to the Father: there is *one* that accuseth you, *even* Moses, in whom ye trust. ₄₆For had ye believed Moses, ye would have believed me: for he wrote of me. ₄₇But if ye believe not his writings, how shall ye believe my words?

THE HARVEST IS PLENTEOUS — Matt. 9:35-38

₃₅And Jesus went about all the cities and villages, teaching in their synagogues, and preaching the gospel of the kingdom, and healing every sickness and every disease among the people.

₃₆But when he saw the multitudes, he was moved with compassion on them, because they ᵃfainted, and were scattered abroad, as sheep having no shepherd.

₃₇Then saith he unto his disciples, The harvest truly *is* plenteous, but the labourers *are* few; ₃₈Pray ye therefore the Lord of the harvest, that he will send forth labourers into his harvest.

a GR: were harassed

MARY CALLED MAGDALENE — Luke 8:1-3

₁And it came to pass afterward, that he went throughout every city and village, preaching and shewing the glad tidings of the kingdom of God: and the twelve *were* with him, ₂And certain women, which had been healed of evil spirits and infirmities, Mary called ᵃMagdalene, out of whom went seven devils, ₃And Joanna the wife of Chuza Herod's steward, and Susanna, and many others, which ministered unto him of their substance.

a IE: of the city Magdala

THE SABBATH MADE FOR MAN — Mark 2:23-28

₂₃And it came to pass, that he went through the corn fields on the sabbath day; and his disciples began, as they went, ᵃto pluck the ears of corn.

₂₄And the Pharisees said unto him, Behold, why do they on the sabbath day that which is not lawful?

₂₅And he said unto them, Have ye never read what David did, when he had need, and was an hungred, he, and they that were with him? ₂₆ᵇHow he went into the house of God in the days of Abiathar the high priest, and did eat the shewbread, which is not lawful to eat but for the priests, and gave also to them which were with him?

₂₇And he said unto them, The sabbath was made for man, and not man for the sabbath: ¹₂₆Wherefore the Sabbath was given unto man for a day of rest; and also that man should glorify God, and not that man should not eat; ₂₇For the Son of Man made the Sabbath day, ₂₈Therefore the Son of man is Lord also of the sabbath.

a GR: occasionally picking some grain

b 1 Sam. 21:1-6

1 JST Mark 2:26-27

SECOND YEAR — THE GALILEAN MINISTRY

THE MAN WITH THE WITHERED HAND — Luke 6:6-11

₆And it came to pass also on another sabbath, that he entered into the synagogue and taught: and there was a man whose right hand was withered. ₇And the scribes and Pharisees watched him, whether he would heal on the sabbath day; that they might find an accusation against him.

₈But he knew their thoughts, and said to the man which had the withered hand, Rise up, and stand forth in the midst. And he arose and stood forth.

₉Then said Jesus unto them, **¹₁₁What man shall there be among you, that shall have one sheep, and if it fall into a pit on the sabbath day, will he not lay hold on it, and lift** *it* **out?** ₁₂How much then is a man better than a sheep? Wherefore it is lawful to do well on the sabbath days.

₁₃Then saith he to the man, Stretch forth thine hand. And he stretched *it* forth; and it was restored whole, like as the other.

₁₄Then the Pharisees went out, and held a council against him, how they might destroy him.

1 Matt. 12:11-14

A MULTITUDE ON THE SEA SHORE — Mark 3:7-12

₇But Jesus withdrew himself with his disciples to the sea: and a great multitude from Galilee followed him, and from Judaea, ₈And from Jerusalem, and from Idumaea, and *from* beyond Jordan; and they about Tyre and Sidon, a great multitude, when they had heard what great things he did, came unto him. ₉And he spake to his disciples, that a small ship should wait on him because of the multitude, lest they should throng him. ₁₀For he had healed many; insomuch that they ᵃpressed upon him for to touch him, as many as had plagues. ₁₁And unclean spirits, when they saw him, fell down before him, and cried, saying, Thou art the Son of God. ₁₂And he straitly charged them that they should not make him known. **¹₁₇That it might be fulfilled which was spoken by Esaias the prophet, saying,** ₁₈ᵇBEHOLD MY ᶜSERVANT, WHOM I HAVE CHOSEN; MY BELOVED, IN WHOM MY SOUL IS WELL PLEASED: I WILL PUT MY SPIRIT UPON HIM, AND HE SHALL SHEW JUDGMENT TO THE GENTILES. ₁₉HE SHALL NOT STRIVE, NOR ᵈCRY; NEITHER SHALL ANY MAN HEAR HIS VOICE IN THE STREETS. ₂₀A BRUISED REED SHALL HE NOT BREAK, AND SMOKING FLAX SHALL HE NOT QUENCH, TILL HE SEND FORTH JUDGMENT UNTO VICTORY. ₂₁AND IN HIS NAME SHALL THE ᵉGENTILES TRUST.

a GR: rushed impetuously
1 Matt. 12:17-21
b Isa. 14:1-4
c GR: son, child
d GR: cry for help
e GR: Nations

SECOND YEAR   THE GALILEAN MINISTRY

BLASPHEMY AGAINST THE HOLY GHOST   Matt. 12:22-37

₂₂Then was brought unto him one possessed with a devil, blind, and dumb: and he healed him, insomuch that the blind and dumb both spake and saw.
₂₃And all the people were amazed, and said, Is not this the son of David? ₂₄But when the Pharisees heard *it*, they said, This *fellow* doth not cast out devils, but by Beelzebub the prince of the devils.
₂₅And Jesus knew their thoughts, and said unto them, Every kingdom divided against itself is brought to desolation; and every city or house divided against itself shall not stand: ₂₆And if Satan cast out Satan, he is divided against himself; how shall then his kingdom stand? ₂₇And if I by Beelzebub cast out devils, by whom do your children cast *them* out? therefore they shall be your judges. ₂₈But if I cast out devils by the Spirit of God, then the kingdom of God is come unto you. ¹For they also cast out devils by the Spirit of God, for unto them is given power over devils, that they may cast them out. ₂₉Or else how can one enter into a strong man's house, and ᵃspoil his goods, except he first bind the strong man? and then he will spoil his house. ₃₀He that is not with me is against me; and he that gathereth not with me scattereth abroad.
₃₁Wherefore I say unto you, All manner of sin and blasphemy shall be forgiven unto men ²who receive me and repent: but the blasphemy *against* the *Holy* Ghost shall not be forgiven unto men. ₃₂And whosoever speaketh a word against the Son of man, it shall be forgiven him: but whosoever speaketh against the Holy Ghost, it shall not be forgiven him, neither in this world, neither in the *world* to come.
₃₃Either make the tree good, and his fruit good; or else make the tree corrupt, and his fruit corrupt: for the tree is known by [his] fruit. ₃₄O generation of vipers, how can ye, being evil, speak good things? for out of the abundance of the heart the mouth speaketh. ₃₅A good man out of the good treasure of the heart bringeth forth good things: and an evil man out of the evil treasure bringeth forth evil things.
₃₆But I say unto you, That every idle word that men shall speak, they shall give account thereof in the day of judgment. ₃₇For by thy words thou shalt be justified, and by thy words thou shalt be condemned.

1 JST Matt. 12:23
a GR: plunder
2 JST Matt. 12:26

WE WOULD SEE A SIGN FROM THEE   Matt. 12:38-42

₃₈Then certain of the scribes and of the Pharisees answered, saying, Master, we would see a sign from thee.
₃₉But he answered and said unto them, An evil and adulterous generation seeketh after a sign; and there shall no sign be given to it, but the sign of the prophet ᵃJonas: ₄₀For as ᵇJONAS WAS THREE DAYS AND THREE NIGHTS IN THE ᶜWHALE'S BELLY; so shall the Son of man be three

a GR: Jonah
b Jonah 1:17
c GR: sea monster, whale or huge fish

44

SECOND YEAR — THE GALILEAN MINISTRY

WE WOULD SEE A SIGN FROM THEE (cont.) — Matt. 12:28-42

days and three nights in the heart of the earth.

₄₁The men of Nineveh shall rise in judgment with this generation, and shall condemn it: because they repented at the preaching of Jonas; and, behold, a greater than Jonas *is* here.

₄₂The queen of the south shall rise up in the judgment with this generation, and shall condemn it: ᵈfor she came from the uttermost parts of the earth to hear the wisdom of Solomon; and, behold, a greater than Solomon *is* here.

d 1 Kings 10:1-13

WHEN THE UNCLEAN SPIRIT IS GONE OUT — Matt. 12:43-45

¹Then came some of the scribes and said unto him, Master, it is written that, Every sin shall be forgiven; but ye say, Whosoever speaketh against the Holy Ghost shall not be forgiven.

And they asked him, saying, How can these things be? ²And then said unto them, ₄₃When the unclean spirit is gone out of a man, he walketh through dry places, seeking rest and findeth none; ²but when a man speaketh against the Holy Ghost, ₄₄then he saith, I will return into my house from whence I came out; and when he is come, he findeth him empty, swept and garnished; ²for the good spirit leaveth him unto himself.

₄₅Then goeth ³the evil spirit, and taketh with himself seven other spirits more wicked than himself, and they enter in and dwell there: and the last *state* of that man is worse than the first. Even so shall it be also unto this wicked generation.

1 JST Matt. 12:37
2 JST Matt. 12:38
3 JST Matt. 12:39; KJV: he

BROTHER, AND SISTER, AND MOTHER — Matt. 12:46-50

₄₆While he yet talked to the people, behold, *his* mother and his brethren stood ªwithout, desiring to speak with him.

₄₇Then one said unto him, Behold, thy mother and thy brethren stand without, desiring to speak with thee.

₄₈But he answered and said unto him that told him, Who is my mother? and who are my brethren? ₄₉And he stretched forth his hand toward his disciples, and said, Behold my mother and my brethren! ₅₀For whosoever shall do the will of my Father which is in heaven, the same is my brother, and sister, and mother.

a IE: outside

PARABLE OF THE SOWER — Mark 4:1-20

₁And he began again to teach by the sea side: and there was gathered unto him a great multitude, so that he entered into a ship, and sat in the sea; and the whole multitude was by the sea on the land.

₂And he taught them many things by parables, and said unto them in his doctrine,

SECOND YEAR — THE GALILEAN MINISTRY

PARABLE OF THE SOWER (cont.) Mark 4:1-20

₃Hearken; Behold, there went out a sower to sow: ₄And it came to pass, as he sowed, some fell by the way side, and the fowls of the air came and devoured it up. ₅And some fell on stony ground, where it had not much earth; and immediately it sprang up, because it had no depth of earth: ₆But when the sun was up, it was scorched; and because it had no root, it withered away. ₇And some fell among thorns, and the thorns grew up, and choked it, and it yielded no fruit. ₈And other fell on good ground, and did yield fruit that sprang up and increased; and brought forth, some thirty, and some sixty, and some an hundred.

₉And he said unto them, He that hath ears to hear, let him hear.

₁₀And when he was alone ¹with the twelve, and they that believed in him, they that were about him with the twelve asked of him the parable. ₁₁And he said unto them, Unto you it is given to know the mystery of the kingdom of God: but unto them that are without, all *these* things are done in parables: ²₁₂**For whosoever** ³receiveth, **to him shall be given, and he shall have more abundance; but whosoever** ⁴continueth not to receive, **from him shall be taken away even that he hath.** ₁₃Therefore speak I to them in parables: because they seeing see not; and hearing they hear not, neither do they understand.

₁₄And in them is fulfilled the prophecy of Esaias, which saith, ᵃBY HEARING YE SHALL HEAR, AND SHALL NOT UNDERSTAND; AND SEEING YE SHALL SEE, AND SHALL NOT PERCEIVE: ₁₅FOR THIS PEOPLE'S HEART IS WAXED GROSS, AND *THEIR* EARS ARE DULL OF HEARING, AND THEIR EYES THEY HAVE CLOSED; LEST AT ANY TIME THEY SHOULD SEE WITH *THEIR* EYES, AND HEAR WITH *THEIR* EARS, AND SHOULD UNDERSTAND WITH *THEIR* HEART, AND SHOULD BE CONVERTED, AND I SHOULD HEAL THEM.

₁₆But blessed *are* your eyes, for they see: and your ears, for they hear. ₁₇For verily I say unto you, That many prophets and righteous *men* have desired to see *those things* which ye see, and have not seen *them*; and to hear *those things* which ye hear, and have not heard *them*.

₁₃And he said unto them, Know ye not this parable? and how then will ye know all parables? The sower soweth the word. ⁵₁₈ᵇ**Hear ye therefore the parable of the sower.**

₁₉When any one heareth the word of the kingdom, and understandeth *it* not, then cometh the wicked *one*, and catcheth away that which was sown in his heart. This is he which received seed by the way side.

₂₀But he that received the seed into stony places, the same is he that heareth the word, and anon with joy receiveth it; ₂₁Yet hath he not root in himself, but dureth for a while: for when tribulation or persecution ariseth because of the word, by and by ᶜhe is offended.

---

1 JST Mark 4:9

2 Matt. 13:12-17

3 JST Matt. 13:10; KJV: hath

4 JST Matt. 13:11; KJV: hath not

a Isa. 6:9-10

5 Matt. 13:18-23

b GR: learn, understand

PARABLE OF THE SOWER (cont.) — Mark 4:1-20

₂₂He also that received seed among the thorns is he that heareth the word; and the care of this world, and the deceitfulness of riches, choke the word, and he becometh unfruitful. ₂₃But he that received seed into the good ground is he that heareth the word, and understandeth ⁶and endureth; which also beareth fruit, and bringeth forth, some an hundredfold, some sixty, some thirty.

c GR: he stumbles, falls away

6 JST Matt. 13:21; KJV: *it*

PARABLE OF THE CANDLE — Mark 4:21-25

₂₁And he said unto them, Is a ᵃcandle brought to be put under a bushel, or under a bed? and not to be set on a ᵇcandlestick? ₂₂For there is nothing hid, which shall not be manifested; neither was any thing kept secret, but that it should come abroad. ₂₃If any man have ears to hear, let him hear.

₂₄And he said unto them, Take heed what ye hear: with what measure ye ᶜmete, it shall be measured to you: and unto you that ¹continue to receive, shall more be given. ₂₅For he that ²receiveth, to him shall be given: ³but he that ⁴continueth not to receive, from him shall be taken even that which he hath.

a GR: lamp

b GR: lampstand

c GR: measure

1 JST Mark 4:20; KJV: hear

2 JST Mark 4:20; KJV: hath

3 JST Mark 4:20; KJV: and

4 JST Mark 4:20; KJV: hath not

PARABLE OF WHEAT AND TARES — Matt. 13:24-30

₂₄Another parable put he forth unto them, saying, The kingdom of heaven is likened unto a man which sowed good seed in his field: ₂₅But while men slept, his enemy came and sowed ᵃtares among the wheat, and went his way. ₂₆But when the blade was sprung up, and brought forth fruit, then appeared the tares also.

₂₇So the servants of the householder came and said unto him, Sir, didst not thou sow good seed in thy field? from whence then hath it tares?

₂₈He said unto them, An enemy hath done this.

The servants said unto him, Wilt thou then that we go and gather them up?

₂₉But he said, Nay; lest while ye gather up the tares, ye root up also the wheat with them. ₃₀Let both grow together until the harvest: and in the time of harvest I will say to the reapers, Gather ye together first the ¹wheat into my barn; and ²the tares are bound in bundles ³to be burned.

a A weed, usually called "darnel."

1 JST Matt. 13:29; KJV: tares

2 JST Matt. 13:29; KJV: bind them

3 JST Matt. 13:29; KJV: to burn them: but gather the wheat into my barn. (The change reverses the order in which the wheat and the tares are gathered.)

PARABLE OF THE MUSTARD SEED — Matt. 13:31-32

₃₁Another parable put he forth unto them, saying, The kingdom of heaven is like to a grain of mustard seed, which a man took, and sowed

SECOND YEAR	THE GALILEAN MINISTRY	
PARABLE OF THE MUSTARD SEED		**Matt. 13:31-32**

in his field: ₃₂Which indeed is the least of all seeds: but when it is grown, it is the greatest among herbs, and becometh a tree, ᵃso that the birds of the air come and lodge in the branches thereof.	**a** An idiomatic Hebrew saying. See Ezek. 17:23; 31:6; Ps. 104:12; Dan. 4:12

PARABLE OF THE LEAVEN	**Matt. 13:33**
₃₃Another parable spake he unto them; The kingdom of heaven is like unto ᵃleaven, which a woman took, and hid in three measures of meal, till the whole was leavened.	**a** GR: yeast

WITHOUT A PARABLE SPAKE HE NOT	**Matt. 13:34-35**
₃₄All these things spake Jesus unto the multitude in parables; and without a parable spake he not unto them: ₃₅That it might be fulfilled which was spoken by the prophet, saying, ᵃI WILL OPEN MY MOUTH IN PARABLES; I WILL UTTER THINGS WHICH HAVE BEEN KEPT SECRET FROM THE FOUNDATION OF THE WORLD.	**a** Ps. 78:2

PARABLE OF WHEAT AND TARES EXPLAINED	**Matt. 13:36-43**
₃₆Then Jesus sent the multitude away, and went into the house: and his disciples came unto him, saying, Declare unto us the parable of the tares of the field. ₃₇He answered and said unto them, He that soweth the good seed is the Son of man; ₃₈The field is the world; the good seed are the children of the kingdom; but the tares are the children of the wicked *one*; ₃₉The enemy that sowed them is the devil; the harvest is the end of the world, ¹or the destruction of the wicked, and the reapers are the angels, ²or the messengers sent of heaven. ₄₀As therefore the tares are gathered and burned in the fire; so shall it be in the end of this world, ³or the destruction of the wicked. ⁴For in that day, before ₄₁the Son of man ⁴shall come, he shall send forth his angels ⁴and messengers of heaven, and they shall gather out of his kingdom all things that offend, and them which do iniquity; ₄₂And shall cast them ⁵out among the wicked; and there shall be wailing and gnashing of teeth. ⁶For the world shall be burned with fire. ₄₃ᵃTHEN SHALL THE RIGHTEOUS SHINE FORTH AS THE SUN in the kingdom of their Father. Who hath ears to hear, let him hear. ⁷₁Verily, thus saith the Lord unto you my servants, concerning the parable of the wheat and of the tares: ₂Behold, verily I say, the field was the world, and the apostles were the sowers of the seed; ₃And after they have fallen asleep the great persecutor of the church, the apostate, the whore, even Babylon, that maketh all nations to drink of her cup, in whose hearts the enemy, even Satan, sitteth to reign—behold he soweth the tares; wherefore, the tares choke the wheat and drive the church into the wilderness.	**a** Dan. 12:3 **1** JST Matt. 13:39 **2** JST Matt. 13:40 **3** JST Matt. 13:41 **4** JST Matt. 13:42 **5** JST Matt. 13:43; into a furnace of fire **6** JST Matt. 13:44 **7** D&C 86:1-7

SECOND YEAR — THE GALILEAN MINISTRY

PARABLE OF WHEAT AND TARES EXPLAINED (cont.) — Matt. 13:36-43

₄But behold, in the last days, even now while the Lord is beginning to bring forth the word, and the blade is springing up and is yet tender—₅Behold, verily I say unto you, the angels are crying unto the Lord day and night, who are ready and waiting to be sent forth to reap down the fields; ₆But the Lord saith unto them, pluck not up the tares while the blade is yet tender (for verily your faith is weak), lest you destroy the wheat also.

₇Therefore, let the wheat and the tares grow together until the harvest is fully ripe; then ye shall first gather out the wheat from among the tares, and after the gathering of the wheat, behold and lo, the tares are bound in bundles, and the field remaineth to be burned.

THE KINGDOM OF HEAVEN IS LIKE UNTO... — Matt. 13:44-53

₄₄Again, the kingdom of heaven is like unto treasure hid in a field; the which when a man hath found, he hideth, and for joy thereof goeth and selleth all that he hath, and buyeth that field.

₄₅Again, the kingdom of heaven is like unto a merchant man, seeking goodly pearls: ₄₆Who, when he had found one pearl of great price, went and sold all that he had, and bought it.

₄₇Again, the kingdom of heaven is like unto a net, that was cast into the sea, and gathered of every kind: ₄₈Which, when it was full, they drew to shore, and sat down, and gathered the good into vessels, but cast the bad away.

₄₉So shall it be at the end of the world: ¹And the world is the children of the wicked. The angels shall come forth, and sever the wicked from among the just, ₅₀And shall cast them ²out into the world to be burned. There shall be wailing and gnashing of teeth.

₅₁Jesus saith unto them, Have ye understood all these things? They say unto him, Yea, Lord.

₅₂Then said he unto them, Therefore every scribe ᵃwhich is instructed unto the kingdom of heaven is like unto a man *that is* an householder, which bringeth forth out of his treasure *things* new and old.

₅₃And it came to pass, *that* when Jesus had finished these parables, he departed thence.

1 JST Matt. 13:50
2 JST Matt. 13:51; kjv: into the furnace of fire
a GR: which has become a disciple in

JESUS IN NAZARETH AGAIN — Mark 6:1-6

₁And he went out from thence, and came into his own country; and his disciples follow him.

₂And when the sabbath day was come, he began to teach in the synagogue: and many hearing *him* were astonished, saying, From whence hath this *man* these things? and what wisdom *is* this which is given unto him, that even such mighty works are wrought by his hands?

₃Is not this the carpenter, the son of Mary, the brother of ᵃJames, and

a GR: Jacob

SECOND YEAR — THE GALILEAN MINISTRY

JESUS IN NAZARETH AGAIN (cont.) — Mark 6:1-6

Joses, and of Juda, and Simon? and are not his sisters here with us? And they were offended at him.

₄But Jesus said unto them, A prophet is not without honour, but in his own country, and among his own kin, and in his own house. ₅And he could there do no mighty work, save that he laid his hands upon a few sick folk, and healed *them*. ₆And he marvelled because of their unbelief. And he went round about the villages, teaching.

THE DEATH OF JOHN THE BAPTIST — Mark 6:14-29

₁₄And king Herod heard *of him*; (for his name was spread abroad:) and he said, That John the Baptist was risen from the dead, and therefore mighty works do shew forth themselves in him. ₁₅Others said, That it is ᵃElias. And others said, That it is a prophet, or as one of the prophets.

₁₆But when Herod heard *thereof*, he said, It is John, whom I beheaded: he is risen from the dead. ₁₇For Herod himself had sent forth and laid hold upon John, and bound him in prison for Herodias' sake, his brother Philip's wife: for he had married her. ₁₈For John had said unto Herod, It is not lawful for thee to have thy brother's wife. ₁₉Therefore Herodias had a quarrel against him, and would have killed him; but she could not: ₂₀For Herod feared John, knowing that he was a ᵇjust man and an holy ¹man, and one who feared God, and ᶜobserved ¹to worship him; and when he heard him, he did many things ¹for him, and heard him gladly.

₂₁And when a convenient day was come, that Herod on his birthday made a supper to his ᵈlords, high captains, and chief *estates* of Galilee; ₂₂And when the daughter of the said Herodias came in, and danced, and pleased Herod and them that sat with him, the king said unto the damsel, Ask of me whatsoever thou wilt, and I will give *it* thee. ₂₃And he sware unto her, Whatsoever thou shalt ask of me, I will give *it* thee, unto the half of my kingdom.

₂₄And she went forth, and said unto her mother, What shall I ask? And she said, The head of John the Baptist.

₂₅And she came in straightway with haste unto the king, and asked, saying, I will that thou give me ᵉby and by in a ᶠcharger the head of John the Baptist.

₂₆And the king was exceeding sorry; *yet* for his oath's sake, and for their sakes which sat with him, he would not reject her.

₂₇And immediately the king sent an executioner, and commanded his head to be brought: and he went and beheaded him in the prison, ₂₈And brought his head in a charger, and gave it to the damsel: and the damsel gave it to her mother.

₂₉And when his disciples heard *of it*, they came and took up his corpse, and laid it in a tomb.

a GR: Elijah
b GR: righteous and holy man
1 JST Mark 6:21
c GR: protected
d GR: nobles, military commanders, and prominent men
e GR: at once
f IE: platter

THIRD YEAR

THE GALILEAN MINISTRY

FEEDING THE FIVE THOUSAND John 6:1-15

₁₃₀And the apostles gathered themselves together unto Jesus, and told him all things, both what they had done, and what they had taught.

₃₁And he said unto them, Come ye yourselves apart into a ²solitary place, and rest a while: for there were many coming and going, and they had no leisure so much as to eat.

₃₂And they departed into a ³solitary place by ship privately ₁over the sea of Galilee, which is *the sea* of Tiberias. ⁴And the people saw them departing, and many knew him, and ran afoot thither out of all cities, and outwent them, and came together unto him.

₃And Jesus went up into a mountain, and there he sat with his disciples. ₄And the passover, a feast of the Jews, was nigh. ₅When Jesus then lifted up *his* eyes, and saw a great company come unto him, ⁵**and was moved with compassion toward them, because they were as sheep not having a shepherd: and he began to teach them many things** ⁶₁₄**and he healed their sick.**

₁₅And when it was evening, his disciples came to him, saying, ⁷₃₅This is a ⁸solitary place, and now the time ⁹for departure is come, ₃₆Send them away, that they may go into the country round about, and into the villages, and buy themselves bread: for they have nothing to eat.

¹⁰**But Jesus said unto them, They need not depart; give ye them to eat.** He saith unto Philip, Whence shall we buy bread, that these may eat? ₆And this he said to prove him: for he himself knew what he would do.

₇Philip answered him, Two hundred pennyworth of bread is not sufficient for them, that every one of them may take a little.

₈One of his disciples, Andrew, Simon Peter's brother, saith unto him, ₉There is a lad here, which hath five barley loaves, and two small fishes: but what are they among so many?

₁₀And Jesus said, Make the men sit down. Now there was much grass in the place. So the men sat down, in number about five thousand.

₁₁And Jesus took the loaves; and when he had given thanks, he distributed to the disciples, and the disciples to them that were set down; and likewise of the fishes as much as they would.

₁₂When they were filled, he said unto his disciples, Gather up the fragments that remain, that nothing be lost. ₁₃Therefore they gathered *them* together, and filled twelve baskets with the fragments of the five barley loaves, which remained over and above unto them that had eaten. ₁₄Then those men, when they had seen the miracle that Jesus did, said, This is of a truth that prophet that should come into the world.

1 Mark 6:30-32
2 JST Mark 6:32; KJV: desert
3 JST Mark 6:33; KJV: desert
4 Mark 6:33
5 Mark 6:34
6 Matt. 14:14-15
7 Mark 6:35-36
8 JST Mark 6:36; KJV: desert
9 JST Mark 6:36; KJV: *is* far passed:
10 Matt. 14:16

THE GALILEAN MINISTRY

WALKING UPON THE SEA — Mark 6:45-52

₄₅And straightway he constrained his disciples to get into the ship, and to go to the other side before unto Bethsaida, while he sent away the people. ₄₆And when he had ᵃsent them away, he departed into a mountain to pray.

₄₇And when even was come, the ship was in the midst of the sea, and he alone on the land. ₄₈And he saw them toiling in rowing; for the wind was contrary unto them: and about the fourth watch of the night he cometh unto them, walking upon the sea, and would have passed by them.

₄₉But when they saw him walking upon the sea, they supposed it had been a spirit, and cried out: ₅₀For they all saw him, and were ᵇtroubled. And immediately he talked with them, and saith unto them, Be of good cheer: it is I; be not afraid.

¹₂₈And Peter answered him and said, Lord, if it be thou, bid me come unto thee on the water.

₂₉And he said, Come.

And when Peter was come down out of the ship, he walked on the water, to go to Jesus. ₃₀But when he saw the wind boisterous, he was afraid; and beginning to sink, he cried, saying, Lord, save me.

₃₁And immediately Jesus stretched forth *his* hand, and caught him, and said unto him, O thou of little faith, wherefore didst thou doubt?

₃₂And when they were come into the ship, the wind ceased. ₃₃Then they that were in the ship came and worshipped him, saying, Of a truth thou art the Son of God.

a GR: bid them farewell
b IE: terrified
1 Matt. 14:28-33

HEALING AT GENNESARET — Mark 6:53-56

₅₃And when they had passed over, they came into the land of ᵃGennesaret, and drew to the shore. ₅₄And when they were come out of the ship, straightway they knew him, ₅₅And ran through that whole region round about, and began to carry about in beds those that were sick, where they heard he was.

₅₆And whithersoever he entered, into villages, or cities, or country, they laid the sick in the streets, and besought him that they might touch if it were but the border of his garment: and as many as touched him were made whole.

a OT: Chimmeroth Refers to the area around the Sea of Galilee.

| THIRD YEAR | THE GALILEAN MINISTRY |

THE BREAD OF LIFE — John 6:22-59

₂₂The day following, when the people which ᵃstood on the other side of the sea saw that there was none other boat there, save that one whereinto his disciples were entered, and that Jesus went not with his disciples into the boat, but *that* his disciples were gone away alone; ₂₃(Howbeit there came other boats from Tiberias nigh unto the place where they did eat bread, after that the Lord had given thanks:) ₂₄When the people therefore saw that Jesus was not there, neither his disciples, they also took shipping, and came to Capernaum, seeking for Jesus.

₂₅And when they had found him on the other side of the sea, they said unto him, Rabbi, when camest thou hither?

₂₆Jesus answered them and said, Verily, verily, I say unto you, Ye seek me, not because ye ¹desire to keep my sayings, neither because ye saw the miracles, but because ye did eat of the loaves, and were filled. ₂₇Labour not for the meat which perisheth, but for that meat which endureth unto everlasting life, which the Son of man shall give unto you: for him hath God the Father sealed.

₂₈Then said they unto him, What shall we do, that we might work the works of God?

₂₉Jesus answered and said unto them, This is the work of God, that ye believe on him whom he hath sent.

₃₀They said therefore unto him, What sign shewest thou then, that we may see, and believe thee? what dost thou work? ₃₁Our fathers did eat manna in the desert; as it is written, ᵇHE GAVE THEM BREAD FROM HEAVEN TO EAT.

₃₂Then Jesus said unto them, Verily, verily, I say unto you, Moses gave you not that bread from heaven; but my Father giveth you the true bread from heaven. ₃₃For the bread of God is he which cometh down from heaven, and giveth life unto the world.

₃₄Then said they unto him, Lord, evermore give us this bread.

₃₅And Jesus said unto them, I am the bread of life: he that cometh to me shall never hunger; and he that believeth on me shall never thirst. ₃₆But I said unto you, That ye also have seen me, and believe not. ₃₇All that the Father giveth me shall come to me; and him that cometh to me I will in no wise cast out. ₃₈For I came down from heaven, not to do mine own will, but the will of him that sent me. ₃₉And this is the Father's will which hath sent me, that of all which he hath given me I should lose nothing, but should raise it up again at the last day. ₄₀And this is the will of him that sent me, that every one which seeth the Son, and believeth on him, may have everlasting life: and I will raise him up ²in the resurrection of the just at the last day.

₄₁The Jews then murmured at him, because he said, I am the bread which came down from heaven. ₄₂And they said, Is not this Jesus, the

---

a IE: stayed

1 JST John 7:26

b This quote is not found in our Old Testament.

2 JST John 7:40

THIRD YEAR — THE GALILEAN MINISTRY

THE BREAD OF LIFE (cont.) — John 6:22-59

son of Joseph, whose father and mother we know? how is it then that he saith, I came down from heaven?

₄₃Jesus therefore answered and said unto them, Murmur not among yourselves. ₄₄No man can come to me, except [3]he doeth the will of my Father which hath sent me. [4]And this is the will of him who hath sent me, that ye receive the Son; for the father beareth record of him; and he who receiveth the testimony, and doeth the will of him who sent me, I will raise up [5]in the resurrection of the just. ₄₅It is written in the prophets, cAnd they shall be all taught of God. Every man therefore that hath heard, and hath learned of the Father, cometh unto me. ₄₆Not that any man hath seen the Father, save he which is of God, he hath seen the Father.

₄₇Verily, verily, I say unto you, He that believeth on me hath everlasting life. ₄₈I am that bread of life. ₄₉Your fathers did eat manna in the wilderness, and are dead. ₅₀This is the bread which cometh down from heaven, that a man may eat thereof, and not die. ₅₁I am the living bread which came down from heaven: if any man eat of this bread, he shall live for ever: and the bread that I will give is my flesh, which I will give for the life of the world.

₅₂The Jews therefore strove among themselves, saying, How can this man give us *his* flesh to eat?

₅₃Then Jesus said unto them, Verily, verily, I say unto you, Except ye eat the flesh of the Son of man, and drink his blood, ye have no life in you. ₅₄Whoso eateth my flesh, and drinketh my blood, hath eternal life; and I will raise him up [6]in the resurrection of the just at the last day. ₅₅For my flesh is meat indeed, and my blood is drink indeed. ₅₆He that eateth my flesh, and drinketh my blood, dwelleth in me, and I in him. ₅₇As the living Father hath sent me, and I live by the Father: so he that eateth me, even he shall live by me. ₅₈This is that bread which came down from heaven: not as your fathers did eat manna, and are dead: he that eateth of this bread shall live for ever.

₅₉These things said he in the synagogue, as he taught in Capernaum.

DISCIPLES TESTED BY JESUS' TEACHING — John 6:60-71

₆₀Many therefore of his disciples, when they had heard *this*, said, This is an hard saying; who can hear it?

₆₁When Jesus knew in himself that his disciples murmured at it, he said unto them, Doth this offend you? ₆₂*What* and if ye shall see the Son of man ascend up where he was before? ₆₃It is the spirit that quickeneth; the flesh profiteth nothing: the words that I speak unto you, *they* are spirit, and *they* are life. ₆₄But there are some of you that believe not. For Jesus knew from the beginning who they were that believed not,

3 JST John 6:44; KJV: the

4 JST John 6:44; KJV: draw him: and

5 JST John 6:44; KJV: at the last day

c An allusion to Jer. 31:34.

6 JST John 6:54

THIRD YEAR THE GALILEAN MINISTRY

DISCIPLES TESTED BY JESUS' TEACHING (cont.) — John 6:60-71

and who should betray him. 65And he said, Therefore said I unto you, that no man can come unto me, except ¹he doeth the will of my Father ¹who hath sent me. 66From that *time* many of his disciples went back, and walked no more with him. 67Then said Jesus unto the twelve, Will ye also go away? 68Then Simon Peter answered him, Lord, to whom shall we go? thou hast the words of eternal life. 69And we believe and are sure that thou art that Christ, the Son of the living God. 70Jesus answered them, Have not I chosen you twelve, and one of you is a devil? 71He spake of Judas Iscariot *the son* of Simon: for he it was that should betray him, being one of the twelve.

1 JST John 6:65

WHAT DEFILES A MAN — Mark 7:1-23

₁Then came together unto him the Pharisees, and certain of the scribes, which came from Jerusalem. ₂And when they saw some of his disciples eat bread with defiled, that is to say, with unwashen, hands, they found fault. ₄For the Pharisees, and all the Jews, except they wash *their* hands oft, eat not, holding the tradition of the elders. And *when they come* from the market, except they wash, they eat not. And many other things there be, which they have received to hold, *as* the washing of cups, and pots, brasen vessels, and of tables. ₅Then the Pharisees and scribes asked him, Why walk not thy disciples according to the tradition of the elders, but eat bread with unwashen hands? ₆He answered and said unto them, Well hath ªEsaias prophesied of you hypocrites, as it is written, ᵇTHIS PEOPLE HONOURETH ME WITH *THEIR* LIPS, BUT THEIR HEART IS FAR FROM ME. ₇HOWBEIT IN VAIN DO THEY WORSHIP ME, TEACHING *FOR* DOCTRINES THE COMMANDMENTS OF MEN. ₈For laying aside the commandment of God, ye hold the tradition of men, *as* the washing of pots and cups: and many other such like things ye do. ₉And he said unto them, Full well ye reject the commandment of God, that ye may keep your own tradition. ¹₁₀Full well is it written of you, by the prophets whom ye have rejected. ₁₁They testified these things of a truth, and their blood shall be upon you. ²Ye have kept not the ordinances of God; ₁₀For Moses said, ᶜHONOUR THY FATHER AND THY MOTHER; and, ᵈWHOSO CURSETH FATHER OR MOTHER, LET HIM DIE THE DEATH ²of the transgressor, as it is written in your law; but ye keep not the law. ₁₁But ye say, If a man shall say to his father or mother, *It is* ᵉCorban, that is to say, a gift, by whatsoever thou mightest be profited by me; *he shall be free.* ₁₂And ye suffer him no more to do ought for his father or his mother; ₁₃Making the word of God of none effect through your tradition, which ye have delivered: and many such like things do ye.

a GR: Isaiah
b Isa. 29:13
1 JST Mark 7:10-11
2 JST Mark 7:12
c Exod. 20:12
d Exod. 21:17 (HEB: being put to death, let him be put to death, IE: shall surely be put to death)
e HEB: sacrificial offering

55

WHAT DEFILES A MAN (cont.) Mark 7:1-23

₁₄And when he had called all the people *unto him*, he said unto them, Hearken unto me every one *of you*, and understand: ₁₅There is nothing from without a man, that entering into him can defile him ³which is food: but the things which come out of him, those are they that defile the man, ³that proceedeth forth out of the heart. ₁₆If any man have ears to hear, let him hear.

₁₇And when he was entered into the house from the people, his disciples asked him concerning the parable. ₁₈And he saith unto them, Are ye so without understanding also? Do ye not perceive, that whatsoever thing from without entereth into the man, *it* cannot defile him; ₁₉Because it entereth not into his heart, but into the belly, and goeth out into the draught, purging all meats?

₂₀And he said, That which cometh out of the man, that defileth the man. ₂₁For from within, out of the heart of men, proceed evil thoughts, adulteries, fornications, murders, ₂₂Thefts, covetousness, wickedness, deceit, lasciviousness, an evil eye, blasphemy, pride, foolishness: ₂₃All these evil things come from within, and defile the man.

3 JST Mark 7:15

THIRD YEAR   THE NORTH GALILEAN MINISTRY

THE WOMAN OF CANAAN   Matt. 15:21-28

₂₁Then Jesus went thence, and departed into the ᵃcoasts of Tyre and Sidon, ¹for he would not walk in Jewry, because the Jews sought to kill him, ²and entered into a house, and would ³that no man should come unto him: but he could not ⁴deny them; for he had compassion upon all men. ⁵For a *certain* woman ₂₂of Canaan came out of the same coasts, and cried unto him, saying, Have mercy on me, O Lord, *thou* Son of David; my daughter is grievously vexed with a devil.
₂₃But he answered her not a word.
And his disciples came and besought him, saying, Send her away; for she crieth after us.
₂₄But he answered and said, I am not sent but unto the lost sheep of the house of Israel.
₂₅Then came she and worshipped him, saying, Lord, help me.
₂₆But he answered and said, It is not meet to take the children's bread, and to cast *it* to dogs.
₂₇And she said, Truth, Lord: yet the dogs eat of the crumbs which fall from their masters' table.
₂₈Then Jesus answered and said unto her, O woman, great *is* thy faith: be it unto thee even as thou wilt.
And her daughter was made whole from that very hour.

a IE: borders
1 John 7:1
2 Mark 7:24
3 JST Mark 7:22; KJV: have no man know it
4 JST Mark 7:23; KJV: be hid
5 Mark 7:25

A HEALING; FEEDING THE FOUR THOUSAND   Matt 15:29-39

₂₉And Jesus departed from thence, and came nigh unto the sea of Galilee; and went up into a mountain, and sat down there.
₃₀And great multitudes came unto him, having with them *those that were* lame, blind, dumb, maimed, and many others, and cast them down at Jesus' feet; and he healed them: ¹₃₂And they bring unto him one that was deaf, and had an impediment in his speech; and they beseech him to put his hand upon him. ₃₃And he took him aside from the multitude, and put his fingers into his ears, and he spit, and touched his tongue; ₃₄And looking up to heaven, he sighed, and saith unto him, Ephphatha, that is, Be opened. ₃₅And straightway his ears were opened, and the string of his tongue was loosed, and he spake plain.
₃₆And he charged them that they should tell no man: but the more he charged them, so much the more a great deal they published *it*; ₃₇And were beyond measure astonished, saying, He hath done all things well: he maketh both the deaf to hear, and the dumb to speak: ₃₁and they glorified the God of Israel.
₃₂Then Jesus called his disciples *unto him*, and said, I have compassion on the multitude, because they continue with me now three days, and have nothing to eat: and I will not send them away fasting, lest they faint in the way.

1 Mark 7:32-37

THIRD YEAR — THE NORTH GALILEAN MINISTRY

A HEALING; FEEDING OF THE FOUR THOUSAND (cont.) — Matt. 15:29-39

33And his disciples say unto him, Whence should we have so much bread in the wilderness, as to fill so great a multitude? 34And Jesus saith unto them, How many loaves have ye? And they said, Seven, and a few little fishes. 35And he commanded the multitude to sit down on the ground. 36And he took the seven loaves and the fishes, and gave thanks, and brake *them*, and gave to his disciples, and the disciples to the multitude. 37And they did all eat, and were filled: and they took up of the [1]broken *meat* that was left seven baskets full. 38And they that did eat were four thousand men, beside women and children.

39And he sent away the multitude, and took ship, and came into the coasts of Magdala.

A SIGN FROM HEAVEN — Matt. 16:1-4

1The Pharisees also with the Sadducees came, and tempting desired him that he would shew them a sign from heaven. 2He answered and said unto them, When it is evening, ye say, *It will be* fair weather: for the sky is red. 3And in the morning, *It will be* foul weather to day: for the sky is red and [a]lowring. O *ye* hypocrites, ye can discern the face of the sky; but can ye not *discern* the signs of the times? 4A wicked and adulterous generation seeketh after a sign; and there shall no sign be given unto it, but the sign of the prophet [b]Jonas. And he left them, and departed.

[a] GR: dark, gloomy
[b] GR: Jonah

BEWARE THE LEAVEN OF THE PHARISEES — Matt. 16:5-12

5And when his disciples were come to the other side, they had forgotten to take bread. 6Then Jesus said unto them, Take heed and beware of the leaven of the Pharisees and of the Sadducees. 7And they reasoned among themselves, saying, *It is* because we have taken no bread. 8*Which* when Jesus perceived, he said unto them, O ye of little faith, why reason ye among yourselves, because ye have brought no bread? 9Do ye not yet understand, neither remember the five loaves of the five thousand, and how many baskets ye took up? 10Neither the seven loaves of the four thousand, and how many baskets ye took up? 11How is it that ye do not understand that I spake *it* not to you concerning bread, that ye should beware of the leaven of the Pharisees and of the Sadducees? 12Then understood they how that he bade *them* not beware of the leaven of bread, but of the doctrine of the Pharisees and of the Sadducees.

THIRD YEAR — THE NORTH GALILEAN MINISTRY

THE BLIND MAN IN BETHSAIDA — Mark 8:22-26

22 And he cometh to Bethsaida; and they bring a blind man unto him, and besought him to touch him.

23 And he took the blind man by the hand, and led him out of the town; and when he had spit on his eyes, and put his hands upon him, he asked him if he saw ought.

24 And he looked up, and said, I see men as trees, walking. 25 After that he put *his* hands again upon his eyes, and made him look up: and he was restored, and saw every man clearly.

26 And he sent him away to his house, saying, Neither go into the town, nor tell *it* to any in the town.

UPON THIS ROCK — Matt. 16:13-20

13 When Jesus came into the coasts of Caesarea Philippi, he asked his disciples, saying, Whom do men say that I the Son of man am?

14 And they said, Some *say that thou art* John the Baptist: some, ªElias; and others, ᵇJeremias, or one of the prophets.

15 He saith unto them, But whom say ye that I am?

16 And Simon Peter answered and said, Thou art the Christ, the Son of the living God.

17 And Jesus answered and said unto him, Blessed art thou, Simon ᶜBarjona: for flesh and blood hath not revealed *it* unto thee, but my Father which is in heaven. 18 And I say also unto thee, That thou art ᵈPeter, and upon this ᵉrock I will build my church; and the gates of hell shall not prevail against it. 19 And I will give unto thee the keys of the kingdom of heaven: and whatsoever thou shalt bind on earth shall be bound in heaven: and whatsoever thou shalt loose on earth shall be loosed in heaven.

20 Then charged he his disciples that they should tell no man that he was Jesus the Christ.

a GR: Elijah
b GR: Jeremiah
c AR: outlaw, IE: Zealot
d GR: small rock
e GR: bedrock

CHRIST REVEALS HIS DEATH — Matt. 16:21-28

21 From that time forth began Jesus to shew unto his disciples, how that he must go unto Jerusalem, and suffer many things of the elders and chief priests and scribes, and be killed, and be raised again the third day.

22 Then Peter took him, and began to rebuke him, saying, Be it far from thee, Lord: this shall not be unto thee.

23 But he turned, and said unto Peter, Get thee behind me, ªSatan: thou art an offence unto me: for thou savourest not the things that be of God, but those that be of men.

24 Then said Jesus unto his disciples, If any *man* will come after me, let him deny himself, and take up his cross, and follow me. ¹And now

a HEB: adversary, opponent

1 JST Matt. 16:26

THIRD YEAR   THE NORTH GALILEAN MINISTRY

CHRIST REVEALS HIS DEATH (cont.)	Matt. 16:21-28
for a man to take up his cross, is to deny himself of all ungodliness, and every worldly lust, and keep my commandments. ²Break not my commandments for to save your lives; ₂₅For whosoever will save his life ²in this world, shall lose it ²in the world to come: and whosoever will lose his life ³in this world for my sake shall find it ³in the world to come. ⁴Therefore, forsake the world, and save your souls; ₂₆For what is a man profited, if he shall gain the whole world, and lose his own soul? Or what shall a man give in exchange for his soul? ₂₇For the Son of man shall come in the glory of his Father with his angels; and ᵇTHEN HE SHALL REWARD EVERY MAN ACCORDING TO HIS WORKS. ₂₈Verily I say unto you, There be some standing here, which shall not taste of death, till they see the Son of man coming in his kingdom.	2 JST Matt. 16:27 3 JST Matt. 16:28 4 JST Matt. 16:29 b Ps. 62:12
THE TRANSFIGURATION	**Matt. 17:1-13**

₁And after six days Jesus taketh Peter, James, and John his brother, and bringeth them up into an high mountain apart, ₂And was transfigured before them: and his face did shine as the sun, and his raiment was white as the light. ₃And, behold, there appeared unto them Moses and ᵃElias talking with him.
    ₄Then answered Peter, and said unto Jesus, Lord, it is good for us to be here: if thou wilt, let us make here three tabernacles; one for thee, and one for Moses, and one for Elias. ₅While he yet spake, behold, a bright cloud overshadowed them: and behold a voice out of the cloud, which said, This is my beloved Son, in whom I am well pleased; hear ye him. ₆And when the disciples heard *it*, they fell on their face, and were sore afraid.
    ₇And Jesus came and touched them, and said, Arise, and be not afraid. ₈And when they had lifted up their eyes, they saw no man, save Jesus only. ₉And as they came down from the mountain, Jesus charged them, saying, Tell the vision to no man, until the Son of man be risen again from the dead.
    ₁₀And his disciples asked him, saying, Why then say the scribes that Elias must first come?
    ₁₁And Jesus answered and said unto them, Elias truly shall first come, and restore all things, ¹as the prophets have written. ²And again ₁₂I say unto you that Elias is come already, ³concerning whom it is written, ᵇBEHOLD, I WILL SEND MY MESSENGER, AND HE SHALL PREPARE THE WAY BEFORE ME; and they knew him not, but have done unto him whatsoever they ᶜlisted. Likewise shall also the Son of Man suffer of them. ⁴But I say unto you, Who is Elias? Behold, this is Elias, whom I send to prepare the way before me. ₁₃Then the disciples understood that he spake unto them of John the Baptist, ⁵and also of another who should come and restore all things, as it is written by the prophets.
	a GR: Elijah
	1 JST Matt. 17:10
	2 JST Matt. 17:11; KJV: But
	3 JST Matt. 17:11
	b Mal. 3:1
	c GR: desired
	4 JST Matt. 17:13
	5 JST Matt. 17:14

60

THOU DUMB AND DEAF SPIRIT　　　　　　　　　　　　　Mark 9:14-29

₁₄And when he came to *his* disciples, he saw a great multitude about them, and the scribes questioning with them. ₁₅And straightway all the people, when they beheld him, were greatly amazed, and running to *him* saluted him.

₁₆And he asked the scribes, What question ye with them?

₁₇And one of the multitude answered and said, Master, I have brought unto thee my son, which hath a dumb spirit; ₁₈And wheresoever he taketh him, he teareth him: and he foameth, and gnasheth with his teeth, and pineth away: and I spake to thy disciples that they should cast him out; and they could not.

₁₉He answereth him, and saith, O faithless generation, how long shall I be with you? how long shall I suffer you? bring him unto me.

₂₀And they brought him unto him: and when he saw him, straightway the spirit tare him; and he fell on the ground, and wallowed foaming. ₂₁And he asked his father, How long is it ago since this came unto him? And he said, Of a child. ₂₂And ofttimes it hath cast him into the fire, and into the waters, to destroy him: but if thou canst do any thing, have compassion on us, and help us.

₂₃Jesus said unto him, If thou canst believe, all things *are* possible to him that believeth.

₂₄And straightway the father of the child cried out, and said with tears, Lord, I believe; help thou mine unbelief.

₂₅When Jesus saw that the people came running together, he rebuked the foul spirit, saying unto him, *Thou* dumb and deaf spirit, I charge thee, come out of him, and enter no more into him.

₂₆And *the spirit* cried, and rent him sore, and came out of him: and he was as one dead; insomuch that many said, He is dead. ₂₇But Jesus took him by the hand, and lifted him up; and he arose.

₂₈And when he was come into the house, his disciples asked him privately, Why could not we cast him out?

¹₂₀And Jesus said unto them, Because of your unbelief: for verily I say unto you, If ye have faith as a grain of mustard seed, ye shall say unto this mountain, Remove hence to yonder place; and it shall remove; and nothing shall be impossible unto you. ₂₁Howbeit this kind goeth not out but by prayer and fasting.

1　Matt. 17:20-21

TAXES PAID WITH MONEY FROM A FISH　　　　　　　Matt. 17:24-27

₂₄And when they were come to Capernaum, they that received tribute *money* came to Peter, and said, Doth not your master pay tribute?

₂₅He saith, Yes.

And when he was come into the house, Jesus ᵃprevented him, saying, What thinkest thou, Simon? of whom do the kings of the earth take

a　GR: spoke to him first

THE NORTH GALILEAN MINISTRY

TAXES PAID WITH MONEY FROM A FISH (cont.) — Matt. 17:24-27

custom or tribute? of their own children, or of strangers? ₂₆Peter saith unto him, Of strangers. Jesus saith unto him, Then are the children free. ₂₇Notwithstanding, lest we should offend them, go thou to the sea, and cast an hook, and take up the fish that first cometh up; and when thou hast opened his mouth, thou shalt find a piece of money: that take, and give unto them for me and thee.

WHO IS THE GREATEST — Matt. 18:1-6

₁₄₆Then there arose a reasoning among them, which of them should be greatest. ₄₇And Jesus, perceiving the thought of their heart, ²₃₃and being in the house he asked them, What was it that ye disputed among yourselves by the way? ₃₄But they held their peace: for by the way they had disputed among themselves, who *should be* the greatest. ₁At the same time came the disciples unto Jesus, saying, Who is the greatest in the kingdom of heaven? ³₃₅**And he sat down, and called the twelve, and saith unto them, If any man desire to be first, *the same* shall be last of all, and servant of all.** ₃₆And he took a child, and set him in the midst of them: and when he had taken him in his arms, he said unto them, ₃Verily I say unto you, Except ye be converted, and become as little children, ye shall not enter into the kingdom of heaven. ₄Whosoever therefore shall humble himself as this little child, the same is greatest in the kingdom of heaven. **⁴Whosoever shall ⁵**humble himself like one of these children, and receiveth me, ye shall receive in my name**: and whosoever shall receive me, receiveth not me ⁶**only**, but him that sent me, ⁶**even the Father**. ₆But whoso shall ᵃoffend one of these little ones which believe in me, it were better for him that a millstone were hanged about his neck, and *that* he were drowned in the depth of the sea.

1 Luke 9:46-47
2 Mark 9:33-34
3 Mark 9:35-36
4 Mark 9:37
5 JST Mark 9:34; KJV: receive one of such children in my name, receiveth me
6 JST Mark 9:35
a cause to stumble

PARABLE OF THE LOST SHEEP — Matt. 18:10-14

₁₀Take heed that ye despise not one of these little ones; for I say unto you, That in heaven their angels do always behold the face of my Father which is in heaven. ₁₁For the Son of man is come to save that which was lost ¹and to call sinners to repentance; but these little ones have no need of repentance, and I will save them.
²₁Then drew near unto him all the publicans and sinners for to hear him.
₂And the Pharisees and scribes murmured, saying, This man receiveth sinners, and eateth with them.
₃And he spake this parable unto them, saying, ₁₂How think ye? if a man have an hundred sheep, and one of them be gone astray, doth he not leave the ninety and nine, and goeth into the ³**wilderness**, and

1 JST Matt. 18:11
2 Luke 15:1-3
3 Luke 15:4

PARABLE OF THE LOST SHEEP — Matt. 18:10-14

seeketh that which is gone astray? ⁴₅And when he hath found *it*, he layeth *it* on his shoulders, rejoicing. ₆And when he cometh home, he calleth together *his* friends and neighbours, saying unto them, Rejoice with me; for I have found my sheep which was lost. ₁₃Verily I say unto you, he rejoiceth more of that *sheep*, than of the ninety and nine which went not astray.

⁵I say unto you, that likewise joy shall be in heaven over one sinner that repenteth, more than over ninety and nine just persons, which need no repentance. ₁₄Even so it is not the will of your Father which is in heaven, that one of these little ones should perish.

4 Luke 15:5-6
5 Luke 15:7

HE THAT IS NOT AGAINST US — Mark 9:38-41

₃₈And John answered him, saying, Master, we saw one casting out devils in thy name, and he followeth not us: and we forbade him, because he followeth not us.

₃₉But Jesus said, Forbid him not: for there is no man which shall do a miracle in my name, that can lightly speak evil of me. ₄₀For he that is not against us is on our part. ₄₁For whosoever shall give you a cup of water to drink in my name, because ye belong to Christ, verily I say unto you, he shall not lose his reward.

IF THY RIGHT HAND OFFEND THEE — Mark 9:43-50

¹₃Take heed to yourselves: If thy brother trespass against thee, rebuke him; and if he repent, forgive him. ₄And if he trespass against thee seven times in a day, and seven times in a day turn again to thee, saying, I repent; thou shalt forgive him.

²Woe unto the world because of offences! for it must needs be that offences come; but woe to that man by whom the offence cometh! ³Therefore, ₄₃if thy hand offend thee, cut it off; ⁴or if thy brother offend thee and confess it not and forsake not, he shall be cut off. It is better for thee to enter into life maimed, than having two hands, to go into hell. ⁵For it is better for thee to enter into life without thy brother, than for thee and thy brother to be cast into hell; into the fire that never shall be quenched: ₄₄ᵃWHERE THEIR WORM DIETH NOT, AND THE FIRE IS NOT QUENCHED.

₄₅And ⁶again, if thy foot offend thee, cut it off; ⁶for he that is thy standard, by whom thou walkest, if he become a transgressor, he shall be cut off: it is better for thee, to enter halt into life, than having two feet to be cast into hell; into the fire that never shall be quenched. ⁷₄₄Therefore, let every man stand or fall, by himself, and not for another; or not trusting another. ₄₅Seek unto my Father, and it shall be done in that very moment what ye shall ask, if ye ask in faith, believing that ye shall receive.

1 Luke 18:3-4
2 Matt. 18:7
3 JST Mark 9:40; KJV: And
4 JST Mark 9:40
5 JST Mark 9:41
a Isa. 66:24
6 JST Mark 9:42
7 JST Mark 9:44-45

THIRD YEAR	THE NORTH GALILEAN MINISTRY	
IF THY RIGHT HAND OFFEND THEE (cont.)		**Mark 9:43-50**

^b₄₇And if thine eye ⁸which seeth for thee, him that is appointed to watch over thee to show thee light, become a transgressor and offend thee, pluck ⁹him out: it is better for thee to enter into the kingdom of God with one eye, than having two eyes to be cast into hell fire:

¹⁰For it is better that thyself should be saved, than to be cast into hell with thy brother, ₄₈WHERE THEIR WORM DIETH NOT, AND THE FIRE IS NOT QUENCHED.

₄₉For every one shall be salted with fire, and every sacrifice shall be salted with salt. ₅₀Salt *is* good: but if the salt have lost his saltness, wherewith will ye season it? Have salt in yourselves, and have peace one with another.

b JST omits KJV Mark 9:46

8 JST Mark 9:46

9 JST Mark 9:46; KJV: it

10 JST Mark 9:48

UNTIL SEVENTY TIMES SEVEN	**Matt. 18:15-22**

₁₅Moreover if thy brother shall trespass against thee, go and tell him his fault between thee and him alone: if he shall hear thee, thou hast gained thy brother. ₁₆But if he will not hear *thee, then* take with thee one or two more, that ªIN THE MOUTH OF TWO OR THREE WITNESSES EVERY WORD MAY BE ESTABLISHED. ₁₇And if he shall neglect to hear them, tell *it* unto the church: but if he neglect to hear the church, let him be unto thee as an heathen man and a publican.

₁₈Verily I say unto you, Whatsoever ye shall bind on earth shall be bound in heaven: and whatsoever ye shall loose on earth shall be loosed in heaven. ₁₉Again I say unto you, That if two of you shall agree on earth as touching any thing that they shall ask, it shall be done for them of my Father which is in heaven. ₂₀For where two or three are gathered together in my name, there am I in the midst of them.

₂₁Then came Peter to him, and said, Lord, how oft shall my brother sin against me, and I forgive him? till seven times?

₂₂Jesus saith unto him, I say not unto thee, Until seven times: but, Until seventy times seven.

a Deut. 19:15

PARABLE OF THE TWO DEBTORS	**Matt. 18:23-35**

₂₃Therefore is the kingdom of heaven likened unto a certain king, which would ªtake account of his servants. ₂₄And when he had begun to reckon, one was brought unto him, which owed him ten thousand talents. ₂₅But forasmuch as he had not to pay, his lord commanded him to be sold, and his wife, and children, and all that he had, and payment to be made.

₂₆The servant therefore fell down, and worshipped him, saying, Lord, have patience with me, and I will pay thee all. ₂₇Then the lord of that servant was moved with compassion, and loosed him, and forgave him the debt.

₂₈But the same servant went out, and found one of his fellowser-

a GR: settle accounts with

THIRD YEAR · THE NORTH GALILEAN MINISTRY

PARABLE OF THE TWO DEBTORS (cont.) — Matt. 18:23-35

vants, which owed him ᵇan hundred pence: and he laid hands on him, and took *him* by the throat, saying, Pay me that thou owest. ₂₉And his fellowservant fell down at his feet, and besought him, saying, Have patience with me, and I will pay thee all. ₃₀And he would not: but went and cast him into prison, till he should pay the debt.

₃₁So when his fellowservants saw what was done, they were very ᶜsorry, and came and told unto their lord all that was done. ₃₂Then his lord, after that he had called him, said unto him, O thou wicked servant, I forgave thee all that debt, because thou desiredst me: ₃₃Shouldest not thou also have had compassion on thy fellowservant, even as I had pity on thee? ₃₄And his lord was wroth, and delivered him to the tormentors, till he should pay all that was due unto him. ₃₅So likewise shall my heavenly Father do also unto you, if ye from your hearts forgive not every one his brother their trespasses.

b over three months' wages for a poor working man

c GR: distressed

PARABLE OF THE LOST COIN — Luke 15:8-10

₈Either what woman having ten ᵃpieces of silver, if she lose one piece, doth not light a candle, and sweep the house, and seek diligently till she find *it*?

₉And when she hath found *it*, she calleth *her* friends and *her* neighbours together, saying, Rejoice with me; for I have found the piece which I had lost.

₁₀Likewise, I say unto you, there is joy in the presence of the angels of God over one sinner that repenteth.

a gr: *drachma*, equal to a *denarius*, a poor workman's daily wage

PARABLE OF THE PRODIGAL SON — Luke 15:11-32

₁₁And he said, A certain man had two sons: ₁₂And the younger of them said to *his* father, Father, give me the portion of goods that falleth *to me*. And he divided unto them *his* living. ₁₃And not many days after the younger son gathered all together, and took his journey into a far country, and there wasted his substance with riotous living. ₁₄And when he had spent all, there arose a mighty famine in that land; and he began to be in want.

₁₅And he went and joined himself to a citizen of that country; and he sent him into his fields to feed swine. ₁₆And he would fain have filled his belly with the ᵃhusks that the swine did eat: and no man gave unto him. ₁₇And when he came to himself, he said, How many hired servants of my father's have bread enough and to spare, and I perish with hunger! ₁₈I will arise and go to my father, and will say unto him, Father, I have sinned against heaven, and before thee, ₁₉And am no more worthy to be called thy son: make me as one of thy hired servants.

₂₀And he arose, and came to his father. But when he was yet a great way off, his father saw him, and had compassion, and ran, and fell on

a GR: pods of the carob tree

PARABLE OF THE PRODIGAL SON (cont.) — Luke 15:11-32

his neck, and kissed him.

₂₁And the son said unto him, Father, I have sinned against heaven, and in thy sight, and am no more worthy to be called thy son.

₂₂But the father said to his servants, Bring forth the best robe, and put *it* on him; and put a ring on his hand, and shoes on *his* feet: ₂₃And bring hither the fatted calf, and kill *it*; and let us eat, and be merry: ₂₄For this my son was dead, and is alive again; he was lost, and is found. And they began to be merry.

₂₅Now his elder son was in the field: and as he came and drew nigh to the house, he heard musick and dancing. ₂₆And he called one of the servants, and asked what these things meant.

₂₇And he said unto him, Thy brother is come; and thy father hath killed the fatted calf, because he hath received him safe and sound.

₂₈And he was angry, and would not go in: therefore came his father out, and intreated him. ₂₉And he answering said to *his* father, Lo, these many years do I serve thee, neither transgressed I at any time thy commandment: and yet thou never gavest me a kid, that I might make merry with my friends: ₃₀But as soon as this thy son was come, which hath devoured thy living with harlots, thou hast killed for him the fatted calf.

₃₁And he said unto him, Son, thou art ever with me, and all that I have is thine. ₃₂It was meet that we should make merry, and be glad: for this thy brother was dead, and is alive again; and was lost, and is found.

THE WORLD HATETH ME — John 7:2-9

₂Now the Jews' feast of tabernacles was at hand. ₃His brethren therefore said unto him, Depart hence, and go into Judaea, that thy disciples also may see the works that thou doest. ₄For *there is* no man *that* doeth any thing in secret, and he himself seeketh to be known openly. If thou do these things, shew thyself to the world. ₅For neither did his brethren believe in him.

₆Then Jesus said unto them, My time is not yet come: but your time is alway ready. ₇The world cannot hate you; but me it hateth, because I testify of it, that the works thereof are evil. ₈Go ye up unto this feast: I go not up yet unto this feast; for my time is not yet full come. ₉When he had said these words unto them, he ᵃabode *still* in Galilee.

a IE: remained

THE LATER JUDEAN MINISTRY

AN EXAMPLE OF NON-VIOLENCE — Luke 9:51-56

₅₁And it came to pass, when the time was come that he should be received up, he stedfastly set his face to go to Jerusalem, ₅₂And sent messengers before his face: and they went, and entered into a village of the Samaritans, to make ready for him. ₅₃And they did not receive him, because his face was as though he would go to Jerusalem.

₅₄And when his disciples James and John saw *this*, they said, Lord, wilt thou that we command fire to come down from heaven, and consume them, ᵃeven as ᵇElias did? ₅₅But he turned, and rebuked them, and said, Ye know not what manner of spirit ye are of. ₅₆For the Son of man is not come to destroy men's lives, but to save *them*.

And they went to another village.

a 2 Kings 1:10-12
b GR: Elijah

THE MISSION OF THE SEVENTY — Luke 10:1-12

₁After these things the Lord appointed other seventy also, and sent them two and two before his face into every city and place, whither he himself would come.

₂Therefore said he unto them, The harvest truly *is* great, but the labourers *are* few: pray ye therefore the Lord of the harvest, that he would send forth labourers into his harvest. ₃Go your ways: behold, I send you forth as lambs among wolves. ₄Carry neither purse, nor scrip, nor shoes: and salute no man by the way. ₅And into whatsoever house ye enter, first say, Peace *be* to this house. ₆And if the son of peace be there, your peace shall rest upon it: if not, it shall turn to you again. ₇And in the same house remain, eating and drinking such things as they give: for the labourer is worthy of his hire. Go not from house to house. ₈And into whatsoever city ye enter, and they receive you, eat such things as are set before you: ₉And heal the sick that are therein, and say unto them, The kingdom of God is come nigh unto you.

₁₀But into whatsoever city ye enter, and they receive you not, go your ways out into the streets of the same, and say, ₁₁Even the very dust of your city, which cleaveth on us, we do wipe off against you: notwithstanding be ye sure of this, that the kingdom of God is come nigh unto you. ₁₂But I say unto you, that it shall be more tolerable in that day for Sodom, than for that city.

CHRIST UPBRAIDS CERTAIN CITIES — Matt. 11:20-24

₂₀Then began he to upbraid the cities wherein most of his mighty works were done, because they repented not: ₂₁Woe unto thee, Chorazin! woe unto thee, Bethsaida! for if the mighty works, which were done in you, had been done in Tyre and Sidon, they would have repented long ago in sackcloth and ashes. ₂₂But I say unto you, It shall be more tolerable for Tyre and Sidon at the day of judgment, than for you. ₂₃And

THIRD YEAR	THE LATER JUDEAN MINISTRY	
CHRIST UPBRAIDS CERTAIN CITIES (cont.)		**Matt. 11:20-24**

thou, Capernaum, which art exalted unto heaven, shalt be brought down to hell: for if the mighty works, which have been done in thee, had been done in Sodom, it would remained until this day. ₂₄But I say unto you, That it shall be more tolerable for the land of Sodom in the day of judgment, than for thee. ¹And he said unto his disciples, ²He that heareth you heareth me; and he that despiseth you despiseth me; and he that despiseth me despiseth him that sent me.	**1** JST Luke 10:17 **2** Luke 10:16

THE SEVENTY RETURN	**Luke 10:17-20**
₁₇And the seventy returned again with joy, saying, Lord, even the devils are subject unto us through thy name. ₁₈And he said unto them, I beheld Satan as lightning fall from heaven. ₁₉Behold, I give unto you power to tread on serpents and scorpions, and over all the power of the enemy: and nothing shall by any means hurt you. ₂₀Notwithstanding in this rejoice not, that the spirits are subject unto you; but rather rejoice, because your names are written in heaven.	

JESUS REJOICES	**Luke 10:21-24**

₂₁In that hour Jesus rejoiced in spirit, and said, I thank thee, O Father, Lord of heaven and earth, that thou hast hid these things from ¹them who think they are wise and prudent, and hast revealed them unto babes: even so, Father; for so it seemed good in thy sight. ₂₂All things are delivered to me of my Father; and no man knoweth ²that the Son is the Father, and the Father is the Son, but him to whom the Son will reveal ³it.
      ₂₃And he turned him unto *his* disciples, and said privately, Blessed *are* the eyes which see the things that ye see: ₂₄For I tell you, that many prophets and kings have desired to see those things which ye see, and have not seen *them*; and to hear those things which ye hear, and have not heard *them*.
      ⁴₂₈Come unto me, all *ye* that labour and are heavy laden, and I will give you rest. ₂₉Take my yoke upon you, and learn of me; for I am meek and lowly in heart: and ᵃYE SHALL FIND REST UNTO YOUR SOULS. ₃₀For my yoke *is* easy, and my burden is light.
	1 JST Luke 10:22; KJV: the
	2 JST Luke 10:23; KJV: who the Son is, but the Father; and who the Father is, but the Son, and *he* (The "wise and prudent" in that Hellenistic age, were especially likely to misinterpret this parable-like statement.)
	3 JST Luke 10:23; KJV: *him*
	4 Matt. 11:28-30
	a Jer. 6:16

PARABLE OF THE GOOD SAMARITAN	**Luke 10:25-37**

₂₅And, behold, a certain lawyer stood up, and tempted him, saying, Master, what shall I do to inherit eternal life?
      ₂₆He said unto him, What is written in the law? how readest thou?
      ₂₇And he answering said, ᵃTHOU SHALT LOVE THE LORD THY GOD WITH ALL THY HEART, AND WITH ALL THY SOUL, AND WITH ALL THY STRENGTH, AND
	a Lev. 19:18; Deut. 6:5

PARABLE OF THE GOOD SAMARITAN (cont.) — Luke 10:25-37

WITH ALL THY MIND; AND THY NEIGHBOUR AS THYSELF.

28And he said unto him, Thou hast answered right: this do, and thou shalt live.

29But he, willing to justify himself, said unto Jesus, And who is my neighbour?

30And Jesus answering said, A certain *man* went down from Jerusalem to Jericho, and fell among thieves, which stripped him of his raiment, and wounded *him*, and departed, leaving *him* half dead. 31And by chance there came down a certain priest that way: and when he saw him, he passed by on the other side. 32And likewise a Levite, when he was at the place, came and looked *on him*, and passed by on the other side.

33But a certain Samaritan, as he journeyed, came where he was: and when he saw him, he had compassion *on him*, 34And went to *him*, and bound up his wounds, pouring in oil and wine, and set him on his own beast, and brought him to an inn, and took care of him. 35And on the morrow when he departed, he took out two pence, and gave *them* to the bhost, and said unto him, Take care of him; and whatsoever thou spendest more, when I come again, I will repay thee.

36Which now of these three, thinkest thou, was neighbour unto him that fell among the thieves?

37And he said, He that shewed mercy on him.

Then said Jesus unto him, Go, and do thou likewise.

b GR: innkeeper

A VISIT WITH MARTHA AND MARY — Luke 10:38-42

38Now it came to pass, as they went, that he entered into a certain village: and a certain woman named Martha received him into her house. 39And she had a sister called Mary, which also sat at Jesus' feet, and heard his word.

40But Martha was cumbered about much serving, and came to him, and said, Lord, dost thou not care that my sister hath left me to serve alone? bid her therefore that she help me.

41And Jesus answered and said unto her, Martha, Martha, thou art acareful and troubled about many things: 42But one thing is needful: and Mary hath chosen that good part, which shall not be taken away from her.

a GR: worried

INSTRUCTION ABOUT PRAYER — Luke 11:1-13

1And it came to pass, that, as he was praying in a certain place, when he ceased, one of his disciples said unto him, Lord, teach us to pray, as John also taught his disciples.

2And he said unto them, aWhen ye pray, say, Our Father which art in heaven, Hallowed be thy name. Thy kingdom come. Thy will be done,

a Christ here reiterates some of his teachings from the Sermon on the Mount. Cf. Matt. 6:9-13

THIRD YEAR	THE LATER JUDEAN MINISTRY	
INSTRUCTION ABOUT PRAYER (cont.)		**Luke 11:1-13**

as in heaven, so in earth. ₃Give us day by day our daily bread. ₄And forgive us our sins; for we also forgive every one that is indebted to us. And ¹let us not be lead into temptation; but deliver us from evil; ²for thine is the kingdom and power. Amen.

₅And he said unto them, ³Your heavenly Father will not fail to give unto you whatsoever ye ask of him. And he spake a parable, saying, Which of you shall have a friend, and shall go unto him at midnight, and say unto him, Friend, lend me three loaves; ₆For a friend of mine in his journey is come to me, and I have nothing to set before him? ₇And he from within shall answer and say, Trouble me not: the door is now shut, and my children are with me in bed; I cannot rise and give thee. ₈I say unto you, Though he will not rise and give him, because he is his friend, yet because of his importunity he will rise and give him as many as he needeth.

₉ᵇAnd I say unto you, Ask, and it shall be given you; seek, and ye shall find; knock, and it shall be opened unto you. ₁₀For every one that asketh receiveth; and he that seeketh findeth; and to him that knocketh it shall be opened.

₁₁ᶜIf a son shall ask bread of any of you that is a father, will he give him a stone? or if *he ask* a fish, will he for a fish give him a serpent? ₁₂Or if he shall ask an egg, will he offer him a scorpion? ₁₃If ye then, being evil, know how to give good gifts unto your children: how much more shall *your* heavenly Father give ⁴good gifts, through the Holy Spirit to them that ask him?

1 JST Luke 11:4; KJV: lead us not

2 JST Luke 11:4; (see note to Matt. 6:13)

3 JST Luke 11:5

b Cf. Matt: 7:7-8

c Cf. Matt: 7:9-11

4 JST Luke 11:14

BLESSINGS	**Luke 11:27-28**

₂₇And it came to pass, as he spake these things, a certain woman of the company lifted up her voice, and said unto him, Blessed *is* the womb that bare thee, and the paps which thou hast sucked.

₂₈But he said, Yea rather, blessed *are* they that hear the word of God, and keep it.

PARABLE OF THE FOOLISH RICH MAN	**Luke 12:13-21**

₁₃And one of the company said unto him, Master, speak to my brother, that he divide the inheritance with me.

₁₄And he said unto him, Man, who made me a judge or a divider over you?

₁₅And he said unto them, Take heed, and beware of covetousness: for a man's life consisteth not in the abundance of the things which he possesseth. ₁₆And he spake a parable unto them, saying, The ground of a certain rich man brought forth plentifully: ₁₇And he thought within himself, saying, What shall I do, because I have no room where to ᵃbestow my fruits?

a GR: gather

THIRD YEAR	THE LATER JUDEAN MINISTRY

PARABLE OF THE FOOLISH RICH MAN (cont.) — Luke 12:13-21

₁₈And he said, This will I do: I will pull down my barns, and build greater; and there will I bestow all my fruits and my goods. ₁₉And I will say to my soul, Soul, thou hast much goods laid up for many years; take thine ease, eat, drink, *and* be merry.

₂₀But God said unto him, *Thou* fool, this night thy soul shall be required of thee: then whose shall those things be, which thou hast provided? ₂₁So *is* he that layeth up treasure for himself, and is not rich toward God.

EXCEPT YE REPENT — Luke 13:1-5

₁There were present at that season some that told him of the Galilaeans, whose blood Pilate had mingled with their sacrifices. ₂And Jesus answering said unto them, Suppose ye that these Galilaeans were sinners above all the Galilaeans, because they suffered such things? ₃I tell you, Nay: but, except ye repent, ye shall all likewise perish. ₄Or those eighteen, upon whom the tower in Siloam fell, and slew them, think ye that they were sinners above all men that dwelt in Jerusalem? ₅I tell you, Nay: but, except ye repent, ye shall all likewise perish.

A WOMAN HEALED ON THE SABBATH — Luke 13:10-17

₁₀And he was teaching in one of the synagogues on the sabbath. ₁₁And, behold, there was a woman which had a spirit of infirmity eighteen years, and was bowed together, and could in no wise lift up *herself*.

₁₂And when Jesus saw her, he called *her to him*, and said unto her, Woman, thou art loosed from thine infirmity. ₁₃And he laid *his* hands on her: and immediately she was made straight, and glorified God.

₁₄And the ruler of the synagogue answered with indignation, because that Jesus had healed on the sabbath day, and said unto the people, There are six days in which men ought to work: in them therefore come and be healed, and not on the sabbath day.

₁₅The Lord then answered him, and said, *Thou* hypocrite, doth not each one of you on the sabbath loose his ox or *his* ass from the stall, and lead *him* away to watering? ₁₆And ought not this woman, being a daughter of Abraham, whom Satan hath bound, lo, these eighteen years, be loosed from this bond on the sabbath day? ₁₇And when he had said these things, all his adversaries were ashamed: and all the people rejoiced for all the glorious things that were done by him.

O JERUSALEM, JERUSALEM * — Luke 13:31-35

₃₁The same day there came certain of the Pharisees, saying unto him, Get thee out, and depart hence: for Herod will kill thee.

₃₂And he said unto them, Go ye, and tell that fox, Behold, I cast out devils, and I do cures to day and to morrow, and the third *day* I shall be

* cf. Matt. 23:37-39

THIRD YEAR	THE LATER JUDEAN MINISTRY	

O JERUSALEM, JERUSALEM (cont.) — Luke 13:31-35

perfected. ₃₃Nevertheless I must walk to day, and to morrow, and the *day* following: for it cannot be that a prophet perish out of Jerusalem.
₁This he spake, signifying of his death. And in this very hour he began to weep over Jerusalem,
₃₄O Jerusalem, Jerusalem, which killest the prophets, and stonest them that are sent unto thee; how often would I have gathered thy children together, as a hen *doth gather* her brood under *her* wings, and ye would not! ₃₅Behold, your house is left unto you desolate: and verily I say unto you, Ye shall not ²know me, ³until ye have received from the hand of the Lord a just recompense for all your sins; until *the time* come when ye shall say, ªBLESSED *IS* HE THAT COMETH IN THE NAME OF THE LORD.

1 JST Luke 13:34
2 JST Luke 13:36; KJV: see
3 JST Luke 13:36
a Ps. 118:26

HEALING A MAN WITH DROPSY — Luke 14:1-6

₁And it came to pass, as he went into the house of one of the chief Pharisees to eat bread on the sabbath day, that they watched him. ₂And, behold, there was a certain man before him which had the dropsy. ₃And Jesus answering spake unto the lawyers and Pharisees, saying, Is it lawful to heal on the sabbath day? And they held their peace. ₄And he took *him*, and healed him, and let him go; ₅And answered them, saying, Which of you shall have an ass or an ox fallen into a pit, and will not straightway pull him out on the sabbath day? ₆And they could not answer him again to these things.

PARABLE OF THE CHIEF WEDDING ROOMS — Luke 14:7-14

₇And he put forth a parable to those which were bidden, when he marked how they chose out the ªchief rooms; saying unto them, ₈When thou art bidden of any *man* to a wedding, sit not down in the highest room; lest a more honourable man than thou be bidden of him; ₉And he that bade thee and him come and say to thee, Give this man place; and thou begin with shame to take the lowest room.
₁₀But when thou art ᵇbidden, go and sit down in the lowest room; that when he that bade thee cometh, he may say unto thee, Friend, go up higher: then shalt thou have ᶜworship in the presence of them that sit at meat with thee. ₁₁For whosoever exalteth himself shall be abased; and he that humbleth himself shall be exalted.
₁₂Then said he also to him that bade him, When thou makest a dinner or a supper, call not thy friends, nor thy brethren, neither thy kinsmen, nor *thy* rich neighbours; lest they also bid thee again, and a recompence be made thee. ₁₃But when thou makest a feast, call the poor, the maimed, the lame, the blind: ₁₄And thou shalt be blessed; for they cannot recompense thee: for thou shalt be recompensed at the resurrection of the just.

a GR: first places
b GR: invited
c GR: honor, glory, respect

THIRD YEAR — THE LATER JUDEAN MINISTRY

PARABLE OF THE GREAT SUPPER — Luke 14:15-24

₁₅And when one of them that sat at meat with him heard these things, he said unto him, Blessed *is* he that shall eat bread in the kingdom of God.

₁₆Then said he unto him, A certain man made a great supper, and bade many: ₁₇And sent his servant at supper time to say to them that were bidden, Come; for all things are now ready. ₁₈And they all with one *consent* began to make excuse.

The first said unto him, I have bought a piece of ground, and I must needs go and see it: I pray thee have me excused.

₁₉And another said, I have bought five yoke of oxen, and I go to prove them: I pray thee have me excused.

₂₀And another said, I have married a wife, and therefore I cannot come.

₂₁So that servant came, and shewed his lord these things. Then the master of the house being angry said to his servant, Go out quickly into the streets and lanes of the city, and bring in hither the poor, and the maimed, and the halt, and the blind.

₂₂And the servant said, Lord, it is done as thou hast commanded, and yet there is room.

₂₃And the lord said unto the servant, Go out into the highways and hedges, and ᵃcompel *them* to come in, that my house may be filled.

₂₄For I say unto you, That none of those men which were bidden shall taste of my supper.

a GR: urge

THE COST OF FOLLOWING JESUS — Luke 14:25-33

₂₅And there went great multitudes with him: and he turned, and said unto them, ₂₆If any *man* come to me, and hate not his father, and mother, and wife, and children, and brethren, and sisters, ¹or husband yea, and his own life also; ¹or in other words, is afraid to lay down his life for my sake, he cannot be my disciple. ₂₇And whosoever doth not bear his cross, and come after me, cannot be my disciple. ²Wherefore, settle this in your hears, that ye will do the things which I shall teach, and command you.

₂₈For which of you, intending to build a tower, sitteth not down first, and counteth the cost, whether he have *sufficient* to finish *it*? ₂₉Lest ᵃhaply, after he hath laid the foundation, and is not able to finish *it*, all that behold *it* begin to mock him, ₃₀Saying, This man began to build, and was not able to finish. ³And this he said, signifying there should not any man follow him, unless he was able to continue; saying, ₃₁Or what king, going to make war against another king, sitteth not down first, and consulteth whether he be able with ten thousand to meet him that cometh against him with twenty thousand? ₃₂Or else, while the other is yet a

1 JST Luke 14:26

2 JST Luke 14:28

a IE: perhaps

3 JST Luke 17:31

THE COST OF FOLLOWING JESUS (cont.) — Luke 14:25-33

great way off, he sendeth an ᵇambassage, and desireth conditions of peace. ₃₃So likewise, whosoever he be of you that forsaketh not all that he hath, he cannot be my disciple.

b IE: embassy

SALT WHICH IS GOOD * — Luke 14:34-35

¹Then certain of them came to him, saying, Good Master, we have Moses and the prophets, and whosoever shall live by them, shall he not have life?
²And Jesus answered, saying, Ye know not Moses, neither the prophets; for if ye had known them, ye would have believed on me; for to this intent they were written. For I am sent that ye might have life. Therefore I will liken it unto ₃₄salt ²which *is* good; but if the salt have lost ³its savour, wherewith shall it be seasoned? ₃₅It is neither fit for the land, nor yet for the dunghill; *but* men cast it out. He who hath ears to hear, let him hear.
⁴These things he said, signifying that which was written, verily must all be fulfilled.

* cf. Matt. 5:13

1 JST Luke 14:35

2 JST Luke 14:36

3 JST Luke 14:37; KJV: his

4 JST Luke 14:38

PARABLE OF THE UNJUST STEWARD — Luke 16:1-15

₁And he said also unto his disciples, There was a certain rich man, which had a steward; and the same was accused unto him that he had wasted his goods. ₂And he called him, and said unto him, How is it that I hear this of thee? give an account of thy stewardship; for ᵃthou mayest be no longer steward.
₃Then the steward said within himself, What shall I do? for my lord taketh away from me the stewardship: I cannot dig; to beg I am ashamed. ₄I am resolved what to do, that, when I am put out of the stewardship, they may receive me into their houses.
₅So he called every one of his lord's debtors *unto him*, and said unto the first, How much owest thou unto my lord?
₆And he said, An hundred measures of oil.
And he said unto him, Take thy bill, and sit down quickly, and write fifty.
₇Then said he to another, And how much owest thou?
And he said, An hundred measures of wheat.
And he said unto him, Take thy bill, and write fourscore.
₈And the lord commended the unjust steward, because he had done wisely: for the children of this world are in their generation wiser than the children of light.
₉And I say unto you, Make to yourselves friends of the ᵇmammon of unrighteousness; that, when ye fail, they may receive you into everlasting habitations.

a IE: it may be you will not continue as steward

b GR: what is trusted in, treasure (The Greek implies that, since the unrighteous trust in treasure, "the mammon of unrighteousness" is a reference to the wealthy.)

THIRD YEAR **THE LATER JUDEAN MINISTRY**

PARABLE OF THE UNJUST STEWARD (cont.) — Luke 16:1-15

₁₀He that is faithful in that which is least is faithful also in much: and he that is unjust in the least is unjust also in much. ₁₁If therefore ye have not been faithful in the unrighteous mammon, who will commit to your trust the true *riches*? ₁₂And if ye have not been faithful in that which is another man's, who shall give you that which is your own?

₁₃No servant can serve two masters: for either he will hate the one, and love the other; or else he will hold to the one, and despise the other. Ye cannot serve God and mammon.

₁₄And the Pharisees also, who were covetous, heard all these things: and they derided him.

₁₅And he said unto them, Ye are they which justify yourselves before men; but God knoweth your hearts: for that which is highly esteemed among men is abomination in the sight of God.

THE LAW AND THE PROPHETS — Luke 16:16-23

¹₁₆And they said unto him, We have the law, and the prophets; but as for this man we will not receive him to be our ruler; for he maketh himself to be a judge over us.

₁₇Then said Jesus unto them, ₁₆ᵃThe law and the prophets ²testify of me; yea, and all the prophets who have written, even until John, ³have foretold of these days: since that time, the kingdom of God is preached, and every man ⁴who seeketh truth presseth into it. ₁₇And it is easier for heaven and earth to pass, than for one tittle of the law to fail. ⁵₂₀And why teach ye the law, and deny that which is written; and condemn him whom the Father hath sent to fulfill the law, that ye might all be redeemed?

₂₁O fools! for you have said in your hearts, There is no God. And you pervert the right way; and the kingdom of heaven suffereth violence of you; and you persecute the meek; and in your violence you seek to destroy the kingdom; and ye take the children of the kingdom by force. Woe unto you, ye adulterers!

₂₂And they reviled him again, being angry for the saying, that they were adulterers. ₂₃But he continued, saying, ₁₈ᵇWhosoever putteth away his wife, and marrieth another, committeth adultery: and whosoever marrieth her who is put away from *her* husband, committeth adultery.

1 JST Luke 16:16-17

a "The law and the prophets" refers to scriptures in the Old Testament: the writings of Moses ("the law"), and the writings of the other prophets.

2 JST Luke 16:17; KJV: *were*

3 JST Luke 16:17

4 JST Luke 16:18

5 JST Luke 16:20-23

b Divorce under the law of Moses was interpreted very loosely by the Jews of that time. See Matt. 19:7.

THIRD YEAR — THE LATER JUDEAN MINISTRY

PARABLE OF THE RICH MAN AND LAZARUS — Luke 16:19-31

¹Verily I say unto you, I will liken you unto the rich man. ₁₉There was a certain rich man, which was clothed in purple and fine linen, and fared sumptuously every day: ₂₀And there was a certain beggar named ªLazarus, which was laid at his gate, full of sores, ₂₁And desiring to be fed with the crumbs which fell from the rich man's table: moreover the dogs came and licked his sores.

₂₂And it came to pass, that the beggar died, and was carried by the angels into Abraham's bosom: the rich man also died, and was buried; ₂₃And in hell he lift up his eyes, being in torments, and seeth Abraham afar off, and Lazarus in his bosom.

₂₄And he cried and said, Father Abraham, have mercy on me, and send Lazarus, that he may dip the tip of his finger in water, and cool my tongue; for I am tormented in this flame.

₂₅But Abraham said, Son, remember that thou in thy lifetime receivedst thy good things, and likewise Lazarus evil things: but now he is comforted, and thou art tormented. ₂₆And beside all this, between us and you there is a great gulf fixed: so that they which would pass from hence to you cannot; neither can they pass to us, that *would come* from thence.

₂₇Then he said, I pray thee therefore, father, that thou wouldest send him to my father's house: ₂₈For I have five brethren; that he may testify unto them, lest they also come into this place of torment.

₂₉Abraham saith unto him, They have Moses and the prophets; let them hear them.

₃₀And he said, Nay, father Abraham: but if one went unto them from the dead, they will repent.

₃₁And he said unto him, If they hear not Moses and the prophets, neither will they be persuaded, though one rose from the dead.

1 JST Luke 16:23
a GR: Eleazar

TEN LEPERS ARE CLEANSED — Luke 17:11-19

₁₁And it came to pass, as he went to Jerusalem, that he passed through the midst of Samaria and Galilee. ₁₂And as he entered into a certain village, there met him ten men that were lepers, which stood afar off: ₁₃And they lifted up *their* voices, and said, Jesus, Master, have mercy on us.

₁₄And when he saw *them*, he said unto them, ªGo shew yourselves unto the priests.

And it came to pass, that, as they went, they were cleansed. ₁₅And one of them, when he saw that he was healed, turned back, and with a loud voice glorified God, ₁₆And fell down on *his* face at his feet, giving him thanks: and he was a Samaritan.

₁₇And Jesus answering said, Were there not ten cleansed? but where *are* the nine? ₁₈There are not found that returned to give glory to

a See Lev. 14:1-32

THIRD YEAR — THE LATER JUDEAN MINISTRY

TEN LEPERS ARE CLEANSED (cont.) — Luke 17:11-19

God, save this stranger. ₁₉And he said unto him, Arise, go thy way: thy faith hath made thee whole.

PARABLE OF THE UNJUST JUDGE — Luke 18:1-8

₁And he spake a parable unto them *to this end*, that men ought always to pray, and not to faint; ₂Saying,

There was in a city a judge, which feared not God, neither regarded man: ₃And there was a widow in that city; and she came unto him, saying, Avenge me of mine adversary. ₄And he would not for a while: but afterward he said within himself, Though I fear not God, nor regard man; ₅Yet because this widow troubleth me, I will avenge her, lest by her continual coming she weary me.

₆And the Lord said, Hear what the unjust judge saith. ₇And shall not God avenge his own elect, which cry day and night unto him, though he bear long with ¹men? ₈I tell you that ²he will come, and when he does come, he will avenge ³his saints speedily. Nevertheless when the Son of man cometh, shall he find faith on the earth?

1 JST Luke 18:7; KJV: them
2 JST Luke 18:8
3 JST Luke 18:8; KJV: them

PARABLE OF THE PHARISEE AND PUBLICAN — Luke 18:9-14

₉And he spake this parable unto certain which trusted in themselves that they were righteous, and despised others: ₁₀Two men went up into the temple to pray; the one a Pharisee, and the other a publican. ₁₁The Pharisee stood and prayed thus with himself, God, I thank thee, that I am not as other men *are*, extortioners, unjust, adulterers, or even as this publican. ₁₂I fast twice in the week, I give tithes of all that I possess.

₁₃And the publican, standing afar off, would not lift up so much as *his* eyes unto heaven, but smote upon his breast, saying, God be merciful to me a sinner.

₁₄I tell you, this man went down to his house justified *rather* than the other: for every one that exalteth himself shall be abased; and he that humbleth himself shall be exalted.

JESUS AT THE FEAST OF TABERNACLES — John 7:10-24

¹And he arose from thence, and cometh into the coasts of Judaea by the farther side of Jordan: and the people resort unto him again; and, as he was wont, he taught them again ²and he healed them there.

₁₀But when his brethren were gone up, then went he also up unto the feast, not openly, but as it were in secret. ₁₁Then the Jews sought him at the feast, and said, Where is he? ₁₂And there was much murmuring among the people concerning him: for some said, He is a good man: others said, Nay; but he deceiveth the people. ₁₃Howbeit no man spake

1 Mark 10:1
2 Matt. 19:2

THIRD YEAR — THE LATER JUDEAN MINISTRY

JESUS IN THE FEAST OF TABERNACLES (cont.) — John 7:10-24

openly of him for fear of the Jews.

₁₄Now about the midst of the feast Jesus went up into the temple, and taught. ₁₅And the Jews marvelled, saying, How knoweth this man letters, having never learned?

₁₆Jesus answered them, and said, My doctrine is not mine, but his that sent me. ₁₇If any man will do his will, he shall know of the doctrine, whether it be of God, or *whether* I speak of myself. ₁₈He that speaketh of himself seeketh his own glory: but he that seeketh his glory that sent him, the same is true, and no unrighteousness is in him. ₁₉Did not Moses give you the law, and *yet* none of you keepeth the law? Why go ye about to kill me?

₂₀The people answered and said, Thou hast a devil: who goeth about to kill thee?

₂₁Jesus answered and said unto them, I have done one work, and ye all marvel. ₂₂Moses therefore gave unto you circumcision; (not because it is of Moses, but of the fathers;) and ye on the sabbath day circumcise a man. ₂₃If a man on the sabbath day receive circumcision, that the law of Moses should not be broken; are ye angry at me, because I have made a man every whit whole on the sabbath day? ₂₄Judge not according to ¹your traditions, but judge righteous judgment.

1 JST John 7:24; KJV: the appearance

I AM NOT COME OF MYSELF — John 7:25-31

₂₅Then said some of them of Jerusalem, Is not this he, whom they seek to kill? ₂₆But, lo, he speaketh boldly, and they say nothing unto him. Do the rulers know indeed that this is the very Christ? ₂₇Howbeit we know this man whence he is: but when Christ cometh, no man knoweth whence he is.

₂₈Then cried Jesus in the temple as he taught, saying, Ye both know me, and ye know whence I am: and I am not come of myself, but he that sent me is true, whom ye know not. ₂₉But I know him: for I am from him, and he hath sent me.

₃₀Then they sought to take him: but no man laid hands on him, because his hour was not yet come. ₃₁And many of the people believed on him, and said, When Christ cometh, will he do more miracles than these which this *man* hath done?

YE SHALL SEEK ME, AND NOT FIND ME — John 7:32-36

₃₂The Pharisees heard that the people murmured such things concerning him; and the Pharisees and the chief priests sent officers to take him.

₃₃Then said Jesus unto them, Yet a little while am I with you, and *then* I go unto him that sent me. ₃₄Ye shall seek me, and shall not find *me*: and where I am, *thither* ye cannot come.

YE SHALL SEEK ME, AND NOT FIND ME (cont.) — John 7:32-36

35 Then said the Jews among themselves, Whither will he go, that we shall not find him? will he go unto the dispersed among the ᵃGentiles, and teach the ᵃGentiles? 36 What *manner of* saying is this that he said, Ye shall seek me, and shall not find *me*: and where I am, *thither* ye cannot come?

a GR: Greeks

RIVERS OF LIVING WATER — John 7:37-39

37 In the last day, that great *day* of the feast, Jesus stood and cried, saying, If any man thirst, let him come unto me, and drink. 38 He that believeth on me, as the scripture hath said, out of his belly shall flow rivers of ᵃliving water. 39 (But this spake he of the Spirit, which they that believe on him should receive: for the Holy Ghost was ¹promised unto them who believe, after that Jesus ²was glorified.)

a Hebrew idiom for running water

1 JST John 7:39; KJV: not yet *given*; because

2 JST John 7:39; KJV: was not yet

A DIVISION AMONG THE PEOPLE — John 7:40-44

40 Many of the people therefore, when they heard this saying, said, Of a truth this is the Prophet. 41 Others said, This is the Christ. But some said, Shall Christ come out of Galilee? 42 Hath not the scripture said, That Christ cometh of the seed of David, and out of the town of ᵃBethlehem, where David was? 43 So there was a division among the people because of him. 44 And some of them would have taken him; but no man laid hands on him.

a 1 Sam. 16:1; Micah 5:2. See also Micah 4:8. (The "tower of the flock" may have been the manger where the lambs without blemish or spot were raised for temple sacrifice, and where Jesus was born.)

NEVER MAN SPAKE LIKE THIS MAN — John 7:45-53

45 Then came the officers to the chief priests and Pharisees; and they said unto them, Why have ye not brought him?
46 The officers answered, Never man spake like this man.
47 Then answered them the Pharisees, Are ye also deceived? 48 Have any of the rulers or of the Pharisees believed on him? 49 But this people who knoweth not the law are cursed.
50 Nicodemus saith unto them, (he that came to Jesus by night, being one of them,) 51 Doth our law judge *any* man, before it hear him, and know what he doeth?
52 They answered and said unto him, Art thou also of Galilee? Search, and look: for out of Galilee ariseth no prophet.
53 And every man went unto his own house.

THE ADULTEROUS WOMAN * John 8:1-11

₁Jesus went unto the mount of Olives. ₂And early in the morning he came again into the temple, and all the people came unto him; and he sat down, and taught them.

₃And the scribes and Pharisees brought unto him a woman taken in adultery; and when they had set her in the midst, ₄They say unto him, Master, this woman was taken in adultery, ᵃin the very act. ₅Now Moses in the law commanded us, that such should be stoned: but what sayest thou? ₆This they said, tempting him, that they might have to accuse him. But Jesus stooped down, and with *his* finger wrote on the ground, *as though he heard them not.*

₇So when they continued asking him, he lifted up himself, and said unto them, He that is without sin among you, let him first cast a stone at her. ₈And again he stooped down, and wrote on the ground.

₉And they which heard *it*, being convicted by *their own* conscience, went out one by one, beginning at the eldest, *even* unto the last: and Jesus was left alone, and the woman standing in the midst.

₁₀When Jesus had lifted up himself, and saw none but the woman, he said unto her, Woman, where are those thine accusers? hath no man condemned thee?

₁₁She said, No man, Lord.

And Jesus said unto her, Neither do I condemn thee: go, and sin no more.

* This event is not found in some early mss.

a Because of the way this feast was celebrated then, it is possible that this woman's accusers were the very men who engaged in the act with her.

THE LIGHT OF THE WORLD John 8:12-20

₁₂Then spake Jesus again unto them, saying, I am the light of the world: he that followeth me shall not walk in darkness, but shall have the light of life.

₁₃The Pharisees therefore said unto him, Thou bearest record of thyself; thy record is not true.

₁₄Jesus answered and said unto them, Though I bear record of myself, *yet* my record is true: for I know whence I came, and whither I go; but ye cannot tell whence I come, and whither I go. Ye judge after the flesh; I judge no man. ₁₆And yet if I judge, my judgment is true: for I am not alone, but I and the Father that sent me. ₁₇It is also written in your law, that ᵃthe testimony of two men is true. ₁₈I am one that bear witness of myself, and the Father that sent me beareth witness of me.

₁₉Then said they unto him, Where is thy Father?

Jesus answered, Ye neither know me, nor my Father: if ye had known me, ye should have known my Father also.

₂₀These words spake Jesus in the treasury, as he taught in the temple: and no man laid hands on him; for his hour was not yet come.

a Deut. 17:6; 19:15

| THIRD YEAR | THE LATER JUDEAN MINISTRY |

WHITHER I GO, YE CANNOT COME — John 8:21-30

21 Then said Jesus again unto them, I go my way, and ye shall seek me, and shall die in your sins: whither I go, ye cannot come. 22 Then said the Jews, Will he kill himself? because he saith, Whither I go, ye cannot come. 23 And he said unto them, Ye are from beneath; I am from above: ye are of this world; I am not of this world. 24 I said therefore unto you, that ye shall die in your sins: for if ye believe not that I am *he*, ye shall die in your sins. 25 Then said they unto him, Who art thou?

And Jesus saith unto them, Even *the same* that I said unto you from the beginning. 26 I have many things to say and to judge of you: but he that sent me is true; and I speak to the world those things which I have heard of him. 27 They understood not that he spake to them of the Father. 28 Then said Jesus unto them, When ye have lifted up the Son of man, then shall ye know that I am *he*, and *that* I do nothing of myself; but as my Father hath taught me, I speak these things. 29 And he that sent me is with me: the Father hath not left me alone; for I do always those things that please him.

30 As he spake these words, many believed on him.

THE TRUTH SHALL MAKE YOU FREE — John 8:31-38

31 Then said Jesus to those Jews which believed on him, If ye continue in my word, *then* are ye my disciples indeed; 32 And ye shall know the truth, and the truth shall make you free. 33 They answered him, We be Abraham's seed, and were never in bondage to any man: how sayest thou, Ye shall be made free? 34 Jesus answered them, Verily, verily, I say unto you, Whosoever committeth sin is the servant of sin. 35 And the servant abideth not in the house for ever: *but* the Son abideth ever. 36 If the Son therefore shall make you free, ye shall be free indeed. 37 I know that ye are Abraham's seed; but ye seek to kill me, because my word hath no place in you. 38 I speak that which I have seen with my Father: and ye do that which ye have seen with your father.

YE ARE OF YOUR FATHER THE DEVIL — John 8:39-47

39 They answered and said unto him, Abraham is our father.

Jesus saith unto them, If ye were Abraham's children, ye would do the works of Abraham. 40 But now ye seek to kill me, a man that hath told you the truth, which I have heard of God: this did not Abraham. 41 Ye do the deeds of your father.

Then said they to him, We be not born of fornication; we have one Father, *even* God.

YE ARE OF YOUR FATHER THE DEVIL (cont.)   John 8:39-47

₄₂Jesus said unto them, If God were your Father, ye would love me: for I proceeded forth and came from God; neither came I of myself, but he sent me. ₄₃Why do ye not understand my speech? *even because ye cannot ¹bear my word.* ₄₄Ye are of *your* father the devil, and the lusts of your father ye will do. He was a murderer from the beginning, and abode not in the truth, because there is no truth in him. When he speaketh a lie, he speaketh of his own: for he is a liar, and the father of it. ₄₅And because I tell *you* the truth, ye believe me not. ₄₆Which of you convinceth me of sin? And if I say the truth, why do ye not believe me? ₄₇He that is of God ²receiveth God's words: ye therefore ³receive *them* not, because ye are not of God.

1 JST John 8:43; KJV: hear

2 JST John 8:47; KJV: heareth

3 JST John 8:47; KJV: hear

BEFORE ABRAHAM WAS I AM   John 8:48-59

₄₈Then answered the Jews, and said unto him, Say we not well that thou art a Samaritan, and hast a devil? ₄₉Jesus answered, I have not a devil; but I honour my Father, and ye do dishonour me. ₅₀And I seek not mine own glory: there is one that seeketh and judgeth. ₅₁Verily, verily, I say unto you, If a man keep my saying, he shall never see death. ₅₂Then said the Jews unto him, Now we know that thou hast a devil. Abraham is dead, and the prophets; and thou sayest, If a man keep my saying, he shall never taste of death. ₅₃Art thou greater than our father Abraham, which is dead? and the prophets are dead: whom makest thou thyself? ₅₄Jesus answered, If I honour myself, my honour is nothing: it is my Father that honoureth me; of whom ye say, that he is your God: ₅₅Yet ye have not known him; but I know him: and if I should say, I know him not, I shall be a liar like unto you: but I know him, and keep his saying. ₅₆Your father Abraham rejoiced to see my day: and he saw *it*, and was glad. ₅₇Then said the Jews unto him, Thou art not yet fifty years old, and hast thou seen Abraham? ₅₈Jesus said unto them, Verily, verily, I say unto you, Before Abraham ªwas, ᵇI AM. ₅₉Then took they up stones to cast at him: but Jesus hid himself, and went out of the temple, going through the midst of them, and so passed by.

a GR: was born, came into being

b These words, in Greek, are used in the Septuigent version of Exod. 3:14 to identify Jehovah

SABBATH HEALING OF A MAN BORN BLIND   John 9:1-12

₁And as *Jesus* passed by, he saw a man which was blind from *his* birth. ₂And his disciples asked him, saying, Master, who did sin, this man, or his parents, that he was born blind? ₃Jesus answered, Neither hath this man sinned, nor his parents: but that the works of God should be made manifest in him. ₄I must work the works of him that sent me, while ¹I am with you: the ²time cometh, when

1 JST John 9:4; KJV: it is day

2 JST John 9:4; KJV: night

82

THIRD YEAR — THE LATER JUDEAN MINISTRY

SABBATH HEALING OF A MAN BORN BLIND (cont.) John 9:1-12

₃I shall have finished my work, then I go unto the Father. ₅As long as I am in the world, I am the light of the world.

₆When he had thus spoken, he spat on the ground, and made clay of the spittle, and he anointed the eyes of the blind man with the clay, ₇And said unto him, Go, wash in the pool of ᵃSiloam, (which is by interpretation, Sent.) He went his way therefore, and washed, and came seeing.

₈The neighbours therefore, and they which before had seen him that he was blind, said, Is not this he that sat and begged? ₉Some said, This is he: others *said*, He is like him: *but* he said, I am *he*.

₁₀Therefore said they unto him, How were thine eyes opened?

₁₁He answered and said, A man that is called Jesus made clay, and anointed mine eyes, and said unto me, Go to the pool of Siloam, and wash: and I went and washed, and I received sight.

₁₂Then said they unto him, Where is he?

He said, I know not.

3 JST John 9:4; KJV: no man can work

a OT: Shiloah (see Isa. 8:6)

WHEREAS I WAS BLIND, NOW I SEE John 9:13-34

₁₃They brought to the Pharisees him that aforetime was blind. ₁₄And it was the sabbath day when Jesus made the clay, and opened his eyes. ₁₅Then again the Pharisees also asked him how he had received his sight.

He said unto them, He put clay upon mine eyes, and I washed, and do see.

₁₆Therefore said some of the Pharisees, This man is not of God, because he keepeth not the sabbath day. Others said, How can a man that is a sinner do such miracles? And there was a division among them. ₁₇They say unto the blind man again, What sayest thou of him, that he hath opened thine eyes?

He said, He is a prophet.

₁₈But the Jews did not believe concerning him, that he had been blind, and received his sight, until they called the parents of him that had received his sight. ₁₉And they asked them, saying, Is this your son, who ye say was born blind? how then doth he now see?

₂₀His parents answered them and said, We know that this is our son, and that he was born blind: ₂₁But by what means he now seeth, we know not; or who hath opened his eyes, we know not: he is of age; ask him: he shall speak for himself. ₂₂These *words* spake his parents, because they feared the Jews: for the Jews had agreed already, that if any man did confess that he was Christ, he should be ᵃput out of the synagogue. ₂₃Therefore said his parents, He is of age; ask him.

₂₄Then again called they the man that was blind, and said unto him,

a IE: excommunicated

WHEREAS I WAS BLIND, NOW I SEE (cont.) John 9:13-34

Give God the praise: we know that this man is a sinner. ₂₅He answered and said, Whether he be a sinner *or no*, I know not: one thing I know, that, whereas I was blind, now I see.

₂₆Then said they to him again, What did he to thee? how opened he thine eyes?

₂₇He answered them, I have told you already, and ye did not hear: ᵇwherefore would ye hear *it* again? will ye also be his disciples?

₂₈Then they reviled him, and said, Thou art his disciple; but we are Moses' disciples. ₂₉We know that God spake unto Moses: *as for* this *fellow*, we know not from whence he is.

₃₀The man answered and said unto them, Why herein is a marvellous thing, that ye know not from whence he is, and *yet* he hath opened mine eyes. ₃₁Now we know that God heareth not sinners: but if any man be a worshipper of God, and doeth his will, him he heareth. ₃₂Since the world began was it not heard that any man opened the eyes of one that was born blind ¹except he be of God. ₃₃If this man were not of God, he could do nothing.

₃₄They answered and said unto him, Thou wast altogether born in sins, and dost thou teach us? And they ᶜcast him out.

b GR: why

1 JST John 9:32

c IE: excommunicated him

THE BLINDNESS OF THE PHARISEES John 9:35-41

₃₅Jesus heard that they had cast him out; and when he had found him, he said unto him, Dost thou believe on the Son of God?

₃₆He answered and said, Who is he, Lord, that I might believe on him?

₃₇And Jesus said unto him, Thou hast both seen him, and it is he that talketh with thee.

₃₈And he said, Lord, I believe. And he worshipped him.

₃₉And Jesus said, For judgment I am come into this world, that they which see not might see; and that they which see might be made blind.

₄₀And *some* of the Pharisees which were with him heard these words, and said unto him, Are we blind also?

₄₁Jesus said unto them, If ye were blind, ye should have no sin: but now ye say, We see; therefore your sin remaineth.

PARABLE OF THE SHEEPFOLD John 10:1-6

₁Verily, verily, I say unto you, He that entereth not by the door into the sheepfold, but climbeth up some other way, the same is a thief and a robber. ₂But he that entereth in by the door is the shepherd of the sheep. ₃To him the ᵃporter openeth; and the sheep hear his voice: and he calleth his own sheep by name, and leadeth them out. ₄And when he putteth forth his own sheep, he goeth before them, and the sheep follow

a GR: doorkeeper

PARABLE OF THE SHEEPFOLD (cont.)   John 10:1-6

him: for they know his voice. ₅And a stranger will they not follow, but will flee from him: for they know not the voice of strangers. ₆This parable spake Jesus unto them: but they understood not what things they were which he spake unto them.

THE GOOD SHEPHERD   John 10:7-21

₇Then said Jesus unto them again, Verily, verily, I say unto you, I am the door of the sheep. ₈All that ever came before me ¹who testified not of me are thieves and robbers: but the sheep did not hear them. ₉I am the door: by me if any man enter in, he shall be saved, and shall go in and out, and find pasture. ₁₀The thief cometh not, but for to steal, and to kill, and to destroy: I am come that they might have life, and that they might have *it* more abundantly.

₁₁ᵃI am the good shepherd: the good shepherd giveth his life for the sheep. ₁₂But he that is an hireling, and not the shepherd, whose own the sheep are not, seeth the wolf coming, and leaveth the sheep, and fleeth: and the wolf catcheth them, and scattereth the sheep. ₁₃The hireling fleeth, because he is an hireling, and careth not for the sheep. ₁₄I am the good shepherd, and know my *sheep*, and am known of mine. ₁₅As the Father knoweth me, even so know I the Father: and I lay down my life for the sheep.

₁₆And other sheep I have, which are not of this fold: them also I must bring, and they shall hear my voice; and there shall be one fold, *and* one shepherd. ₁₇Therefore doth my Father love me, because I lay down my life, that I might take it again. ₁₈No man taketh it from me, but I lay it down of myself. I have power to lay it down, and I have ᵇpower to take it again. This commandment have I received of my Father.

₁₉There was a division therefore again among the Jews for these sayings. ₂₀And many of them said, He hath a devil, and is mad; why hear ye him? ₂₁Others said, These are not the words of him that hath a devil. Can a devil open the eyes of the blind?

1 JST John 10:8

a Ps. 23:1

b GR: authority, full power

ABOUT MARRIAGE AND DIVORCE   Matt. 19:3-12

₃The Pharisees also came unto him, tempting him, and saying unto him, Is it lawful for a man to ᵃput away his wife for every cause? ₄And he answered and said unto them, Have ye not read, that he which made *them* at the beginning ᵇMADE THEM MALE AND FEMALE, ₅And said, ᶜFOR THIS CAUSE SHALL A MAN LEAVE FATHER AND MOTHER, AND SHALL CLEAVE TO HIS WIFE: AND THEY TWAIN SHALL BE ONE FLESH? ₆Wherefore they are no more twain, but one flesh. What therefore God hath joined together, let not man ᵈput asunder.

a GR: divorce

b Gen. 1:27

c Gen. 2:24. (Note that Christ here affirms the Genesis narrative of man's creation.)

d IE: divide, separate

ABOUT MARRIAGE AND DIVORCE (cont.) — Matt. 19:3-12

₇They say unto him, Why did Moses then command to ᵉGIVE A ᶠWRITING OF DIVORCEMENT, AND TO PUT HER AWAY? ₈He saith unto them, Moses because of the hardness of your hearts suffered you to put away your wives: but from the beginning it was not so. ₉And I say unto you, Whosoever shall put away his wife, except *it be* for fornication, and shall marry another, committeth adultery: and whoso marrieth her which is put away doth commit adultery.

¹And in the house his disciples asked him again of the same matter. ₁₀His disciples say unto him, If the case of the man be so with *his* wife, it is not good to marry.

₁₁But he said unto them, All *men* cannot receive this saying, save *they* to whom it is given. ₁₂For there are some eunuchs, which were so born from *their* mother's womb: and there are some eunuchs, which were made eunuchs of men: and there be eunuchs, which have made themselves eunuchs for the kingdom of heaven's sake. He that is able to receive *it*, let him receive *it*.

e Deut. 24:1-4
f GR: certificate of divorce
1 Mark 10:10

BLESSING THE LITTLE CHILDREN — Mark 10:13-16

₁₃And they brought young children to him, that he should touch them: and *his* disciples rebuked those that brought *them*. ₁₄But when Jesus saw *it*, he was much displeased, and said unto them, Suffer the little children to come unto me, and forbid them not: for of such is the kingdom of God. ₁₅Verily I say unto you, Whosoever shall not receive the kingdom of God as a little child, he shall not enter therein. ₁₆And he took them up in his arms, put *his* hands upon them, and blessed them.

THE RICH YOUNG MAN — Mark 10:17-31

₁₇And when he was gone forth into the way, there came one running, and kneeled to him, and asked him, Good Master, what shall I do that I may inherit eternal life?

¹ ₁₇And he said unto him, ᵃWhy callest thou me good? *there is* none good but one, *that is*, God: but if thou wilt enter into life, keep the commandments.

₁₈He saith unto him, Which?

Jesus said, ᵇTHOU SHALT DO NO MURDER, THOU SHALT NOT COMMIT ADULTERY, THOU SHALT NOT STEAL, THOU SHALT NOT BEAR FALSE WITNESS, ₁₉ᶜHONOUR THY FATHER AND *THY* MOTHER: and, ᵈTHOU SHALT LOVE THY NEIGHBOUR AS THYSELF.

₂₀The young man saith unto him, All these things have I kept from my youth up: what lack I yet?

₂₁Then Jesus beholding him loved him, and said unto him, One thing thou lackest: go thy way, sell whatsoever thou hast, and give to the poor, and thou shalt have treasure in heaven: and come, take up the

1 Matt. 19:17-20
a This may have been an question about this young man's testimony of Christ's deity.
b Exod. 20:13-16
c Exod. 20:12
d Lev. 19:18

THIRD YEAR — THE LATER JUDEAN MINISTRY

THE RICH YOUNG MAN (cont.) — Mark 10:17-31

cross, and follow me.

₂₂And he was sad at that saying, and went away grieved: for he had great possessions.

₂₃And Jesus looked round about, and saith unto his disciples, How hardly shall they that have riches enter into the kingdom of God!

₂₄And the disciples were astonished at his words. But Jesus answereth again, and saith unto them, Children, how hard is it for them that trust in riches to enter into the kingdom of God! ₂₅It is easier for a camel to go through the eye of a needle, than for a rich man to enter into the kingdom of God.

₂₆And they were astonished out of measure, saying among themselves, Who then can be saved?

₂₇And Jesus looking upon them saith, With men *it is* impossible, but not with God: for with God all things are possible.

²₂₇**Then answered Peter and said unto him, Behold, we have forsaken all, and followed thee; what shall we have therefore?**

₂₈**And Jesus said unto them, Verily I say unto you, That ye which have followed me, in the ³resurrection when the Son of man shall sit in the throne of his glory, ye also shall sit upon twelve thrones, judging the twelve tribes of Israel.** ₂₉And every one that hath forsaken houses, or brethren, or sisters, or father, or mother, or wife, or children, or lands, for my name's sake, shall receive an hundredfold, and shall inherit everlasting life. ₃₀But many *that are* first shall be last; and the last *shall be* first.

2 Matt. 19:27-30
3 JST Matt. 19:28; KJV: regeneration

PARABLE OF THE LABORERS IN THE VINEYARD — Matt. 20:1-16

₁For the kingdom of heaven is like unto a man *that is* an householder, which went out early in the morning to hire labourers into his vineyard. ₂And when he had agreed with the labourers for a penny a day, he sent them into his vineyard. ₃And he went out about the third hour, and saw others standing idle in the marketplace, ₄And said unto them; Go ye also into the vineyard, and whatsoever is right I will give you. And they went their way. ₅Again he went out about the sixth and ninth hour, and did likewise. ₆And about the eleventh hour he went out, and found others standing idle, and saith unto them, Why stand ye here all the day idle?

₇They say unto him, Because no man hath hired us.

He saith unto them, Go ye also into the vineyard; and whatsoever is right, *that* shall ye receive. ₈So when even was come, the lord of the vineyard saith unto his steward, Call the labourers, and give them *their* hire, beginning from the last unto the first.

₉And when they came that *were hired* about the eleventh hour, they received every man a penny. ₁₀But when the first came, they supposed

THIRD YEAR	THE LATER JUDEAN MINISTRY	

PARABLE OF THE LABORERS IN THE VINEYARD (cont.) — Matt. 20:1-16

that they should have received more; and they likewise received every man a penny. ₁₁And when they had received *it*, they murmured against the goodman of the house, ₁₂Saying, These last have wrought *but* one hour, and thou hast made them equal unto us, which have borne the burden and heat of the day.

₁₃But he answered one of them, and said, Friend, I do thee no wrong: didst not thou agree with me for a penny? ₁₄Take *that* thine *is*, and go thy way: I will give unto this last, even as unto thee. ₁₅Is it not lawful for me to do what I will with mine own? Is thine eye evil, because I am good? ₁₆So the last shall be first, and the first last: for many be called, but few chosen.

DECLARATION AT THE FEAST OF THE DEDICATION — John 10:22-42

₂₂And it was at Jerusalem the feast of the dedication, and it was winter. ₂₃And Jesus walked in the temple in Solomon's porch. ₂₄Then came the Jews round about him, and said unto him, How long dost thou make us to doubt? If thou be the Christ, tell us plainly.

₂₅Jesus answered them, I told you, and ye believed not: the works that I do in my Father's name, they bear witness of me. ₂₆But ye believe not, because ye are not of my sheep, as I said unto you. ₂₇My sheep hear my voice, and I know them, and they follow me: ₂₈And I give unto them eternal life; and they shall never perish, neither shall any *man* pluck them out of my hand. ₂₉My Father, which gave *them* me, is greater than all; and no *man* is able to pluck *them* out of my Father's hand. ₃₀I and *my* Father are one.

₃₁Then the Jews took up stones again to stone him. ₃₂Jesus answered them, Many good works have I shewed you from my Father; for which of those works do ye stone me?

₃₃The Jews answered him, saying, For a good work we stone thee not; but for blasphemy; and because that thou, being a man, makest thyself God.

₃₄Jesus answered them, Is it not written in your law, a I SAID, YE ARE GODS? ₃₅If he called them gods, b unto whom the word of God came, and the scripture cannot be broken; ₃₆Say ye of him, whom the Father hath sanctified, and sent into the world, Thou blasphemest; because I said, I am the Son of God? ₃₇If I do not the works of my Father, believe me not. ₃₈But if I do, though ye believe not me, believe the works: that ye may know, and believe, that the Father *is* in me, and I in him.

₃₉Therefore they sought again to take him: but he escaped out of their hand, ₄₀And went away again beyond Jordan into the place where John at first baptized; and there he abode. ₄₁And many resorted unto him, and said, John did no miracle: but all things that John spake of this man were true. ₄₂And many believed on him there.

a Ps. 82:6

b Christ here identifies those to whom the statements in Ps. 82 were made.

| THIRD YEAR | THE PEREAN MINISTRY | |

THE DEATH OF LAZARUS — John 11:1-16

₁Now a certain *man* was sick, *named* Lazarus, of Bethany, the town of Mary and her sister Martha. ₂(It was *that* Mary which anointed the Lord with ointment, and wiped his feet with her hair, whose brother Lazarus was sick.) ₃Therefore his sisters sent unto him, saying, Lord, behold, he whom thou lovest is sick.

₄When Jesus heard *that*, he said, This sickness is not unto death, but for the glory of God, that the Son of God might be glorified thereby. ₅Now Jesus loved Martha, and her sister, and Lazarus. ₆When he had heard therefore that he was sick, he abode two days still in the same place where he was. ₇Then after that saith he to *his* disciples, Let us go into Judaea again.

₈*His* disciples say unto him, Master, the ᵃJews of late sought to stone thee; and goest thou thither again?

₉Jesus answered, Are there not twelve hours in the day? If any man walk in the day, he stumbleth not, because he seeth the light of this world. ₁₀But if a man walk in the night, he stumbleth, because there is no light in him. ₁₁These things said he: and after that he saith unto them, Our friend Lazarus sleepeth; but I go, that I may awake him out of sleep.

₁₂Then said his disciples, Lord, if he sleep, he shall ᵇdo well. ₁₃Howbeit Jesus spake of his death: but they thought that he had spoken of taking of rest in sleep.

₁₄Then said Jesus unto them plainly, Lazarus is dead. ₁₅And I am glad for your sakes that I was not there, to the intent ye may believe; nevertheless let us go unto him.

₁₆Then said Thomas, which is called Didymus, unto his fellowdisciples, Let us also go, that we may die with him; ¹for they feared lest the Jews should take Jesus and put him to death, for as yet they did not understand the power of God.

a IE: Judeans
b GR: be cured or saved
1 JST John 11:16

JESUS' COMING DEATH AND RESURRECTION — Mark 10:32-34

₃₂And they were in the way going up to Jerusalem; and Jesus went before them: and they were amazed; and as they followed, they were afraid. And he took again the twelve, and began to tell them what things should happen unto him, ₃₃*Saying*, Behold, we go up to Jerusalem; ¹and all things that are written by the prophets concerning the Son of Man shall be accomplished. For he shall be delivered unto the chief priests, and unto the scribes; and they shall condemn him to death, and shall deliver him to the Gentiles: ₃₄And they shall mock him, and shall scourge him, and shall spit upon him, and shall kill him: and the third day he shall rise again. ²And they understood none of these things: and this saying was hid from them, neither knew they the things which were spoken.

1 Luke 18:31
2 Luke 18:34

THIRD YEAR — THE PEREAN MINISTRY

THE PETITION OF THE SONS OF ZEBEDEE — Matt. 20:20-24

₂₀Then came to him the mother of Zebedee's children with her sons, worshipping *him*, and desiring a certain thing of him.
₂₁And he said unto her, What wilt thou?
She saith unto him, Grant that these my two sons may sit, the one on thy right hand, and the other on the left, in thy kingdom.

1 Mark 10:35-37

**¹₃₅And James and John, the sons of Zebedee, come unto him, saying, Master, we would that thou shouldest do for us whatsoever we shall desire.
₃₆And he said unto them, What would ye that I should do for you?
₃₇They said unto him, Grant unto us that we may sit, one on thy right hand, and the other on thy left hand, in thy glory.**

₂₂But Jesus answered and said, Ye know not what ye ask. Are ye able to drink of the cup that I shall drink of, and to be baptized with the baptism that I am baptized with?
They say unto him, We are able.
₂₃And he saith unto them, Ye shall drink indeed of my cup, and be baptized with the baptism that I am baptized with: but to sit on my right hand, and on my left, is not mine to give, but *it shall be given to them* for whom it is prepared of my Father.
₂₄And when the ten heard *it*, they were moved with indignation against the two brethren.

HE THAT IS GREATEST AMONG YOU — Luke 22:24-30

₂₄And there was also a strife among them, which of them should be accounted the greatest.
₂₅And he said unto them, The kings of the Gentiles exercise lordship over them; and they that exercise authority upon them are called benefactors. ₂₆But ye *shall* not *be* so: but he that is greatest among you, let him be as the younger; and he that is chief, as he that doth serve.
¹₂₇And whosoever ᵃwill be chief among you, let him be your servant: ₂₈Even as the Son of man came not to be ministered unto, but to minister, and to give his life a ransom for many.
₂₇For whether *is* greater, he that sitteth at meat, or he that serveth? *is* not he that sitteth at meat? but I am among you as he that serveth. ₂₈Ye are they which have continued with me in my temptations. ₂₉And I appoint unto you a kingdom, as my Father hath appointed unto me; ₃₀That ye may eat and drink at my table in my kingdom, and sit on thrones judging the twelve tribes of Israel.

1 Matt. 20:27-28

a GR: desires to be

THE PEREAN MINISTRY

THE HEALING OF BARTIMAEUS   Mark 10:46-52

₄₆And they came to Jericho: and as he went out of Jericho with his disciples and a great number of people, blind Bartimaeus, the son of Timaeus, sat by the highway side begging. ¹₃₆**And hearing the multitude pass by, he asked what it meant.** ₃₇**And they told him, that Jesus of Nazareth passeth by.** ₄₇And when he heard that it was Jesus of Nazareth, he began to cry out, and say, Jesus, *thou* Son of David, have mercy on me. ²**And they which went before rebuked him, that he should hold his peace: but he cried so much the more, Thou Son of David, have mercy on me.**

₄₉And Jesus stood still, and commanded him to be called. And they call the blind man, saying unto him, Be of good comfort, rise; he calleth thee. ₅₀And he, casting away his garment, rose, and came to Jesus. ³₄₀**And when he was come near, he asked him,** ₄₁**Saying, What wilt thou that I shall do unto thee?**

And he said, Lord, that I may receive my sight.

₅₂And Jesus said unto him, Go thy way; thy faith hath made thee whole. And immediately he received his sight, and followed Jesus in the way, ⁴**glorifying God: and all the people, when they saw** *it,* **gave praise unto God.**

1 Luke 18:36-37
2 Luke 18:39
3 Luke 18:40-41
4 Luke 18:43

THE HOUSE OF ZACCHAEUS   Luke 19:1-10

₁And *Jesus* entered and passed through Jericho. ₂And, behold, *there was* a man named Zacchaeus, which was the chief among the publicans, and he was rich. ₃And he sought to see Jesus who he was; and could not for the press, because he was little of stature. ₄And he ran before, and climbed up into a sycomore tree to see him: for he was to pass that *way.*

₅And when Jesus came to the place, he looked up, and saw him, and said unto him, Zacchaeus, make haste, and come down; for to day I must abide at thy house. ₆And he made haste, and came down, and received him joyfully. ₇And when they saw *it,* they all murmured, saying, That he was gone to be guest with a man that is a sinner.

₈And Zacchaeus stood, and said unto the Lord; Behold, Lord, the half of my goods I give to the poor; and if I have taken any thing from any man by false accusation, I restore *him* fourfold.

₉And Jesus said unto him, This day is salvation come to this house, forsomuch as he also is a son of Abraham. ₁₀For the Son of man is come to seek and to save that which was lost.

PARABLE OF THE POUNDS *   Luke 19:11-28

₁₁And as they heard these things, he added and spake a parable, because he was nigh to Jerusalem, and because they thought that the kingdom of God should immediately appear.

* cf. Matt. 25:14-30

THIRD YEAR — THE PEREAN MINISTRY

PARABLE OF THE POUNDS (cont.) — Luke 19:11-28

₁₂He said therefore, A certain nobleman went into a far country to receive for himself a kingdom, and to return. ₁₃And he called his ten servants, and delivered them ten pounds, and said unto them, Occupy till I come.

₁₄But his citizens hated him, and sent a ᵃmessage after him, saying, We will not have this *man* to reign over us. ₁₅And it came to pass, that when he was returned, having received the kingdom, then he commanded these servants to be called unto him, to whom he had given the money, that he might know how much every man had gained by trading.

₁₆Then came the first, saying, Lord, thy pound hath gained ten pounds.

₁₇And he said unto him, Well, thou good servant: because thou hast been faithful in a very little, have thou authority over ten cities.

₁₈And the second came, saying, Lord, thy pound hath gained five pounds.

₁₉And he said likewise to him, Be thou also over five cities.

₂₀And another came, saying, Lord, behold, *here is* thy pound, which I have kept laid up in a napkin: ₂₁For I feared thee, because thou art an ᵇaustere man: thou takest up that thou layedst not down, and reapest that thou didst not sow.

₂₂And he saith unto him, Out of thine own mouth will I judge thee, *thou* wicked servant. Thou knewest that I was an austere man, taking up that I laid not down, and reaping that I did not sow: ₂₃Wherefore then gavest not thou my money into the bank, that at my coming I might have ᶜrequired mine own with usury?

₂₄And he said unto them that stood by, Take from him the pound, and give *it* to him that hath ten pounds. ₂₅(And they said unto him, Lord, he hath ten pounds.) ₂₆For I say unto you, That unto every one which ¹occupieth shall be given; and from him that ¹occupieth not, even that he ¹received shall be taken away from him. ₂₇But those mine enemies, which would not that I should reign over them, bring hither, and slay *them* before me.

₂₈And when he had thus spoken, he went before, ascending up to Jerusalem.

a GR: ambassador
b IE: harsh, ungenerous
c GR: collected
1 JST: Luke 19:25; KJV: hath

I AM THE RESURRECTION, AND THE LIFE — John 11:17-27

₁₇Then when Jesus came ¹to Bethany, to Martha's house, Lazarus had already been in the grave four days. ₁₈Now Bethany was nigh unto Jerusalem, about fifteen ᵃfurlongs off: ₁₉And many of the Jews came to Martha and Mary, to comfort them concerning their brother. ₂₀Then Martha, as soon as she heard that Jesus was coming, went and met him: but Mary sat *still* in the house. ₂₁Then said Martha unto Jesus, Lord, if thou hadst been here, my brother had not died. ₂₂But I know, that even

1 JST John 11:17; KJV: he found that he had *lain*
a GR: *stadium* (equivalent to 607' or 185 m.; fifteen *stadia* is about two miles)

I AM THE RESURRECTION, AND THE LIFE (cont.)	John 11:17-27

now, whatsoever thou wilt ask of God, God will give *it* thee.

$_{23}$Jesus saith unto her, Thy brother shall rise again.

$_{24}$Martha saith unto him, I know that he shall rise again in the resurrection at the last day.

$_{25}$Jesus said unto her, I am the resurrection, and the life: he that believeth in me, though he were dead, yet shall he live: $_{26}$And whosoever liveth and believeth in me shall never die. Believest thou this?

$_{27}$She saith unto him, Yea, Lord: I believe that thou art the Christ, the Son of God, which should come into the world.

JESUS WEEPS	John 11:28-37

$_{28}$And when she had so said, she went her way, and called Mary her sister secretly, saying, The Master is come, and calleth for thee. $_{29}$As soon as she heard *that*, she arose quickly, and came unto him. $_{30}$Now Jesus was not yet come into the town, but was in that place where Martha met him.

$_{31}$The Jews then which were with her in the house, and comforted her, when they saw Mary, that she rose up hastily and went out, followed her, saying, She goeth unto the grave to weep there.

$_{32}$Then when Mary was come where Jesus was, and saw him, she fell down at his feet, saying unto him, Lord, if thou hadst been here, my brother had not died.

$_{33}$When Jesus therefore saw her weeping, and the Jews also weeping which came with her, he groaned in the spirit, and was troubled,

$_{34}$And said, Where have ye laid him?

They said unto him, Lord, come and see.

$_{35}$Jesus wept.

$_{36}$Then said the Jews, Behold how he loved him! $_{37}$And some of them said, Could not this man, which opened the eyes of the blind, have caused that even this man should not have died?

LAZARUS, COME FORTH	John 11:38-44

$_{38}$Jesus therefore again groaning in himself cometh to the grave. It was a cave, and a stone lay upon it. $_{39}$Jesus said, Take ye away the stone.

Martha, the sister of him that was dead, saith unto him, Lord, by this time he stinketh: for he hath been *dead* four days.

$_{40}$Jesus saith unto her, Said I not unto thee, that, if thou wouldest believe, thou shouldest see the glory of God? $_{41}$Then they took away the stone *from the place* where the dead was laid.

And Jesus lifted up *his* eyes, and said, Father, I thank thee that thou hast heard me. $_{42}$And I knew that thou hearest me always: but because of the people which stand by I said *it*, that they may believe that thou

LAZARUS, COME FORTH (cont.) — John 11:38-44

hast sent me. ₄₃And when he thus had spoken, he cried with a loud voice, ᵃLazarus, come forth. ₄₄And he that was dead came forth, bound hand and foot with graveclothes: and his face was bound about with a napkin. Jesus saith unto them, Loose him, and let him go.

a GR: Eleazar

PLOTTING TO KILL JESUS — John 11:45-57

₄₅Then many of the Jews which came to Mary, and had seen the things which Jesus did, believed on him. ₄₆But some of them went their ways to the Pharisees, and told them what things Jesus had done. ₄₇Then gathered the chief priests and the Pharisees a council, and said, What do we? for this man doeth many miracles. ₄₈If we let him thus alone, all *men* will believe on him: and the Romans shall come and take away both our place and nation.

₄₉And one of them, *named* Caiaphas, being the high priest that same year, said unto them, Ye know nothing at all, ₅₀Nor consider that it is expedient for us, that one man should die for the people, and that the whole nation perish not. ₅₁And this spake he not of himself: but being high priest that year, he prophesied that Jesus should die for that nation; ₅₂And not for that nation only, but that also he should gather together in one the children of God that were scattered abroad.

₅₃Then from that day forth they took counsel together for to put him to death. ₅₄Jesus therefore walked no more openly among the Jews; but went thence unto a country near to the wilderness, into a city called Ephraim, and there continued with his disciples.

₅₅And the Jews' passover was nigh at hand: and many went out of the country up to Jerusalem before the passover, to purify themselves. ₅₆Then sought they for Jesus, and spake among themselves, as they stood in the temple, What think ye, that he will not come to the feast? ₅₇Now both the chief priests and the Pharisees had given a commandment, that, if any man knew where he were, he should shew *it*, that they might take him.

ANOINTING JESUS' FEET — John 12:1-8

₁Then Jesus six days before the passover came to Bethany, where Lazarus was which had been dead, whom he raised from the dead. ₂There they made him a supper; and Martha served: but Lazarus was one of them that sat at the table with him.

₃Then took Mary a pound of ointment of spikenard, very costly, and anointed the feet of Jesus, and wiped his feet with her hair: and the house was filled with the odour of the ointment. ₄Then saith one of his disciples, Judas Iscariot, Simon's *son*, which should betray him, ₅Why was not this ointment sold for three hundred pence, and given to the

ANOINTING JESUS' FEET (cont.) — John 12:1-8

poor? 6This he said, not that he cared for the poor; but because he was a thief, and had the bag, and bare what was put therein.

7Then said Jesus, Let her alone: [1]<u>for she hath preserved this ointment until now, that she might anoint me in token of my burial</u>. 8For the poor always ye have with you; but me ye have not always.

1 JST John 12:7; KJV: against the day of my burying hath she kept this.

A PLOT AGAINST LAZARUS — John 12:9-11

9Much people of the Jews therefore knew that he was there: and they came not for Jesus' sake only, but that they might see [a]Lazarus also, whom he had raised from the dead.

10But the chief priests consulted that they might put Lazarus also to death; 11Because that by reason of him many of the Jews went away, and believed on Jesus.

a GR: Eleazar

SUNDAY — THE WEEK OF THE ATONING SACRIFICE

THY KING COMETH
Mark 11:1-11

₁And when they came nigh to Jerusalem, unto Bethphage and Bethany, at the mount of Olives, he sendeth forth two of his disciples, ₂And saith unto them, Go your way into the village over against you: and as soon as ye be entered into it, ye shall find a colt tied, whereon never man sat; loose him, and bring *him*. ₃And if any man say unto you, Why do ye this? say ye that the Lord hath need of him; and straightway he will send him hither.

₄And they went their way, and found the colt tied by the door without in a place where two ways met; and they loose him. ₅And certain of them that stood there said unto them, What do ye, loosing the colt? ₆And they said unto them even as Jesus had commanded: and they let them go.

₇And they brought the colt to Jesus, and cast their garments on him; and he sat upon him; ¹₁₄**as it is written,** ₁₅ᵃ**FEAR NOT,** ᵇ**DAUGHTER OF SION: BEHOLD, THY KING COMETH, SITTING ON AN ASS'S COLT.**

²And a very great multitude ³that were come to the feast, when they heard that Jesus was coming to Jerusalem, ₂ᶜ**spread their garments in the way; others cut down branches from the ⁴palm trees,** ¹**and strawed** *them* **in the way. ⁵And when he was come nigh, even now at the descent of the mount of Olives, the whole multitude of the disciples began to rejoice and praise God with a loud voice for all the mighty works that they had seen;** ⁶**And the multitudes that went before, and that followed, cried, saying,** ᵈ**Hosanna to the Son of David;** ᵉ**BLESSED** *IS* **HE THAT COMETH IN THE NAME OF THE LORD;** ⁷That bringeth ₁₀the kingdom of our father David; ⁶Hosanna in the highest.

⁸₃₉**And some of the Pharisees from among the multitude said unto him, Master, rebuke thy disciples.**

₄₀**And he answered and said unto them, I tell you that, if these should hold their peace, the stones would immediately cry out.** ₄₁**And when he was come near, he beheld the city, and wept over it,** ₄₂**Saying, If thou hadst known, even thou, at least in this thy day, the things** *which belong* **unto thy peace! but now they are hid from thine eyes.** ₄₃**For the days shall come upon thee, that thine enemies shall cast a trench about thee, and compass thee round, and keep thee in on every side,** ₄₄**And shall lay thee even with the ground, and thy children within thee; and they shall not leave in thee one stone upon another; because thou knewest not the time of thy visitation.**

₁₁And Jesus entered into Jerusalem, and into the temple: and when he had looked round about upon all things, and now the eventide was come, he went out unto Bethany with the twelve.

1 John 12:14-15
a Isa. 40:9
b Zech. 9:9
2 Matt. 21:8
3 John 12:12
c See 2 Kings 9:13
4 John 12:13
5 Luke 19:37
6 Matt. 21:9
d GR: Save now, see Ps. 118:25
e Ps. 118:26
7 JST Mark 11:11; KJV: Blessed be
8 Luke 19:39-44

SUNDAY — THE WEEK OF THE ATONING SACRIFICE

HE THAT LOVETH HIS LIFE SHALL LOSE IT — John 12:20-26

₂₀And there were certain Greeks among them that came up to worship at the feast: ₂₁The same came therefore to Philip, which was of Bethsaida of Galilee, and desired him, saying, Sir, we would see Jesus. ₂₂Philip cometh and telleth Andrew: and again Andrew and Philip tell Jesus. ₂₃And Jesus answered them, saying, The hour is come, that the Son of man should be glorified. ₂₄Verily, verily, I say unto you, Except a ᵃcorn of wheat fall into the ground and die, it abideth alone: but if it die, it bringeth forth much fruit. ₂₅He that loveth his life shall lose it; and he that hateth his life in this world shall keep it unto life eternal. ₂₆If any man serve me, let him follow me; and where I am, there shall also my servant be: if any man serve me, him will *my* Father honour.

a GR: grain, seed

A VOICE FROM HEAVEN — John 12:27-36

₂₇Now is my soul troubled; and what shall I say? Father, save me from this hour: but for this cause came I unto this hour. ₂₈Father, glorify thy name.

Then came there a voice from heaven, *saying*, I have both glorified *it*, and will glorify *it* again. ₂₉The people therefore, that stood by, and heard *it*, said that it thundered: others said, An angel spake to him.

₃₀Jesus answered and said, This voice came not because of me, but for your sakes. ₃₁Now is the judgment of this world: now shall the prince of this world be cast out. ₃₂And I, if I be lifted up from the earth, will draw all *men* unto me. ₃₃This he said, signifying what death he should die.

₃₄The people answered him, We have heard out of the law that Christ abideth for ever: and how sayest thou, The Son of man must be lifted up? who is this Son of man?

₃₅Then Jesus said unto them, Yet a little while is the light with you. Walk while ye have the light, lest darkness come upon you: for he that walketh in darkness knoweth not whither he goeth. ₃₆While ye have light, believe in the light, that ye may be the children of light.

These things spake Jesus, and departed, and did hide himself from them.

BLINDED THEIR EYES, HARDENED THEIR HEART — John 12:37-43

₃₇But though he had done so many miracles before them, yet they believed not on him: ₃₈That the saying of ᵃEsaias the prophet might be fulfilled, which he spake, ᵇLORD, WHO HATH BELIEVED OUR REPORT? AND TO WHOM HATH THE ARM OF THE LORD BEEN REVEALED?

₃₉Therefore they could not believe, because that Esaias said again, ₄₀ᶜHE HATH BLINDED THEIR EYES, AND HARDENED THEIR HEART; THAT THEY SHOULD NOT SEE WITH *THEIR* EYES, NOR UNDERSTAND WITH *THEIR* HEART, AND BE CONVERTED, AND I SHOULD HEAL THEM. ₄₁These things said

a GR: Isaiah
b Isa. 53:1
c Isa. 6:10

* MONDAY   THE WEEK OF THE ATONING SACRIFICE

| BLINDED THEIR EYES, HARDENED THEIR HEART (cont.) | John 12:37-43 |

Esaias, when he saw his glory, and spake of him.
₄₂Nevertheless among the chief rulers also many believed on him; but because of the Pharisees they did not confess *him*, lest they should be ᵈput out of the synagogue: ₄₃For they loved the praise of men more than the praise of God.

d IE: excommunicated

HE THAT SEETH ME SEETH HIM THAT SENT ME — John 12:44-50

₄₄Jesus cried and said, He that believeth on me, believeth not on me, but on him that sent me. ₄₅And he that seeth me seeth him that sent me. ₄₆I am come a light into the world, that whosoever believeth on me should not abide in darkness. ₄₇And if any man hear my words, and believe not, I judge him not: for I came not to judge the world, but to save the world. ₄₈He that rejecteth me, and receiveth not my words, hath one that judgeth him: the word that I have spoken, the same shall judge him in the last day. ₄₉For I have not spoken of myself; but the Father which sent me, he gave me a commandment, what I should say, and what I should speak. ₅₀And I know that his commandment is life everlasting: whatsoever I speak therefore, even as the Father said unto me, so I speak.

* CURSING THE FIG TREE — Mark 11:12-14

₁₂And on the morrow, when they were come from Bethany, he was hungry: ₁₃And seeing a fig tree afar off having leaves, he came, if haply he might find any thing thereon: and when he came to it, he found nothing but leaves; for the time of figs was not *yet*.
₁₄And Jesus answered and said unto it, No man eat fruit of thee hereafter for ever. And his disciples heard *it*.

DEN OF THIEVES * — Mark 11:15-19

₁₅And they come to Jerusalem: and Jesus went into the temple, and began to cast out them that sold and bought in the temple, and overthrew the tables of the moneychangers, and the seats of them that sold doves; ₁₆And would not suffer that any man should carry *any* vessel through the temple.
₁₇And he taught, saying unto them, Is it not written, ᵃMY HOUSE SHALL BE CALLED OF ALL NATIONS THE HOUSE OF PRAYER? but ye have made it ᵇA DEN OF THIEVES.
¹₁₄And the blind and the lame came to him in the temple; and he healed them. ₁₅And when the chief priests and scribes saw the wonderful things that he did, and the children ²of the kingdom crying in the temple, and saying, Hosanna to the Son of David; they were sore displeased, ₁₆And said unto him, Hearest thou what these say?

* cf. John 2:13-25
a Isa. 56:7
b Jer. 7:11
1 Matt. 21:14-16
2 JST Matt. 21:13

* TUESDAY — THE WEEK OF THE ATONING SACRIFICE

DEN OF THIEVES (cont.) — Mark 11:15-19

And Jesus saith unto them, Yea; have ye never read, ᶜOUT OF THE MOUTH OF BABES AND SUCKLINGS THOU HAST PERFECTED PRAISE? ₁₈And the scribes and chief priests heard *it*, and sought how they might destroy him: for they feared him, because all the people was astonished at his doctrine. ₁₉And when even was come, ³he left them, and went out of the city into Bethany; and he lodged there.

c Ps. 8:2

3 Matt. 21:17

* FAITH TO MOVE MOUNTAINS — Mark 11:20-26

₂₀And in the morning, as they passed by, they saw the fig tree dried up from the roots. ₂₁And Peter calling to remembrance saith unto him, Master, behold, the fig tree which thou cursedst is withered away. ₂₂And Jesus answering saith unto them, Have faith in God. ₂₃For verily I say unto you, That whosoever shall say unto this mountain, Be thou removed, and be thou cast into the sea; and shall not doubt in his heart, but shall believe that those things which he saith shall come to pass; he shall have whatsoever he saith. ₂₄Therefore I say unto you, What things soever ye desire, when ye pray, believe that ye receive *them*, and ye shall have *them*. ₂₅And when ye stand praying, forgive, if ye have ought against any: that your Father also which is in heaven may forgive you your trespasses. ₂₆But if ye do not forgive, neither will your Father which is in heaven forgive your trespasses.

PARABLE OF THE BARREN FIG TREE — Luke 13:6-9

₆He spake also this parable; A certain *man* had a fig tree planted in his vineyard; and he came and sought fruit thereon, and found none. ₇Then said he unto the dresser of his vineyard, Behold, these three years I come seeking fruit on this fig tree, and find none: cut it down; why cumbereth it the ground? ₈And he answering said unto him, Lord, let it alone this year also, till I shall dig about it, and dung *it*: ₉And if it bear fruit, *well*: and if not, *then* after that thou shalt cut it down.

BY WHAT AUTHORITY? — Mark 11:27-33

₂₇And they come again to Jerusalem: and as he was walking in the temple, there come to him the chief priests, and the scribes, and the elders, ₂₈And say unto him, By what authority doest thou these things? and who gave thee this authority to do these things? ₂₉And Jesus answered and said unto them, I will also ask of you one question, and answer me, and I will tell you by what authority I do these things. ₃₀The baptism of John, was *it* from heaven, or of men? answer me. ₃₁And they reasoned with themselves, saying, If we shall say, From heaven; he will say, Why then did ye not believe him? ¹₆**But and if we**

1 Luke 20:6-8

TUESDAY — THE WEEK OF THE ATONING SACRIFICE

BY WHAT AUTHORITY? (cont.) — Mark 11:27-33

say, Of men; all the people will stone us: for they be persuaded that John was a prophet. ₇And they answered, that they could not tell whence *it was*. ₈And Jesus said unto them, Neither tell I you by what authority I do these things.

PARABLE OF THE TWO SONS — Matt. 21:28-32

₂₈But what think ye? A *certain* man had two sons; and he came to the first, and said, Son, go work to day in my vineyard. ₂₉He answered and said, ᵃI will not: but afterward he repented, and went. ₃₀And he came to the second, and said likewise. And he answered and said, I *go*, sir: and went not. ₃₁Whether of them twain did the will of *his* father? They say unto him, The first. Jesus saith unto them, Verily I say unto you, That the publicans and the harlots go into the kingdom of God before you. ₃₂For John came unto you in the way of righteousness, and ye believed him not: but the publicans and the harlots believed him: and ye, when ye had seen ¹me, repented not afterward, that ye might believe him. ²₃₃<u>For he that believed not John concerning me, cannot believe me, except he first repent.</u> ₃₄<u>And except ye repent, the preaching of John shall condemn you in the day of judgment.</u>

a GR: I don't want to go

1 JST Matt. 21:32; KJV: *it*

2 JST Matt. 21:33-34

PARABLE OF THE WICKED HUSBANDMEN — Matt. 21:33-46

¹<u>And again,</u> ₃₃Hear another parable: ¹<u>for unto you that believe not, I speak in parables; that your unrighteousness may be rewarded unto you.</u> There was a certain householder, which ᵃPLANTED A VINEYARD, AND HEDGED IT ROUND ABOUT, AND DIGGED A WINEPRESS IN IT, AND BUILT A TOWER, and let it out to husbandmen, and went into a far country: ₃₄And when the time of the fruit drew near, he sent his servants to the husbandmen, that they might receive the fruits of it. ₃₅And the husbandmen took his servants, and beat one, and killed another, and stoned another. ₃₆Again, he sent other servants more than the first: and they did unto them likewise. ₃₇But last of all he sent unto them his son, saying, They will reverence my son. ₃₈But when the husbandmen saw the son, they said among themselves, This is the heir; come, let us kill him, and let us seize on his inheritance. ₃₉And they caught him, and cast *him* out of the vineyard, and slew *him*. ₄₀When the lord therefore of the vineyard cometh, what will he do unto those husbandmen? ₄₁They say unto him, He will miserably destroy those wicked men, and will let out *his* vineyard unto other husbandmen, which shall render

1 JST Matt. 21:34

a Isa. 5:1-2

100

TUESDAY — THE WEEK OF THE ATONING SACRIFICE

PARABLE OF THE WICKED HUSBANDMEN (cont.)   Matt. 21:33-46

him the fruits in their seasons.

₄₂Jesus saith unto them, Did ye never read in the scriptures, ᵇTHE STONE WHICH THE BUILDERS REJECTED, THE SAME IS BECOME THE HEAD OF THE CORNER: THIS IS THE LORD'S DOING, AND IT IS MARVELLOUS IN OUR EYES? ₄₃Therefore say I unto you, The kingdom of God shall be taken from you, and given to a nation bringing forth the fruits thereof. ₄₄And whosoever shall fall on this stone shall be broken: but on whomsoever it shall fall, it will grind him to powder.

₄₅And when the chief priests and Pharisees had heard his parables, they perceived that he spake of them. ²And they said among themselves, Shall this man think that he alone can spoil this great kingdom? And they were angry with him. ₄₆But when they sought to lay hands on him, they feared the multitude, because they took him for a prophet.

³ ₅₀And now his disciples came to him, and Jesus said unto them, Marvel ye at the words of the parable which I spake unto them? ₅₁Verily I say unto you, I am the stone, and those wicked ones reject me. ₅₂I am the head of the corner. These Jews shall fall upon me, and shall be broken. ₅₃And the kingdom of God shall be taken from them, and shall be given to a nation bringing forth the fruits thereof; (meaning the Gentiles.) ₅₄Wherefore on whomsoever this stone shall fall, it shall grind him to powder. ₅₅And when the Lord therefore of the vineyard cometh, he will destroy those miserable, wicked men, and will let again his vineyard unto other husbandmen, even in the last days, who shall render him the fruits in their seasons.

₅₆And then understood they the parable which he spake unto them, that the Gentiles should be destroyed also, when the Lord should descend out of heaven to reign in his vineyard, which is the earth and the inhabitants thereof.

b Ps. 118:22-23
2 JST Matt. 21:48
3 JST Matt. 21:50-56

PARABLE OF THE MARRIAGE FEAST   Matt. 22:1-14

₁And Jesus answered and spake unto them again by parables, and said, ₂The kingdom of heaven is like unto a certain king, which ᵃmade a marriage for his son, ₃And sent forth his servants to call them that were bidden to the wedding: and ᵇthey would not come.

₄Again, he sent forth other servants, saying, Tell them which are bidden, Behold, I have prepared my dinner: my oxen and *my* fatlings *are* killed, and all things *are* ready: come unto the marriage. ₅But they made light of *it*, and went their ways, one to his farm, another to his merchandise: ₆And the remnant took his servants, and entreated *them* spitefully, and slew *them*.

₇But when the king heard *thereof*, he was wroth: and he sent forth his armies, and destroyed those murderers, and burned up their city.

₈Then saith he to his servants, The wedding is ready, but they which

a GR: gave a wedding celebration
b GR: they did not want to come

TUESDAY	THE WEEK OF THE ATONING SACRIFICE	

PARABLE OF THE MARRIAGE FEAST (cont.)	Matt. 22:1-14
were bidden were not worthy. ₉Go ye therefore into the highways, and as many as ye shall find, bid to the marriage. ₁₀So those servants went out into the highways, and gathered together all as many as they found, both bad and good: and the wedding was furnished with guests. ₁₁And when the king came in to see the guests, he saw there a man which had not on a wedding garment: ₁₂And he saith unto him, Friend, how camest thou in hither not having a wedding garment? And he was speechless. ₁₃Then said the king to the servants, Bind him hand and foot, and take him away, and cast *him* into outer darkness; there shall be weeping and gnashing of teeth. ₁₄For many are called, but few *are* chosen ¹wherefore all do not have on the wedding garment.	**1** JST Matt. 22:14

THE QUESTION OF TRIBUTE	Matt. 22:15-22
₁₅Then went the Pharisees, and took counsel how they might entangle him in *his* talk. ₁₆And they sent out unto him their disciples with the Herodians, saying, Master, we know that thou art true, and teachest the way of God in truth, ᵃneither carest thou for any *man*: for thou regardest not the person of men. ₁₇Tell us therefore, What thinkest thou? Is it lawful to give tribute unto Caesar, or not? ₁₈But Jesus perceived their wickedness, and said, Why tempt ye me, *ye* hypocrites? ₁₉Shew me the tribute money. And they brought unto him a penny. ₂₀And he saith unto them, Whose *is* this image and superscription? ₂₁They say unto him, Caesar's. Then saith he unto them, Render therefore unto Caesar the things which are Caesar's; and unto God the things that are God's. ₂₂When they had heard *these words*, they marvelled, and left him, and went their way.	**a** IE: you court no man's favor

THE SADDUCEES' QUESTION	Luke 20:27-40
¹**The same day came to him the Sadducees, which say that there is no resurrection, and asked him,** ₂₈Saying, Master, Moses wrote unto us, ᵃIF ANY MAN'S BROTHER DIE, HAVING A WIFE, AND HE DIE WITHOUT CHILDREN, THAT HIS BROTHER SHOULD TAKE HIS WIFE, AND RAISE UP SEED UNTO HIS BROTHER. ₂₉There were therefore seven brethren: and the first took a wife, and died without children. ₃₀And the second took her to wife, and he died childless. ₃₁And the third took her; and in like manner the seven also: and they left no children, and died. ₃₂Last of all the woman died also. ₃₃Therefore in the resurrection whose wife of them is she? for seven had her to wife. ₃₄And Jesus answering said unto them, ²**Ye do err,** ᵇ**not knowing**	**1** Matt. 22:23 **a** Deut. 25:5-6 **2** Matt. 22:29 **b** This may refer to the book of Tobit, still in Catholic Bibles, which contains this very story.

| TUESDAY | THE WEEK OF THE ATONING SACRIFICE |

THE SADDUCEES' QUESTION (cont.) — Luke 20:28-40

the scriptures, nor the power of God. The children of this world marry, and are given in marriage: ₃₅But they which shall be accounted worthy to obtain that world ³through resurrection from the dead, neither marry, nor are given in marriage: ₃₆Neither can they die any more: for they are equal unto the angels; and are the children of God, being the children of the resurrection.

⁴But as touching the resurrection of the dead, ₃₇even Moses shewed at the bush, when he calleth the Lord the God of Abraham, and the God of Isaac, and the God of Jacob. ₃₈For he is not a God of the dead, but of the living: for all live unto him. ⁵And when the multitude heard *this*, they were astonished at his doctrine.

₃₉Then certain of the scribes answering said, Master, thou hast well said. ₄₀And after that they durst not ask him any *question at all.*

3 JST Luke 20:35; KJV: and the
4 Matt. 22:31
5 Matt. 22:33

THE GREAT COMMANDMENT — Mark 12:28-34

¹₃₄But when the Pharisees had heard that he had put the Sadducees to silence, they were gathered together. ₃₅Then one of them, *which was* a lawyer, asked *him a question*, tempting him, and saying, ₃₆Master, which *is* the great commandment in the law?

₂₉And Jesus answered him, The first of all the commandments *is,* ªHEAR, O ISRAEL; THE LORD OUR GOD IS ONE LORD: ₃₀And THOU SHALT LOVE THE LORD THY GOD WITH ALL THY HEART, AND WITH ALL THY SOUL, AND WITH ALL THY MIND, AND WITH ALL THY STRENGTH: ²This is the first and great commandment. ₃₁And the second *is* like ³unto it, namely this, ᵇTHOU SHALT LOVE THY NEIGHBOUR AS THYSELF. There is none other commandment greater than these.

₃₂And the scribe said unto him, Well, Master, thou hast said the truth: for ᶜTHERE IS ONE GOD; AND THERE IS NONE OTHER BUT HE: ₃₃ᵈAND TO LOVE HIM WITH ALL THE HEART, AND WITH ALL THE UNDERSTANDING, AND WITH ALL THE SOUL, AND WITH ALL THE STRENGTH, ᵇAND TO LOVE *HIS* NEIGHBOUR AS HIMSELF, is more than all whole burnt offerings and sacrifices.

₃₄And when Jesus saw that he answered discreetly, he said unto him, Thou art not far from the kingdom of God. And no man after that durst ask him *any question.*

1 Matt. 22:34-36
a Deut 6:4-5
2 Matt. 22:38
3 Matt. 22:39
b Lev. 19:18
c Deut. 4:35; Isa. 44:6, 8; 45:5
d Deut. 6:5

WHOSE SON IS HE? — Matt. 22:41-46

₄₁While the Pharisees were gathered together, ¹while he taught in the temple, Jesus asked them, ₄₂Saying, What think ye of Christ? whose son is he?

They say unto him, *The Son* of David.

₄₃He saith unto them, How then doth David in spirit call him Lord, saying, ₄₄ªTHE LORD SAID UNTO MY LORD, SIT THOU ON MY RIGHT HAND, TILL I MAKE THINE ENEMIES THY FOOTSTOOL? ₄₅If David then call him Lord,

1 Mark 12:35
a Ps. 110:1

| TUESDAY | THE WEEK OF THE ATONING SACRIFICE |

WHOSE SON IS HE? — Matt. 22:41-46

how is he his son? ₄₆And no man was able to answer him a word, neither ᵇdurst any *man* from that day forth ask him any more *questions*. **²And the common people heard him gladly.**

b GR: dared

2 Mark 12:37

THE WIDOWS OFFERING — Mark 12:41-44

₄₁And Jesus sat over against the treasury, and beheld how the people cast money into the treasury: and many that were rich cast in much. ₄₂And there came a certain poor widow, and she threw in two mites, which make a farthing. ₄₃And he called *unto him* his disciples, and saith unto them, Verily I say unto you, That this poor widow hath cast more in, than all they which have cast into the treasury: ₄₄For all *they* did cast in of their abundance; but she of her want did cast in all that she had, *even* all her living.

WOE UNTO YOU PHARISEES — Matt. 23:1-36

₁Then spake Jesus to the multitude, and to his disciples, ₂Saying, The scribes and the Pharisees sit in Moses' ᵃseat: ₃All therefore whatsoever they bid you observe, *that* observe and do; but do not ye after their works: for they say, and do not. ₄For they bind heavy burdens and grievous to be borne, and lay *them* on men's shoulders; but they *themselves* will not move them with one of their fingers. ₅But all their works they do for to be seen of men: they ᵇmake broad their phylacteries, and enlarge the borders of their garments, ₆And love the uppermost rooms at feasts, and the chief seats in the synagogues, ₇And greetings in the markets, and to be called of men, ᶜRabbi, Rabbi. ₈But be not ye called Rabbi: for one is your Master, *even* Christ; and all ye are brethren. ₉And call no ¹one your ²creator upon the earth, ³or your heavenly Father: for one is your ³creator and heavenly Father, ⁴even he who is in heaven. ₁₀Neither be ye called masters: for one is your Master, *even* ⁵he whom your heavenly Father sent, which is Christ; ⁵for he hath sent him among you that ye might have life. ₁₁But he that is greatest among you shall be your servant. ₁₂And whosoever shall exalt himself shall be abased; and he that shall humble himself shall be exalted.

₁₃But woe unto you, scribes and Pharisees, hypocrites! for ye shut up the kingdom of heaven against men: for ye neither go in *yourselves*, neither suffer ye them that are entering to go in. ₁₄Woe unto you, scribes and Pharisees, hypocrites! for ye devour widows' houses, and for a pretence make long prayer: therefore ye shall receive the greater damnation.

₁₅Woe unto you, scribes and Pharisees, hypocrites! for ye compass sea and land to make one proselyte, and when he is made, ye make him twofold more the child of hell than ⁶he was before, like unto yourselves.

a GR: a chair occupied by a teacher, judge or other respected or eminent person

b GR: enlarge

c HEB and AR: master or my master

1 JST Matt. 23:6; KJV: man

2 JST Matt. 23:6; KJV: father

3 JST Matt. 23:6

4 JST Matt. 23:6; KJV: which

5 JST Matt. 23:7

6 JST Matt. 23:12

104

TUESDAY THE WEEK OF THE ATONING SACRIFICE

WOE UNTO YOU PHARISEES (cont.)   Matt. 23:1-36

16 Woe unto you, *ye* blind guides, which say, Whosoever shall swear by the temple, it is nothing; but whosoever shall swear by the gold of the temple, he is a debtor! 17 Ye fools and blind: for whether is greater, the gold, or the temple that sanctifieth the gold? 18 And, Whosoever shall swear by the altar, it is nothing; but whosoever sweareth by the gift that is upon it, he is guilty. 19 Ye fools and blind: for whether *is* greater, the gift, or the altar that sanctifieth the gift? 20 Whoso therefore shall swear by the altar, sweareth by it, and by all things thereon. 21 And whoso shall swear by the temple, sweareth by it, and by him that dwelleth therein. 22 And he that shall swear by heaven, sweareth by the throne of God, and by him that sitteth thereon.

23 Woe unto you, scribes and Pharisees, hypocrites! for ye pay tithe of mint and anise and cummin, and have omitted the weightier *matters* of the law, judgment, mercy, and faith: these ought ye to have done, and not to leave the other undone. 24 Ye blind guides, which strain at a gnat, and swallow a camel; [7]who make yourselves appear unto men that ye would not commit the least sin, and yet ye yourselves, transgress the whole law.

25 Woe unto you, scribes and Pharisees, hypocrites! for ye make clean the outside of the cup and of the platter, but within they are full of ᵈextortion and ᵉexcess. 26 *Thou* blind Pharisee, cleanse first that *which is* within the cup and platter, that the outside of them may be clean also. 27 Woe unto you, scribes and Pharisees, hypocrites! for ye are like unto whited sepulchres, which indeed appear beautiful outward, but are within full of dead *men's* bones, and of all uncleanness. 28 Even so ye also outwardly appear righteous unto men, but within ye are full of hypocrisy, and iniquity.

29 Woe unto you, scribes and Pharisees, hypocrites! because ye build the tombs of the prophets, and garnish the sepulchres of the righteous, 30 And say, If we had been in the days of our fathers, we would not have been partakers with them in the blood of the prophets. 31 Wherefore ye be witnesses unto yourselves, that ye are the children of them which killed the prophets. 32 Fill ye up then the measure of your fathers. 33 Ye serpents, *ye* generation of vipers, how can ye escape the damnation of hell? 34 Wherefore, behold, I send unto you prophets, and wise men, and scribes: and *some* of them ye shall kill and crucify; and *some* of them shall ye scourge in your synagogues, and persecute *them* from city to city: 35 That upon you may come all the righteous blood shed upon the earth, from the blood of righteous Abel unto the blood of ᶠZacharias son of ᵍBarachias, whom ye slew between the temple and the altar. 36 Verily I say unto you, All these things shall come upon this generation. [8]34 Ye

---

7 JST Matt. 23:21

d GR: greediness

e GR: self-indulgence, lack of self-control

f GR: Zechariah

g Jerome's Hebrew copy of Matt. has "Jehoiada," consistent with 2 Chron. 24:20.

8 JST Matt. 23:34-35

TUESDAY THE WEEK OF THE ATONING SACRIFICE

WOE UNTO YOU PHARISEES (cont.) Matt. 23:1-36

bear testimony against your fathers, when ye, yourselves, are partakers of the same wickedness. ₃₅Behold your fathers did it through ignorance, but ye do not; wherefore, their sins shall be upon your heads.

JESUS LAMENTS OVER JERUSALEM * Matt. 23:37-39

₃₇O Jerusalem, Jerusalem, *thou* that killest the prophets, and stonest them which are sent unto thee, how often would I have gathered thy children together, even as a hen gathereth her chickens under *her* wings, and ye would not! ₃₈Behold, your house is left unto you desolate. ₃₉For I say unto you, Ye shall not see me henceforth, **¹and know that I am he of whom it is written by the prophets,** till ye shall say, ªBLESSED *IS* HE THAT COMETH IN THE NAME OF THE LORD, **¹ᵇIN THE CLOUDS OF HEAVEN, and ᶜALL THE HOLY ANGELS WITH HIM.**

¹Then understood his disciples that he should come again on the earth, after that he was glorified and crowned on the right hand of God.

* cf. Luke 13:31-35

a Ps. 118:26

1 JS-M. 1:1

b Dan. 7:13

c Zech. 14:5

NOT ONE STONE UPON ANOTHER Matt. *24:1-2

₁And Jesus went out, and departed from the temple; and his disciples came to *him* for to **¹hear** him, **²saying, Master, show us concerning** the buildings of the temple; **²as thou hast said—They shall be thrown down and left unto you desolate.**

₂And Jesus said unto them, See ye not all these things? **³And do ye not understand them them?** Verily I say unto you, There shall not be left here **³upon this temple**, one stone upon another, that shall not be thrown down.

* The verses in Matt. 24 have been arranged in the order they appear in JS-M.

1 JS-M. 1:2; KJV: shew

2 JS-M. 1:2

3 JS-M. 1:3

WHAT IS THE SIGN OF THY COMING

Matt. 24:3-6, 9-13, 15-28

¹And Jesus left them, and went upon the Mount of Olives. ₃And as he sat upon the Mount of Olives, the disciples came unto him privately, saying: Tell us when shall these things be **¹which thou hast said concerning the destruction of the temple, and the Jews?** and what **¹is** the sign of thy coming, and of the end of the world? **¹(or the destruction of the wicked, which is the end of the world.)**

₄And Jesus answered, and said unto them: Take heed that no man deceive you; ₅For many shall come in my name, saying, I am Christ;and shall deceive many. ₉Then shall they deliver you up to be afflicted, and shall kill you: and ye shall be hated of all nations, for my name's sake; ₁₀And then shall many be offended, and shall betray one another, and shall hate one another. ₁₁And many false prophets shall arise, and shall deceive many. ₁₂And because iniquity shall abound, the love of many shall wax cold. ₁₃But he that **²remaineth steadfast and is not over-**

1 JS-M. 1:4

2 JS-M. 1:11; KJV: shall endure unto the end

106

TUESDAY   THE WEEK OF THE ATONING SACRIFICE

WHAT IS THE SIGN OF THY COMING (cont.) Matt. 24:3-6, 9-13, 15-28

come, the same shall be saved.

₁₅When ye therefore shall see the abomination of desolation, spoken of by Daniel the prophet, **³concerning the destruction of Jerusalem, then you shall** stand in the holy place, (whoso readeth, let him understand:) ₁₆Then let them which be in Judea flee into the mountains: ₁₇Let him which is on the housetop **⁴flee, and not return** to take any thing out of his house; ₁₈Neither let him which is in the field return back to take his clothes. ₁₉And woe unto them that are with child, and to them that give suck in those days! **⁵Therefore, pray ye the Lord** ₂₀that your flight be not in the winter, neither on the sabbath day:

₂₁For then, **⁶in those days**, shall be great tribulation **⁶on the Jews, and upon the inhabitants of Jerusalem**, such as was not **⁶before sent upon Israel, of God**, since the beginning of **⁷their kingdom** to this time; no, nor ever shall be **⁶sent again upon Israel. ⁸All things which have befallen them are only the beginning of the sorrows which shall come upon them.** ₂₂And except those days should be shortened, there should **⁹none of their** flesh be saved: but for the elect's sake, **¹⁰according to the covenant**, those days shall be shortened.

¹¹Behold, these things I have spoken unto you concerning the Jews; and again, after the tribulation of those days which shall come upon Jerusalem, ₂₃if any man shall say unto you, Lo, here is Christ, or there; believe *it* not; ₂₄For **¹²in those days** there shall **¹²also** arise false Christs, and false prophets, and shall shew great signs and wonders; insomuch that, if ᵃ*it were* possible, they shall deceive the very elect, **¹²who are the elect according to the covenant. ¹³Behold, I speak these things unto you for the elect's sake.** ₆And ye shall hear of wars and rumours of wars: see that ye be not ᵇtroubled, for all **¹⁴I have told you** must come to pass, but the end is not yet.

₂₅Behold, I have told you before. ₂₆Wherefore if they shall say unto you, Behold, he is in the desert; go not forth: behold, *he is* in the secret chambers; believe *it* not; ₂₇For as the **¹⁵light of the morning** cometh out of the east, and shineth even unto the west; **¹⁶and covereth the whole earth**, so shall also the coming of the Son of Man be.

¹⁷And now I show unto you a parable. Behold, ₂₈wheresoever the carcase is, there will the eagles be gathered together; **¹⁸so likewise shall mine elect be gathered from the four quarters of the earth.**

THE SECOND COMING OF THE SON OF MAN

¹₂₈And they shall hear of wars, and rumors of wars. ₂₉Behold I speak for mine elect's sake; ₇For nation shall rise against nation, and kingdom against kingdom: ᵃand there shall be famines, and pestilences, and earthquakes, in divers places. ₁₂And because iniquity shall abound,

3	JS-M. 1:12
4	JS-M. 1:14; KJV: not come down
5	JS-M. 1:17; KJV: But pray ye
6	JS-M. 1:18
7	JS-M. 1:18; KJV: the world
8	JS-M. 1:19
9	JS-M. 1:20; KJV: no
10	JS-M. 1:20
11	JS-M. 1:21; KJV: Then
12	JS-M. 1:22
a	omitted from JS-M. 1:23
13	JS-M. 1:23
b	GR: frightened
14	JS-M. 1:23; KJV: these things
15	JS-M. 1:26; KJV: lightning
16	JS-M. 1:26
17	JS-M. 1:27; KJV: For
18	JS-M. 1:27

Matt. 24:7, 12-14, 29-51

1	JS-M. 1:28-29
a	omitted from JS-M. 1:29

TUESDAY — THE WEEK OF THE ATONING SACRIFICE

THE SECOND COMING OF THE SON OF MAN (cont.)   Matt. 24:6-7, 12-15, 29-51

the love of ²men shall wax cold. ₁₃But he that shall ³not be overcome, the same shall be saved.
₁₄And this gospel of the kingdom shall be preached in all the world for a witness unto all nations; and then shall the end come, ⁴or the destruction of the wicked. ⁵And again shall the abomination of desolation, spoken of by Daniel the prophet, be fulfilled. ₂₉Immediately after the tribulation of those days ᵇSHALL THE SUN BE DARKENED, AND THE MOON SHALL NOT GIVE HER LIGHT, AND THE STARS SHALL FALL from heaven, and the powers of heaven shall be shaken:
₃₄Verily, I say unto you, This generation, ⁶in which these things shall be shown forth, shall not pass ⁶away till all ⁶I have told you shall be fulfilled. ⁷Although, the days will come, that ₃₅heaven and earth shall pass away, but my words shall not pass away, ⁷but all shall be fulfilled.
₃₀And, ⁸as I said before, after the tribulation of those days, and the powers of the heavens shall be shaken, then shall appear the sign of the Son of man in heaven: and then shall all the tribes of the earth mourn, and they shall see the ᶜSON OF MAN COMING IN THE CLOUDS OF HEAVEN with power and great glory. ⁹And whoso treasureth up my word, shall not be deceived, for the Son of Man shall come, ₃₁And he shall send his angels ⁹before him with a great sound of ᵈA TRUMPET, AND THEY SHALL GATHER TOGETHER ⁹the remainder of his elect from the four winds, from one end of heaven to the other.
₃₂Now learn a parable of the fig-tree; When his branch is yet tender, and ¹⁰it begins to put forth leaves, ye know that summer *is* nigh; ₃₃So likewise, ¹¹mine elect, when ¹¹they shall see all these things, ¹²they shall know that ¹³he is near, *even* at the doors. ₃₆But of that day and hour, knoweth no *man*; no, not the angels of ¹⁴God in heaven, but my Father only.
₃₇But as the days of ᵉNoe *were*, so ¹⁵it shall ¹⁵be also ¹⁵at the coming of ᶠthe Son of man. ₃₈For ¹⁶it shall be with them, as ¹⁶it was in the days that were before the flood; they were eating and drinking, marrying and giving in marriage, until the day that ᵉNoe entered into the ark, ₃₉And knew not until the flood came, and took them all away; so shall also the coming of the Son of man be.
₄₀Then shall ¹⁷be fulfilled that which is written, that in the last days, ᵍtwo ¹⁷shall be in the field; the one shall be taken, and the other left, ₄₁Two ʰ<u>women</u> *shall be* grinding at the mill; the one shall be taken, and the other left. ¹⁸And what I say unto one, I say unto all men; ₄₂Watch therefore: for ye know not what hour your Lord doth come. ₄₃But know this, if the goodman of the house had known in what watch the thief would come, he would have watched, and would not have suffered his house to be broken up, ¹⁹but would have been ready.

2 JS-M. 1:30; KJV: many
3 JS-M. 1:30; KJV: endure unto the end
4 JS-M. 1:31
5 JS-M. 1:32
b Isa. 13:10; Joel 3:15
6 JS-M. 1:34
7 JS-M. 1:35
8 JS-M. 1:36
c Dan. 7:13
9 JS-M. 1:37
d Isa. 27:13; Deut. 30:4
10 JS-M. 1:38; KJV: putteth
11 JS-M. 1:39; KJV: ye
12 JS-M. 1:39
13 JS-M. 1:39; KJV: it
14 JS-M. 1:40
e IE: Noah
15 JS-M. 1:41
f KJV ends this phrase with "be"
16 JS-M. 1:42
17 JS-M. 1:44
g The source of this quote is unknown.
h omitted from JS-M. 1:45
18 JS-M. 1:46
19 JS-M. 1:47

TUESDAY   THE WEEK OF THE ATONING SACRIFICE

THE COMING OF THE SON OF MAN (cont.) Matt. 24:6-7, 12-15, 29-51

₄₄Therefore be ye also ready: for in such an hour as ye think not the Son of man cometh. ₄₅Who then is a faithful and wise servant, whom his lord hath made ruler over his household, to give them meat in due season? ₄₆Blessed is that servant, whom his lord when he cometh shall find so doing. ₄₇Verily I say unto you, ⁱ*That* he shall make him ruler over all his goods. ₄₈But ʲ*and* if that evil servant shall say in his heart, My lord delayeth his coming; ₄₉And shall begin to smite his fellowservants, and to eat and drink with the drunken; ₅₀The lord of that servant shall come in a day when he looketh not for *him*, and in an hour that he is not aware of, ₅₁And shall cut him asunder, and shall appoint *him* his portion with the hypocrites: there shall be weeping and gnashing of teeth.

²⁰**And thus cometh the end of the wicked, according to the prophecy of Moses, saying:** ᵏTHEY SHALL BE CUT OFF FROM AMONG THE PEOPLE; **but the end of the earth is not yet, but by and by.**

i	omitted from JS-M. 1:50
j	omitted from JS-M. 1:51
20	JS-M. 1:55
k	Deut. 18:18 (See also Acts 3:22-23; 1 Ne. 22:20; 3 Ne. 20:23; D&C 133:63; JS-H. 1:40)

PARABLE OF THE TEN VIRGINS Matt. 25:1-13

₁Then, ¹*at that day, before the Son of Man comes*, shall the kingdom of heaven be likened unto ten virgins, which took their lamps, and went forth to meet the bridegroom. ₂And five of them were wise, and five *were* foolish. ₃They that *were* foolish took their lamps, and took no oil with them: ₄But the wise took oil in their vessels with their lamps.

₅While the bridegroom tarried, they all slumbered and slept. ₆And at midnight there was a cry made, Behold, the bridegroom cometh; go ye out to meet him. ₇Then all those virgins arose, and trimmed their lamps.

₈And the foolish said unto the wise, Give us of your oil; for our lamps are ᵃgone out.

₉But the wise answered, saying, *Not so*; lest there be not enough for us and you: but go ye rather to them that sell, and buy for yourselves.

₁₀And while they went to buy, the bridegroom came; and they that were ready went in with him to the marriage: and the door was ᵇshut.

₁₁Afterward came also the other virgins, saying, Lord, Lord, open to us.

₁₂But he answered and said, Verily I say unto you, I know you not.

₁₃Watch therefore, for ye know neither the day nor the hour wherein the Son of man cometh.

1	JST Matt. 25:1
a	GR: going
b	GR: locked

PARABLE OF THE TALENTS * Matt. 25:14-30

₁₄For *the kingdom of heaven is* as a man travelling into a far country, *who* called his own servants, and delivered unto them his goods. ₁₅And unto one he gave five talents, to another two, and to another one; to every man according to his several ability; and straightway took his journey. Then he that had received the five talents went and traded with the same, and made *them* other five talents. ₁₇And likewise he that *had* re-

* This parable and the parable of the pounds (Luke 19:11-27), are similar but appear to have different teaching objectives.

TUESDAY — THE WEEK OF THE ATONING SACRIFICE

PARABLE OF THE TALENTS (cont.) — Matt. 25:14-30

ceived two, he also gained other two. ₁₈But he that had received one went and digged in the earth, and hid his lord's money. ₁₉After a long time the lord of those servants cometh, and ᵃreckoneth with them.

₂₀And so he that had received five talents came and brought other five talents, saying, Lord, thou ᵇdeliveredst unto me five talents: behold, I have gained beside them five talents more.

₂₁His lord said unto him, Well done, *thou* good and faithful servant: thou hast been faithful over a few things, I will make thee ruler over many things: enter thou into the joy of thy lord.

₂₂He also that had received two talents came and said, Lord, thou deliveredst unto me two talents: behold, I have gained two other talents beside them.

₂₃His lord said unto him, Well done, good and faithful servant; thou hast been faithful over a few things, I will make thee ruler over many things: enter thou into the joy of thy lord.

₂₄Then he which had received the one talent came and said, Lord, I knew thee that thou art an ᶜhard man, reaping where thou hast not sown, and gathering where thou hast not strawed: ₂₅And I was afraid, and went and hid thy talent in the earth: lo, *there* thou hast *that is* thine.

₂₆His lord answered and said unto him, *Thou* wicked and slothful servant, thou knewest that I reap where I sowed not, and gather where I have not strawed: ₂₇Thou oughtest therefore to have put my money to the exchangers, and *then* at my coming I should have received mine own with usury. ₂₈Take therefore the talent from him, and give *it* unto him which hath ten talents. ₂₉For unto every one that hath ¹obtained other talents shall be given, and he shall have abundance: but from him that hath not ²obtained other talents shall be taken away even that which he hath ²received.

₃₀And cast ye the unprofitable servant into outer darkness: there shall be weeping and gnashing of teeth.

a GR: settled accounts
b GR: entrusted
c GR: strict
1 JST: Matt. 25:29
2 JST: Matt. 25:30

PARABLE OF THE SHEEP AND THE GOATS — Matt. 25:31-46

₃₁When the Son of man shall come in his glory, and all the holy angels with him, then shall he sit upon the throne of his glory: ₃₂And before him shall be gathered all nations: and he shall separate them one from another, as a shepherd divideth *his* sheep from the goats: ₃₃And he shall set the sheep on his right hand, but the goats on the left.

₃₄Then shall the King say unto them on his right hand, Come, ye blessed of my Father, inherit the kingdom prepared for you from the foundation of the world: ₃₅For I was an hungred, and ye gave me meat: I was thirsty, and ye gave me drink: I was a stranger, and ye took me in: ₃₆Naked, and ye clothed me: I was sick, and ye ᵃvisited me: I was in prison, and ye came unto me.

a GR: cared for

110

PARABLE OF THE SHEEP AND THE GOATS (cont.) — Matt. 25:31-46

₃₇Then shall the righteous answer him, saying, Lord, when saw we thee an hungred, and fed *thee*? or thirsty, and gave *thee* drink? ₃₈When saw we thee a stranger, and took *thee* in? or naked, and clothed *thee*? ₃₉Or when saw we thee sick, or in prison, and came unto thee?

₄₀And the King shall answer and say unto them, Verily I say unto you, Inasmuch as ye have done *it* unto one of the least of these my brethren, ye have done *it* unto me. ₄₁Then shall he say also unto them on the left hand, Depart from me, ye ᵇcursed, into everlasting fire, prepared for the devil and his angels: ₄₂For I was an hungred, and ye gave me no meat: I was thirsty, and ye gave me no drink: ₄₃I was a stranger, and ye took me not in: naked, and ye clothed me not: sick, and in prison, and ye visited me not.

₄₄Then shall they also answer him, saying, Lord, when saw we thee an hungred, or athirst, or a stranger, or naked, or sick, or in prison, and did not minister unto thee?

₄₅Then shall he answer them, saying, Verily I say unto you, Inasmuch as ye did *it* not to one of the least of these, ye did *it* not to me. ₄₆And these shall go away into everlasting punishment: but the righteous into life eternal.

b GR: who have come under a curse

BETRAYAL BY CRAFT — Matt. 26:1-5

₁And it came to pass, when Jesus had finished all these sayings, he said unto his disciples, ₂Ye know that after two days is *the feast of* the passover, and the Son of man is betrayed to be crucified.

₃Then assembled together the chief priests, and the scribes, and the elders of the people, unto the palace of the high priest, who was called Caiaphas, ₄And ᵃconsulted ¹how they might take him by craft, and put *him* to death. ₅But they said, Not on the feast *day*, lest there be an uproar among the people.

1 Mark 14:1

a GR: plotted

ANOINTING JESUS' HEAD — Mark 14:3-9

₃And being in Bethany in the house of Simon the ᵃleper, as he sat at meat, there came a woman having an alabaster box of ointment of spikenard very precious; and she brake the box, and poured *it* on his head. ₄And there were some that had indignation within themselves, and said, Why was this waste of the ointment made? ₅For it might have been sold for more than three hundred pence, and have been given to the poor. And they murmured against her.

¹**When Jesus understood *it*, he said unto them,** ₆Let her alone; why trouble ye her? she hath wrought a good work on me. ₇For ye have the poor with you always, and whensoever ye will ye may do them good: but me ye have not always. ₈She hath done what she could: ²<u>and this which she has done unto me, shall be had in remembrance in genera-</u>

a This is an error in the text. If Simon were a leper, Christ could not have returned to the temple or taken Passover. This is likely Simon the Pharisee from Luke 7:36-50.

1 Matt. 26:10

2 JST Mark 14:8

* THURSDAY — **THE WEEK OF THE ATONING SACRIFICE**

ANOINTING OF CHRIST'S HEAD (cont.) — Mark 14:3-9

tions to come, wheresoever my gospel shall be preached; for verily she is come aforehand to anoint my body to the burying. ₉Verily I say unto you, Wheresoever this gospel shall be preached throughout the whole world, *this* also that she hath done shall be spoken of for a memorial of her.

SATAN INFLUENCES JUDAS — Luke 22:1-6

₁Now the feast of unleavened bread drew nigh, which is called the Passover. ₂And the chief priests and scribes sought how they might kill him; for they feared the people. ₃Then entered Satan into Judas surnamed Iscariot, being of the number of the twelve. And he went his way, and communed with the chief priests and captains, how he might betray him unto them. **¹And said** *unto them***, What will ye give me, and I will deliver him unto you?** ₅And they were glad, and covenanted to give him **¹thirty pieces of silver.** ₆And he promised, and **²from that time he** sought opportunity to betray him unto them in the absence of the multitude.

1 Matt. 26:15
2 Matt. 26:16

* THE UPPER ROOM – THE SACRAMENT — Luke 22:7-25

₇Then came the day of unleavened bread, when the passover must be killed. ₈And he sent Peter and John, saying, Go and prepare us the passover, that we may eat. ₉And they said unto him, **¹Where wilt thou that we prepare for thee to eat the passover?** ₁₀And he said unto them, **²Go ye into the city, and there shall meet you a man bearing a pitcher of water:** follow him into the house where he entereth in. ₁₁And ye shall say unto the goodman of the house, **³The Master saith, My time is at hand; I will keep the passover at thy house,** Where is the guestchamber, where I shall eat the passover with my disciples? ₁₂And he shall shew you a large upper room furnished **⁴₁₅and prepared: there make ready for us.** ₁₆**And his disciples went forth, and came into the city,** ₁₃and found as he had said unto them: and they made ready the passover. ⁵**And in the evening** ₁₄when the hour was come, he sat down, and the twelve apostles with him. ₁₅And he said unto them, With desire I have desired to eat this passover with you before I suffer: ₁₆For I say unto you, I will not any more eat thereof, until it be fulfilled ⁶**which is written in the prophets concerning me. Then I will partake with you,** in the kingdom of God. ⁷**And as they were eating, Jesus took bread and** ⁸**brake it, and blessed it, and gave** *it* **to the disciples, and said,** ⁹**Take, eat; this is** ¹⁰**for you to do in remembrance of my body** ¹¹**which I give a ransom for you;** ¹²**for as oft as ye do this ye will remember this hour that I was with**

1 Matt. 26:17
2 Mark 14:13
3 Matt. 26:18
4 Mark 14:15-16
5 Mark 14:17
6 JST Luke 22:16
7 Matt. 26:26
8 JST Matt. 26: 22; KJV: blessed it, and brake *it*
9 Mark 14:22
10 JST Mark 14:21
11 JST Matt. 26:22
12 JST Mark 14:21

THURSDAY   THE WEEK OF THE ATONING SACRIFICE

THE UPPER ROOM – THE SACRAMENT (cont.)   Luke 22:7-25

you. ¹³₂₃And he took the cup, and when he had given thanks, he gave *it* to them: and they all drank of it. ₂₄And he said unto them, This is ¹⁴in remembrance of my blood ¹⁵which is shed for ¹⁶as many as shall believe on my name for the remission of sins, ¹⁷₂₃and the new testament which I give unto you; for of me ye shall bear record unto all the world. ₂₄And as oft as ye do this ordinance, ye will remember me in this hour that I was with you and drank with you of this cup, even the last time in my ministry. ¹⁸And I give unto you a commandment, that ye shall observe to do the things which ye have seen me do.

¹⁹Verily I say unto you, ²⁰Of this ye shall bear record; for I will drink no more of the fruit of the vine ²⁰with you, until that day ²¹when I ²²shall come and drink it new with you in my Father's kingdom.

13	Mark 14:23-24
14	JST Mark 14:23
15	Matt. 26:28 ("of the new testament" is omitted here; see insert # 20)
16	JST Matt. 26:24; KJV: many
17	JST Mark 14:23-24
18	JST Matt. 26:25
19	Mark 14:25
20	JST Mark 14:25
21	Matt. 26:29
22	JST Matt. 26:26

THE UPPER ROOM – WASHING THE FEET   John 13:2-20

₂And supper being ended, the devil having now put into the heart of Judas Iscariot, Simon's *son*, to betray him; ₃Jesus knowing that the Father had given all things into his hands, and that he was come from God, and went to God; ₄He riseth from supper, and laid aside his garments; and took a towel, and girded himself. ₅After that he poureth water into a bason, and began to wash the disciples' feet, and to wipe *them* with the towel wherewith he was girded.

₆Then cometh he to Simon Peter: and Peter saith unto him, Lord, dost thou wash my feet?

₇Jesus answered and said unto him, What I do thou knowest not now; but thou shalt know hereafter.

₈Peter saith unto him, Thou ¹needest not to wash my feet.

Jesus answered him, If I wash thee not, thou hast no part with me.

₉Simon Peter saith unto him, Lord, not my feet only, but also *my* hands and *my* head.

₁₀Jesus saith to him, He that ²has washed ³his hands and his head, needeth not save to wash *his* feet, but is clean every whit: and ye are clean, but not all. ³Now this was the custom of the Jews under their law; wherefore, Jesus did this that the law might be fulfilled. ₁₁For he knew who should betray him; therefore said he, Ye are not all clean.

₁₂So after he had washed their feet, and had taken his garments, and was set down again, he said unto them, Know ye what I have done to you? ₁₃Ye call me Master and Lord: and ye say well; for *so* I am. ₁₄If I then, *your* Lord and Master, have washed your feet; ye also ought to

1	JST John 13:8; KJV: shalt never
2	JST John 13:10; KJV: is
3	JST John 13:10

THURSDAY — **THE WEEK OF THE ATONING SACRIFICE**

THE UPPER ROOM – WASHING THE FEET (cont.) John 13:2-20

wash one another's feet. ₁₅For I have given you an example, that ye should do as I have done to you. ₁₆Verily, verily, I say unto you, The servant is not greater than his lord; neither he that is sent greater than he that sent him. ₁₇If ye know these things, happy are ye if ye do them.

₁₈I speak not of you all: I know whom I have chosen: but that the scripture may be fulfilled, ᵃHE THAT EATETH BREAD WITH ME HATH LIFTED UP HIS HEEL AGAINST ME. ₁₉Now I tell you before it come, that, when it is come to pass, ye may believe that I am **4the Christ**. ₂₀Verily, verily, I say unto you, He that receiveth whomsoever I send receiveth me; and he that receiveth me receiveth him that sent me.

a Ps. 41:9

4 JST John 13:19; KJV: *he*

THE UPPER ROOM – JUDAS REVEALED, DEPARTS John 13:21-30

₂₁When Jesus had thus said, **¹as they did eat,** he was troubled in spirit, and testified, and said, Verily, verily, I say unto you, that one of you shall betray me.

₂₂Then the disciples looked one on another, doubting of whom he spake. **²And they were exceeding sorrowful, and began every one of them to say unto him ³one by one, *Is* it I? and another *said, Is* it I?**

₂₃Now there was leaning on Jesus' bosom one of his disciples, ᵃwhom Jesus loved. ₂₄Simon Peter therefore beckoned to him, that he should ask who it should be of whom he spake.

₂₅He then lying on Jesus' breast saith unto him, Lord, who is it? ₂₆Jesus answered, He it is, to whom I shall give a sop, when I have dipped *it*. **⁴The Son of man indeed goeth, as it is written of him: but woe to that man by whom the Son of man is betrayed! good were it for that man if he had never been born.**

And when he had dipped the sop, he gave *it* to Judas Iscariot, *the son* of Simon. ₂₇And after the sop Satan entered into him. **⁵Then Judas, which betrayed him, answered and said, Master, is it I?**

He said unto him, Thou hast said. Then said Jesus unto him, That thou doest, do quickly.

₂₈Now no man at the table knew for what intent he spake this unto him. ₂₉For some *of them* thought, because Judas had the bag, that Jesus had said unto him, Buy *those things* that we have need of against the feast; or, that he should give something to the poor. ₃₀He then having received the sop went immediately out: and it was night.

1 Matt. 26:21

2 Matt. 26:22

3 Mark 14:19

a In the Gospel of John, the unnamed disciple "whom Jesus loved" is John.

4 Mark 14:21

5 Matt. 26:25

THE UPPER ROOM – A NEW COMMANDMENT John 13:31-35

₃₁Therefore, when he was gone out, Jesus said, Now is the Son of man glorified, and God is glorified in him. If God be glorified in him, God shall also glorify him in himself, and shall straightway glorify him. ₃₃Little children, yet a little while I am with you. Ye shall seek me: and as I said unto the Jews, Whither I go, ye cannot come; so now I say to you.

THURSDAY — **THE WEEK OF THE ATONING SACRIFICE**

THE UPPER ROOM – A NEW COMMANDMENT (cont.) — John 13:31-35

34 A new commandment I give unto you, That ye love one another; as I have loved you, that ye also love one another. 35 By this shall all *men* know that ye are my disciples, if ye have love one to another.

THE UPPER ROOM – THE WAY, THE TRUTH, THE LIFE — John 14:1-14

1 Let not your heart be troubled: ye believe in God, believe also in me. 2 In my Father's house are many mansions: if *it were* not *so*, I would have told you. I go to prepare a place for you. 3 And if I go and prepare a place for you, I will come again, and receive you unto myself; that where I am, *there* ye may be also.

4 And whither I go ye know, and the way ye know.

5 Thomas saith unto him, Lord, we know not whither thou goest; and how can we know the way?

6 Jesus saith unto him, I am the way, the truth, and the life: no man cometh unto the Father, but by me. 7 If ye had known me, ye should have known my Father also: and from henceforth ye know him, and have seen him.

8 Philip saith unto him, Lord, shew us the Father, and it sufficeth us.

9 Jesus saith unto him, Have I been so long time with you, and yet hast thou not known me, Philip? he that hath seen me hath seen the Father; and how sayest thou *then*, Shew us the Father? 10 Believest thou not that I am in the Father, and the Father in me? the words that I speak unto you I speak not of myself: but the Father that dwelleth in me, he doeth the works. 11 Believe me that I *am* in the Father, and the Father in me: or else believe me for the very works' sake.

12 Verily, verily, I say unto you, He that believeth on me, the works that I do shall he do also; and greater *works* than these shall he do; be-

THE UPPER ROOM – THE COMFORTER — John 14:15-31

15 If ye love me, keep my commandments. 16 And I will pray the Father, and he shall give you another Comforter, that he may abide with you for ever; 17 *Even* the Spirit of truth; whom the world cannot receive, because it seeth him not, neither knoweth him: but ye know him; for he dwelleth with you, and shall be in you.

18 I will not leave you comfortless: I will come to you. 19 Yet a little while, and the world seeth me no more; but ye see me: because I live, ye shall live also. 20 At that day ye shall know that I *am* in my Father, and ye in me, and I in you. 21 He that hath my commandments, and keepeth them, he it is that loveth me: and he that loveth me shall be loved of my Father, and I will love him, and will manifest myself to him.

22 Judas saith unto him, not Iscariot, Lord, how is it that thou wilt manifest thyself unto us, and not unto the world?

23 Jesus answered and said unto him, If a man love me, he will keep

THURSDAY   The Week Of The Atoning Sacrifice

THE UPPER ROOM – THE COMFORTER (cont.)   John 14:15-31

my words: and my Father will love him, and we will come unto him, and make our abode with him. 24He that loveth me not keepeth not my sayings: and the word which ye hear is not mine, but the Father's which sent me.

25These things have I spoken unto you, being *yet* present with you. 26But the Comforter, *which is* the Holy Ghost, whom the Father will send in my name, he shall teach you all things, and bring all things to your remembrance, whatsoever I have said unto you. 27Peace I leave with you, my peace I give unto you: not as the world giveth, give I unto you. Let not your heart be troubled, neither let it be afraid.

28Ye have heard how I said unto you, I go away, and come *again* unto you. If ye loved me, ye would rejoice, because I said, I go unto the Father: for my Father is greater than I. 29And now I have told you before it come to pass, that, when it is come to pass, ye might believe. 30Hereafter I will not talk much with you: for the prince ¹of darkness, who is of this world cometh, and hath ²no power over me but he hath power over you. 31But that the world may know that I love the Father; and as the Father gave me commandment, even so I do.

1 JST John 14:30

2 JST John 14:30; kjv: nothing in me

THE UPPER ROOM – I AM THE TRUE VINE   John 15:1-17

1I am the true vine, and my Father is the husbandman. 2Every branch in me that beareth not fruit he taketh away: and every *branch* that beareth fruit, he purgeth it, that it may bring forth more fruit. 3Now ye are clean through the word which I have spoken unto you. 4Abide in me, and I in you. As the branch cannot bear fruit of itself, except it abide in the vine; no more can ye, except ye abide in me. 5I am the vine, ye *are* the branches: He that abideth in me, and I in him, the same bringeth forth much fruit: for without me ye can do nothing. 6If a man abide not in me, he is cast forth as a branch, and is withered; and men gather them, and cast *them* into the fire, and they are burned. 7If ye abide in me, and my words abide in you, ye shall ask what ye will, and it shall be done unto you. 8Herein is my Father glorified, that ye bear much fruit; so shall ye be my disciples.

9As the Father hath loved me, so have I loved you: continue ye in my love. 10If ye keep my commandments, ye shall abide in my love; even as I have kept my Father's commandments, and abide in his love. 11These things have I spoken unto you, that my joy might remain in you, and *that* your joy might be full.

12This is my commandment, That ye love one another, as I have loved you. 13Greater love hath no man than this, that a man lay down his life for his friends. 14Ye are my friends, if ye do whatsoever I command you. 15Henceforth I call you not servants; for the servant knoweth not what his lord doeth: but I have called you friends; for all things that I

THE UPPER ROOM – I AM THE TRUE VINE (cont.) — John 15:1-17

have heard of my Father I have made known unto you. ₁₆Ye have not chosen me, but I have chosen you, and ordained you, that ye should go and bring forth fruit, and *that* your fruit should remain: that whatsoever ye shall ask of the Father in my name, he may give it you. ₁₇These things I command you, that ye love one another.

THE UPPER ROOM – NOT OF THE WORLD — John 15:18-16:4

₁₈If the world hate you, ye know that it hated me before *it hated* you. ₁₉If ye were of the world, the world would love his own: but because ye are not of the world, but I have chosen you out of the world, therefore the world hateth you. ₂₀Remember the word that I said unto you, The servant is not greater than his lord. If they have persecuted me, they will also persecute you; if they have kept my saying, they will keep yours also.

₂₁But all these things will they do unto you for my name's sake, because they know not him that sent me. ₂₂If I had not come and spoken unto them, they had not had sin: but now they have no cloke for their sin. ₂₃He that hateth me hateth my Father also. ₂₄If I had not done among them the works which none other man did, they had not had sin: but now have they both seen and hated both me and my Father. ₂₅But *this cometh to pass*, that the word might be fulfilled that is written in their law, ᵃTHEY HATED ME WITHOUT A CAUSE.

₂₆But when the Comforter is come, whom I will send unto you from the Father, *even* the Spirit of truth, which proceedeth from the Father, he shall testify of me: ₂₇And ye also shall bear witness, because ye have been with me from the beginning. ₁₆:₁These things have I spoken unto you, that ye should not be offended. ₂They shall ᵇput you out of the synagogues: yea, the time cometh, that whosoever killeth you will think that he doeth God service. ₃And these things will they do unto you, because they have not known the Father, nor me. ₄But these things have I told you, that when the time shall come, ye may remember that I told you of them

a Ps. 35:19

b IE: excommunicate you

THE UPPER ROOM – A GUIDE TO ALL TRUTH — John 16:4-15

₄And these things I said not unto you at the beginning, because I was with you. ₅But now I go my way to him that sent me; and none of you asketh me, Whither goest thou? ₆But because I have said these things unto you, sorrow hath filled your heart.

₇Nevertheless I tell you the truth; It is expedient for you that I go away: for if I go not away, the Comforter will not come unto you; but if I depart, I will send him unto you. ₈And when he is come, he will reprove the world of sin, and of righteousness, and of judgment: ₉Of sin, be-

THURSDAY THE WEEK OF THE ATONING SACRIFICE

THE UPPER ROOM – A GUIDE TO ALL TRUTH (cont.) — John 16:4-15

cause they believe not on me; ₁₀Of righteousness, because I go to my Father, and ye see me no more; ₁₁Of judgment, because the prince of this world is judged.

₁₂I have yet many things to say unto you, but ye cannot bear them now. ₁₃Howbeit when he, the Spirit of truth, is come, he will guide you into all truth: for he shall not speak of himself; but whatsoever he shall hear, *that* shall he speak: and he will shew you things to come. ₁₄He shall glorify me: for he shall receive of mine, and shall shew *it* unto you. ₁₅All things that the Father hath are mine: therefore said I, that he shall take of mine, and shall shew *it* unto you.

THE UPPER ROOM – SORROW SHALL TURN TO JOY — John 16:16-24

₁₆A little while, and ye shall not see me: and again, a little while, and ye shall see me, because I go to the Father. **1** JST John 16:23

₁₇Then said *some* of his disciples among themselves, What is this that he saith unto us, A little while, and ye shall not see me: and again, a little while, and ye shall see me: and, Because I go to the Father?

₁₈They said therefore, What is this that he saith, A little while? we cannot tell what he saith.

₁₉Now Jesus knew that they were desirous to ask him, and said unto them, Do ye enquire among yourselves of that I said, A little while, and ye shall not see me: and again, a little while, and ye shall see me? ₂₀Verily, verily, I say unto you, That ye shall weep and lament, but the world shall rejoice: and ye shall be sorrowful, but your sorrow shall be turned into joy. ₂₁A woman when she is in travail hath sorrow, because her hour is come: but as soon as she is delivered of the child, she remembereth no more the anguish, for joy that a man is born into the world. ₂₂And ye now therefore have sorrow: but I will see you again, and your heart shall rejoice, and your joy no man taketh from you.

₂₃And in that day ye shall ask me nothing **1**<u>but it shall be done unto you</u>. Verily, verily, I say unto you, Whatsoever ye shall ask the Father in my name, he will give *it* you. ₂₄Hitherto have ye asked nothing in my name: ask, and ye shall receive, that your joy may be full.

THE UPPER ROOM – I HAVE OVERCOME THE WORLD — John 16:25-33

₂₅These things have I spoken unto you in proverbs: but the time cometh, when I shall no more speak unto you in proverbs, but I shall shew you plainly of the Father. ₂₆At that day ye shall ask in my name: and I say not unto you, that I will pray the Father for you: ₂₇For the Father himself loveth you, because ye have loved me, and have believed that I came out from God.

₂₈I came forth from the Father, and am come into the world: again, I leave the world, and go to the Father.

THE WEEK OF THE ATONING SACRIFICE

THE UPPER ROOM – I HAVE OVERCOME THE WORLD (cont.) — John 16:25-33

₂₉His disciples said unto him, Lo, now speakest thou plainly, and speakest no proverb. ₃₀Now are we sure that thou knowest all things, and needest not that any man should ask thee: by this we believe that thou camest forth from God.

₃₁Jesus answered them, Do ye now believe? ₃₂Behold, the hour cometh, yea, is now come, that ye shall be scattered, every man to his own, and shall leave me alone: and yet I am not alone, because the Father is with me. ₃₃These things I have spoken unto you, that in me ye might have peace. In the world ye shall have tribulation: but be of good cheer; I have overcome the world.

THE UPPER ROOM – THE GREAT INTERCESSORY PRAYER — John 17:1-26

₁These words spake Jesus, and lifted up his eyes to heaven, and said, Father, the hour is come; glorify thy Son, that thy Son also may glorify thee: ₂As thou hast given him power over all flesh, that he should give eternal life to as many as thou hast given him. ₃And this is life eternal, that they might know thee the only true God, and Jesus Christ, whom thou hast sent. ₄I have glorified thee on the earth: I have finished the work which thou gavest me to do. ₅And now, O Father, glorify thou me with thine own self with the glory which I had with thee before the world was.

₆I have manifested thy name unto the men which thou gavest me out of the world: thine they were, and thou gavest them me; and they have kept thy word. ₇Now they have known that all things whatsoever thou hast given me are of thee. ₈For I have given unto them the words which thou gavest me; and they have received *them*, and have known surely that I came out from thee, and they have believed that thou didst send me. ₉I pray for them: I pray not for the world, but for them which thou hast given me; for they are thine. ₁₀And all mine are thine, and thine are mine; and I am glorified in them.

₁₁And now I am no more in the world, but these are in the world, and I come to thee. Holy Father, keep through thine own name those whom thou hast given me, that they may be one, as we *are*. ₁₂While I was with them in the world, I kept them in thy name: those that thou gavest me I have kept, and none of them is lost, but the son of perdition; that the scripture might be fulfilled. ₁₃And now come I to thee; and these things I speak in the world, that they might have my joy fulfilled in themselves. ₁₄I have given them thy word; and the world hath hated them, because they are not of the world, even as I am not of the world. ₁₅I pray not that thou shouldest take them out of the world, but that thou shouldest keep them from the evil. ₁₆They are not of the world, even as I am not of the world.

₁₇Sanctify them through thy truth: thy word is truth. ₁₈As thou hast

THURSDAY — **THE WEEK OF THE ATONING SACRIFICE**

THE UPPER ROOM – THE GREAT INTERCESSORY PRAYER (cont.) — John 17:1-26

sent me into the world, even so have I also sent them into the world. ₁₉And for their sakes I sanctify myself, that they also might be sanctified through the truth.

₂₀Neither pray I for these alone, but for them also which shall believe on me through their word; ₂₁That they all may be one; as thou, Father, *art* in me, and I in thee, that they also may be one in us: that the world may believe that thou hast sent me. ₂₂And the glory which thou gavest me I have given them; that they may be one, even as we are one: ₂₃I in them, and thou in me, that they may be made perfect in one; and that the world may know that thou hast sent me, and hast loved them, as thou hast loved me.

₂₄Father, I will that they also, whom thou hast given me, be with me where I am; that they may behold my glory, which thou hast given me: for thou lovedst me before the foundation of the world. ₂₅O righteous Father, the world hath not known thee: but I have known thee, and these have known that thou hast sent me. ₂₆And I have declared unto them thy name, and will declare *it*: that the love wherewith thou hast loved me may be in them, and I in them.

THE UPPER ROOM – PURSE AND SCRIPT — Luke 22:35-38

₃₅And he said unto them, When I sent you without purse, and scrip, and shoes, lacked ye any thing?
And they said, Nothing.
₃₆Then said he unto them, But now, he that hath a purse, let him take *it*, and likewise *his* scrip: and he that hath no sword, let him sell his garment, and buy one. ₃₇For I say unto you, that this that is written must yet be accomplished in me, ᵃAND HE WAS RECKONED AMONG THE TRANSGRESSORS: for the things concerning me have an end.
₃₈And they said, Lord, behold, here *are* two swords.
And he said unto them, It is enough. ¹**Arise, let us go hence.**

²**And when they had sung an hymn, ³he came out, and went, as he was wont, to the mount of Olives; and his disciples also followed him.**

- a Isa. 53:12
- 1 John 14:31
- 2 Matt. 26:30
- 3 Luke 22:39

PETER TO DENY CHRIST — Luke 22:31-34

¹₃₆Simon Peter said unto him, Lord, whither goest thou?
Jesus answered him, Whither I go, thou canst not follow me now; but thou shalt follow me afterwards.
₃₇Peter said unto him, Lord, why cannot I follow thee now? I will lay down my life for thy sake.
₃₈Jesus answered him, Wilt thou lay down thy life for my sake? ²₃₁Then saith Jesus unto them, All ye shall be offended because of me this night: for it is written, ᵃI WILL SMITE THE SHEPHERD, AND THE SHEEP OF THE FLOCK SHALL BE SCATTERED ABROAD. ₃₂But after I am

- 1 John 13:36-38
- 2 Matt. 26:31-33
- a Zech. 13:7

THURSDAY   THE WEEK OF THE ATONING SACRIFICE

PETER TO DENY CHRIST (cont.)   Luke 22:31-34

risen again, I will go before you into Galilee. ₃₃Peter answered and said unto him, Though all *men* shall be offended because of thee, *yet* will I never be offended. ₃₁And the Lord said, Simon, Simon, behold, Satan hath desired *to have* you, that he may sift *you* as wheat: ₃₂But I have prayed for thee, that thy faith fail not: and when thou art converted, strengthen thy brethren. ₃₃And he said unto him, Lord, I am ready to go with thee, both into prison, and to death. ₃₄And he said, I tell thee, Peter, the cock shall not ᵇcrow this day, before that thou shalt thrice deny that thou knowest me. ³But he spake the more vehemently, If I should die with thee, I will not deny thee in any wise. Likewise also said they all.	**b** Mark notes the number of times the cock will crow (twice). Mark 14:30 **3** Mark 14:31

THE GARDEN OF GETHSEMANE   Matt. 26:36-46

¹When Jesus had spoken these words, he went forth with his disciples over the brook Cedron, ²And they came to a place which was named Gethsemane: ¹where was a garden, into the which he entered, and his disciples; ³and ⁴the disciples began to be sore amazed, and to be very heavy; ⁴and to complain in their hearts, wondering if this be the Messiah. ⁵And Jesus knowing their hearts ²saith to his disciples, Sit ye here, while I shall pray. ³And he taketh with him, Peter, and James, and John, ⁶and rebuked them, ⁷And saith unto them, My soul is exceeding sorrowful, ⁶even unto death: tarry ye here and watch. ⁸₄₀Pray that ye enter not into temptation. ₄₁And he was withdrawn from them about a stone's cast, and kneeled down, ₃₉and fell on his face, and prayed, saying, O my Father, if it be possible, let this cup pass from me: nevertheless not as I will, but as thou *wilt*. ₄₀And he cometh unto the disciples, and findeth them asleep, and saith unto Peter, What, could ye not watch with me one hour? ₄₁Watch and pray, that ye enter not into temptation: the spirit indeed *is* willing, but the flesh *is* weak. ₄₂He went away again the second time, and prayed, saying, O my Father, if this cup may not pass away from me, except I drink it, thy will be done. ₄₃And he came and found them asleep again: for their eyes were heavy, ⁹neither ᵃwist they what to answer him. ₄₄And he left them, and went away again, and prayed the third time, saying ¹⁰Abba, Father, all things *are* possible unto thee; ¹¹₄₂if thou be willing, remove this cup from me: nevertheless, not my will, but thine be done. ₄₃And there appeared an angel unto him from heaven, strengthening him. ₄₄And being in an agony he prayed more earnestly: and ¹²he sweat as it were great drops of blood falling down to the ground.	**1** John 18:1 **2** Mark 14:32 (Phrases in this verse and Mark 14:33 appear out of order here. The sequence is that in JST Mark 14:36-38.) **3** Mark 14:33 **4** JST Mark 14:36 **5** JST Mark 14:37 **6** JST Mark 14:38 **7** Mark 14:34 **8** Luke 22:40-41 **9** Mark 14:40 **a** IE: knew **10** Mark 14:36 **11** Luke 22:42-45 **12** JST Luke 22:44; kjv: his sweat was

THURSDAY	THE WEEK OF THE ATONING SACRIFICE	

THE GARDEN OF GETHSEMANE (cont.)	Matt. 26:36-46

₄₅And when he rose up from prayer, and was come to his disciples, he found them sleeping for sorrow, ₄₅and saith unto them, Sleep on now, and take *your* rest: behold, the hour is at hand, and the Son of man is betrayed into the hands of sinners. ₄₆Rise, let us be going: behold, he is at hand that doth betray me.

WHOMSOEVER I SHALL KISS IS HE	John 18:2-11

₂And Judas also, which betrayed him, knew the place: for Jesus ofttimes resorted thither with his disciples. ₃Judas then, having received a band *of men* and officers from the chief priests and Pharisees, cometh thither with lanterns and torches and weapons. ¹₄₈**Now he that betrayed him gave them a sign, saying, Whomsoever I shall kiss, that same is he: hold him fast.** ₄₉**And forthwith he came to Jesus, and said, Hail, master; and kissed him.**

₄Jesus therefore, knowing all things that should come upon him, went forth, and said unto them, Whom seek ye?

₅They answered him, Jesus of Nazareth.

Jesus saith unto them, I am *he*.

And Judas also, which betrayed him, stood with them. ₆As soon then as he had said unto them, I am *he*, they went backward, and fell to the ground. ₇Then asked he them again, Whom seek ye?

And they said, Jesus of Nazareth.

₈Jesus answered, I have told you that I am *he*: if therefore ye seek me, let these go their way: ₉That the saying might be fulfilled, which he spake, Of them which thou gavest me have I lost none.

²**Then came they, and laid hands on Jesus, and took him.**

₁₀Then Simon Peter having a sword drew it, and smote the high priest's servant, and cut off his right ear. The servant's name was Malchus.

³**And Jesus answered and said, Suffer ye thus far. And he touched his ear, and healed him.** ⁴₅₂**Then said Jesus unto him, Put up again thy sword into his place: for all they that take the sword shall perish with the sword.** ₅₃**Thinkest thou that I cannot now pray to my Father, and he shall presently give me more than twelve legions of angels?** ₅₄**But how then shall the scriptures be fulfilled, that thus it must be?** ₁₁The cup which my Father hath given me, shall I not drink it?

⁵₅₂Then Jesus said unto the chief priests, and captains of the temple, and the elders, which were come to him, Be ye come out, as against a thief, with swords and staves? ₅₃When I was daily with you in the temple, ye stretched forth no hands against me: but this is your hour, and the power of darkness. ⁶But all this was done, that the scriptures of the prophets might be fulfilled.

Then all the disciples forsook him, and fled.

1 Matt. 26:48-49
2 Matt. 26:50
3 Luke 22:51
4 Matt. 26:52-54
5 Luke 22:52-53
6 Matt. 26:56

FRIDAY   **THE WEEK OF THE ATONING SACRIFICE**

(About Midnight) **TAKEN BEFORE ANNAS THE HIGH PRIEST**	John 18:12-14
₁₂Then the band and the captain and officers of the Jews took Jesus, and bound him, ₁₃And led him away to Annas first; for he was father in law to Caiaphas, which was the high priest that same year. ₁₄Now Caiaphas was he, which gave counsel to the Jews, that it was expedient that one man should die for the people. ¹₅₁And there followed him a certain young man, ²a disciple having a linen cloth cast about *his* naked *body*; and the young men laid hold on him: ₅₂And he left the linen cloth, and fled from them naked.	1 Mark 14:51-52 2 JST Mark 14:57
QUESTIONED BY ANNAS	John 18:19-24
₁₉The high priest then asked Jesus of his disciples, and of his doctrine. ₂₀Jesus answered him, I spake openly to the world; I ever taught in the synagogue, and in the temple, whither the Jews always resort; and in secret have I said nothing. ₂₁Why askest thou me? ask them which heard me, what I have said unto them: behold, they know what I said. ₂₂And when he had thus spoken, one of the officers which stood by struck Jesus with the palm of his hand, saying, Answerest thou the high priest so? ₂₃Jesus answered him, If I have spoken evil, bear witness of the evil: but if well, why smitest thou me? ₂₄Now Annas had sent him bound unto Caiaphas the high priest, ¹where the scribes and the elders were assembled.	1 Matt. 26:57
BEFORE THE COUNSEL	Matt. 26:58-67
₅₈But Peter followed him afar off unto the high priest's palace, and went in, and ¹when they had kindled a fire in the midst of the hall, and were set down together, Peter sat down among the servants, to see the end. ₅₉Now the chief priests, and elders, and all the council, sought false witness against Jesus, to put him to death; ₆₀But found none: yea, though many false witnesses came, *yet* found they none. At the last came two false witnesses, ₆₁And said, ²₅₈We heard him say, I will destroy this temple that is made with hands, and within three days I will build another made without hands. ₅₉But neither so did their witness agree together. ₆₂And the high priest arose, and said unto him, Answerest thou nothing? what *is it which* these witness against thee? ₆₃But Jesus held his peace. And the high priest answered and said unto him, I adjure thee by the living God, that thou tell us whether thou be the Christ, the Son of God. ₆₄Jesus saith unto him, Thou hast said: nevertheless I say unto you, Hereafter shall ye see ᵃTHE SON OF MAN ᵇSITTING ON THE RIGHT HAND OF	1 Luke 22:55 2 Mark 14:58-59 a Dan. 7:13 b Ps. 110:1

FRIDAY　　　　　THE WEEK OF THE ATONING SACRIFICE

BEFORE THE COUNSEL (cont.)	Matt. 26:58-67
POWER, and ^cCOMING IN THE CLOUDS OF HEAVEN. ₆₅Then the high priest rent his clothes, saying, He hath spoken blasphemy; what further need have we of witnesses? behold, now ye have heard his blasphemy. ₆₆What think ye? They answered and said, He is guilty of death. ₆₇Then did they spit in his face, and buffeted him; ³₆₄**And when they had blindfolded him, they struck him on the face, and asked him, saying, Prophesy, who is it that smote thee?** ₆₅And many other things blasphemously spake they against him.	c Dan. 7:13 3 Luke 22:64-65

BEFORE THE COCK CREW	Mark 14:66-72
₆₆And as Peter was beneath in the palace, there cometh one of the maids of the high priest: ₆₇And when she saw Peter **¹as he sat by the fire** warming himself, she **¹earnestly looked upon him, and said, This man** also wast with Jesus of Nazareth.	1 Luke 22:56 2 Matt. 26:70 3 Luke 22:57
₆₈But he denied **²before *them* all**, saying, **³Woman** I know not, neither understand I what thou sayest.	4 Luke 22:58
And he went out into the porch; and the cock crew.	5 John 18:26
⁴And after a little while another saw him, ⁵One of the servants of the high priest, being *his* kinsman whose ear Peter cut off, ⁴and said, **⁵Did not I see thee in the garden with him? ⁴Thou art also of them.**	6 Matt. 26:72 7 Luke 22:59
And Peter said, Man, I am not. **⁶And again he denied with an oath, I do not know the man.**	8 Matt. 26:73
⁷And about the space of one hour after another confidently affirmed, saying, Of a truth this *fellow* also was with him: for he is a Galilaean, ₇₀they that stood by said again to Peter, Surely thou art *one* of them: for thou art a Galilaean, **⁸thy speech ªbewrayeth thee.**	a GR: reveals 9 Matt. 26:75
₇₁But he began to curse and to swear, *saying*, I know not this man of whom ye speak. ₇₂And the second time the cock crew. And Peter called to mind the word that Jesus said unto him, Before the cock crow twice, thou shalt deny me thrice. And when he thought thereon, **⁹he went out, and wept bitterly.**	

THE TRIAL BEFORE PILATE	John 18:28-38
¹And straightway in the morning the chief priests held a consultation with the elders and scribes and the whole council ²to put him to death: And when they had bound him, they led *him* away ₂₈from Caiaphas unto the hall of judgment: **²and delivered him to Pontius Pilate the governor.** And it was early; and they themselves went not into the judgment hall, lest they should be defiled; but that they might eat the passover.	1 Mark 15:1 2 Matt. 27:2
₂₉Pilate then went out unto them, and said, What accusation bring ye against this man?	

124

FRIDAY THE WEEK OF THE ATONING SACRIFICE

THE TRIAL BEFORE PILATE (cont.) John 18:28-38

$_{30}$They answered and said unto him, If he were not a malefactor, we would not have delivered him up unto thee. $_{31}$Then said Pilate unto them, Take ye him, and judge him according to your law. The Jews therefore said unto him, It is not lawful for us to put any man to death: $_{32}$That the saying of Jesus might be fulfilled, which he spake, signifying what death he should die.

3 And they began to accuse him, saying, We found this *fellow* perverting the nation, and forbidding to give tribute to Caesar, saying that he himself is Christ a King.

$_{33}$Then Pilate entered into the judgment hall again, and called Jesus, and said unto him, Art thou the King of the Jews?

$_{34}$Jesus answered him, Sayest thou this thing of thyself, or did others tell it thee of me?

$_{35}$Pilate answered, Am I a Jew? Thine own nation and the chief priests have delivered thee unto me: what hast thou done?

$_{36}$Jesus answered, My kingdom is not of this world: if my kingdom were of this world, then would my servants fight, that I should not be delivered to the Jews: but now is my kingdom not from hence.

$_{37}$Pilate therefore said unto him, Art thou a king then? Jesus answered, Thou sayest that I am a king. To this end was I born, and for this cause came I into the world, that I should bear witness unto the truth. Every one that is of the truth heareth my voice.

$_{38}$Pilate saith unto him, What is truth? And when he had said this, he went out again unto the Jews, and saith unto them, I find in him no fault *at all*.

4 5 And they were the more fierce, saying, He stirreth up the people, teaching throughout all Jewry, beginning from Galilee to this place. 6 When Pilate heard of Galilee, he asked whether the man were a Galilaean. 7 And as soon as he knew that he belonged unto Herod's jurisdiction, he sent him to Herod, who himself also was at Jerusalem at that time.

3 Luke 23:2

4 Luke 23:5-7

BEFORE HEROD Luke 23:8-12

$_{8}$And when Herod saw Jesus, he was exceeding glad: for he was desirous to see him of a long *season*, because he had heard many things of him; and he hoped to have seen some miracle done by him. $_{9}$Then he questioned with him in many words; but he answered him nothing. $_{10}$And the chief priests and scribes stood and vehemently accused him. $_{11}$And Herod with his men of war set him at nought, and mocked *him*, and arrayed him in a gorgeous robe, and sent him again to Pilate.

$_{12}$And the same day Pilate and Herod were made friends together: for before they were at enmity between themselves.

FRIDAY · THE WEEK OF THE ATONING SACRIFICE

THE SENTENCING · John 18:38-19:16

¹Now at *that* feast the governor was ªwont to release unto the people a prisoner, whom they would. ²₁₃And Pilate, when he had called together the chief priests and the rulers and the people, ₁₄Said unto them, Ye have brought this man unto me, as one that perverteth the people: and, behold, I, having examined *him* before you, have found no fault in this man touching those things whereof ye accuse him: ₁₅No, nor yet Herod: for I sent you to him; and, lo, nothing worthy of death is done ᵇunto him. ₁₆I will therefore chastise him, and release *him*. ₃₉But ye have a custom, that I should release unto you one at the passover: will ye therefore that I release unto you the King of the Jews? ³For he knew that the chief priests had delivered him for envy.
⁴And they had then a notable prisoner, called Barabbas. ₄₀Now Barabbas was a robber, ⁵which lay bound with them that had made insurrection with him, who had committed murder in the insurrection. ⁶But the chief priests and elders persuaded the multitude that they should ask Barabbas, and destroy Jesus. ⁷And they cried out all at once, saying, Away with this *man*, and release unto us Barabbas:
⁸When he was set down on the judgment seat, his wife sent unto him, saying, Have thou nothing to do with that just man: for I have suffered many things this day in a dream because of him. ⁹Pilate therefore, willing to release Jesus, spake again to them. ¹⁰What will ye then that I shall do *unto him* whom ye call the King of the Jews?
¹¹*They* all say unto him, Let him be crucified.
And the governor said, Why, what evil hath he done?
But they cried out ᶜthe more, saying, Let him be crucified.
¹²And he said unto them the third time, Why, what evil hath he done? I have found no cause of death in him: I will therefore chastise him, and let *him* go. ₁₉:₁Then Pilate therefore took Jesus, and scourged *him*. ¹³₁₆And the soldiers led him away into the hall, called Praetorium; and they call together the whole band. ₁₇And they clothed him with purple, and platted a crown of thorns, and put it about his *head*, ₁₈And began to salute him, Hail, King of the Jews! ₁₉And they smote him on the head with a reed, and did spit upon him, and bowing *their* knees worshipped him.
  ₄Pilate therefore went forth again, and saith unto them, Behold, I bring him forth to you, that ye may know that I find no fault in him. ₅Then came Jesus forth, wearing the crown of thorns, and the purple robe. And *Pilate* saith unto them, Behold the man!
  ₆When the chief priests therefore and officers saw him, they cried out, saying, Crucify *him*, crucify *him*. ¹⁴And the voices of them and of

1 Matt. 27:15
a IE: accustomed
2 Luke 23:13-16
b GR: by
3 Mark 15:10
4 Matt. 27:16
5 Mark 15:7
6 Matt. 27:20
7 Luke 23:18
8 Matt. 27:19
9 Luke 23:20
10 Mark 15:12
11 Matt. 27:23
c GR: exceedingly, beyond measure
12 Luke 23:22
13 Mark 15:16-19
14 Luke 23:23

126

FRIDAY THE WEEK OF THE ATONING SACRIFICE

THE SENTENCING (cont.)   John 18:39-19:16

the chief priests prevailed.
15 24When Pilate saw that he ᵈcould prevail nothing, but *that* rather a tumult was made, he took water, and washed *his* hands before the multitude, saying, I am innocent of the blood of this just person: see ye *to it.*
25Then answered all the people, and said, His blood *be* on us, and on our children. 7We have a law, and by our law he ought to die, because he made himself the Son of God.

8When Pilate therefore heard that saying, he was the more afraid; 9And went again into the judgment hall, and saith unto Jesus, Whence art thou?

But Jesus gave him no answer.

10Then saith Pilate unto him, Speakest thou not unto me? knowest thou not that I have power to crucify thee, and have power to release thee?

11Jesus answered, Thou couldest have no power *at all* against me, except it were given thee from above: therefore he that delivered me unto thee hath the greater sin.

12And from thenceforth Pilate sought to release him: but the Jews cried out, saying, If thou let this man go, thou art not Caesar's friend: whosoever maketh himself a king speaketh against Caesar.

13When Pilate therefore heard that saying, he brought Jesus forth, and sat down in the judgment seat in a place that is called the Pavement, but in the Hebrew, Gabbatha. 14And it was the preparation of the passover, and about the sixth hour: and he saith unto the Jews, Behold your King!

15But they cried out, Away with *him,* away with *him,* crucify him.
Pilate saith unto them, Shall I crucify your King?
The chief priests answered, We have no king but Caesar.

16Then delivered he him therefore unto them to be crucified. And **16they took the robe off from him, and put his own raiment on him, and led him away to crucify** *him.*

15 Matt. 27:24-25

d GR: was accomplishing nothing

16 Matt. 27:31

THE DEATH OF JUDAS   Matt. 27:3-10

3Then Judas, which had betrayed him, when he saw that he was condemned, repented himself, and brought again the thirty pieces of silver to the chief priests and elders, 4Saying, I have sinned in that I have betrayed the innocent blood. And they said, What *is that* to us? see thou *to* ¹it; thy sins be upon thee. 5And he cast down the pieces of silver in the temple, and departed, and went and hanged himself ²on a tree. And straightway he fell down, and his bowels gushed out, and he died. 6And the chief priests took the silver pieces, and said, It is not lawful for to put them into the treasury, because it is the price of blood. 7And

1 JST Matt. 27:5; KJV: *that*

2 JST Matt. 27:6 (see Acts 1:18)

127

| FRIDAY | THE WEEK OF THE ATONING SACRIFICE |

THE DEATH OF JUDAS (cont.) — Matt. 27:3-10

they took counsel, and bought with them the potter's field, to bury strangers in. ₈Wherefore that field was called, The field of blood, unto this day. ₉Then was fulfilled that which was spoken by ᵃJeremy the prophet, saying, ᵇAND THEY TOOK THE THIRTY PIECES OF SILVER, THE PRICE OF HIM THAT WAS VALUED, whom they of the children of Israel did value; ₁₀ᶜAND THEY GAVE THEM FOR THE POTTER'S FIELD, AS THE LORD APPOINTED ME.

a GR: Jeremiah (an error in the text; possibly based on Jer. 32:9-10)
b Zech. 11:12
c Zech. 11:13

THE CRUCIFIXION — Luke 23:26-49

₂₆And as they led him away, they laid hold upon one Simon, a Cyrenian, coming out of the country, and on him they laid the cross, that he might bear *it* after Jesus. ₂₇And there followed him a great company of people, and of women, which also bewailed and lamented him. ₂₈But Jesus turning unto them said, Daughters of Jerusalem, weep not for me, but weep for yourselves, and for your children. ₂₉For, behold, the days are coming, in the which they shall say, Blessed *are* the barren, and the wombs that never bare, and the paps which never gave suck. ₃₀ᵃTHEN SHALL THEY BEGIN TO SAY TO THE MOUNTAINS, FALL ON US; AND TO THE HILLS, COVER US. ₃₁For if they do these things in a green tree, what shall be done in the dry? ¹This he spake, signifying the scattering of Israel, and the desolation of the heathen, or in other words, the Gentiles.

²₃₃And when they were come unto a place called ᵇGolgotha, that is to say, a place of ³burial, ₃₄They gave him vinegar to drink mingled with gall: and when he had tasted *thereof*, he would not drink.

⁴₂₅And it was the third hour, and they crucified him. ₂₇And with him they crucify two thieves; the one on his right hand, and the other on his left. ₂₈And the scripture was fulfilled, which saith, ᶜAND HE WAS NUMBERED WITH THE TRANSGRESSORS.

⁵₂₃Then the soldiers, when they had crucified Jesus, took his garments, and made four parts, to every soldier a part; and also *his* coat: now the coat was without seam, woven from the top throughout. ₂₄They said therefore among themselves, Let us not rend it, but cast lots for it, whose it shall be: that the scripture might be fulfilled, which saith, ᵈTHEY PARTED MY RAIMENT AMONG THEM, AND FOR MY VESTURE THEY DID CAST LOTS. These things therefore the soldiers did.

₃₅And the people stood beholding. And the rulers also with them derided *him*, saying, He saved others; let him save himself, if he be Christ, the chosen of God. ₃₆And the soldiers also mocked him, coming to him, and offering him vinegar, ₃₇And saying, If thou be the king of the Jews, save thyself.

⁶And Pilate wrote a title, and put *it* on the cross ₃₈over him in

a Hos. 10:8
1 JST Luke 23:32
2 Matt. 27:33-34
b GR: a skull (according to the Greek text, "place of a skull")
3 JST Matt. 27:35; KJV: a skull
4 Mark 15:25, 27-28
c Isa. 53:12
5 John 19:23-24
d Ps. 22:18
6 John 19:19

FRIDAY   THE WEEK OF THE ATONING SACRIFICE

THE CRUCIFIXION (cont.)   Luke 23:26-48

letters of Greek, and Latin, and Hebrew, ⁶And the writing was, ⁷THIS IS ⁸₁₉JESUS OF NAZARETH THE KING OF THE JEWS. ₂₀This title then read many of the Jews: for the place where Jesus was crucified was nigh to the city: ₂₁Then said the chief priests of the Jews to Pilate, Write not, The King of the Jews; but that he said, I am King of the Jews.

  ₂₂Pilate answered, What I have written I have written.

  ⁹₂₉And they that passed by railed on him, wagging their heads, and saying, Ah, thou that destroyest the temple, and buildest *it* in three days, ₃₀Save thyself, and come down from the cross.

  ₃₁Likewise also the chief priests mocking said among themselves with the scribes, He saved others; himself he cannot save. ₃₂Let Christ the King of Israel descend now from the cross, that we may see and believe.

  ₃₉And one of the malefactors which were hanged railed on him, saying, If thou be Christ, save thyself and us.

  ₄₀But the other answering rebuked him, saying, Dost not thou fear God, seeing thou art in the same condemnation? ₄₁And we indeed justly; for we receive the due reward of our deeds: but this man hath done nothing amiss.

  ₄₂And he said unto Jesus, Lord, remember me when thou comest into thy kingdom.

  ₄₃And Jesus said unto him, Verily I say unto thee, To day shalt thou be with me in paradise.

  ¹⁰₂₅Now there stood by the cross of Jesus his mother, and his mother's sister, Mary the *wife* of Cleophas, and Mary Magdalene. ₂₆When Jesus therefore saw his mother, and the disciple standing by, whom he loved, he saith unto his mother, Woman, behold thy son! ₂₇Then saith he to the disciple, Behold thy mother! And from that hour that disciple took her unto his own *home*.

  ₄₄And it was about the sixth hour, and there was a darkness over all the earth until the ninth hour. ₄₅And the sun was darkened, and the veil of the temple was rent in ¹¹twain from the top to the bottom;.and the earth did quake, and the rocks rent; ¹²₄₆And about the ninth hour Jesus cried with a loud voice, saying, ᶜELI, ELI, LAMA SABACHTHANI? that is to say, ᵈMY GOD, MY GOD, WHY HAST THOU FORSAKEN ME?

  ₄₇Some of them that stood there, when they heard *that*, said, This *man* calleth for ᵈElias.

  ¹³₂₈After this, Jesus knowing that all things were now accomplished, that the scripture might be fulfilled, saith, I thirst.

  ₂₉Now there was set a vessel full of vinegar: ¹⁴₄₈And straightway one of them ran, and took a spunge, and filled *it* with vinegar, and put *it* on a reed, and gave him to drink.

---

7   Matt. 27:37

8   John 19:19-22

9   Mark 15:29-32

10   John 19:25-27

11   Matt. 27:51

12   Matt. 27:46-47

c   These words are in Aramaic.

d   Ps. 22:1

e   GR: Elijah

13   John 19:28-29

14   Matt. 27:48-49

129

| FRIDAY | THE WEEK OF THE ATONING SACRIFICE |

THE CRUCIFIXION (cont.) — Luke 23:26-49

₄₉The rest said, Let be, let us see whether Elias will come to save him. ₄₆And when Jesus had cried with a loud voice, he said, Father, ¹⁵it is finished, thy will is done, ᶠINTO THY HANDS I COMMEND MY SPIRIT: and having said thus, he ᵍgave up the ghost.

¹⁶₅₄Now when the centurion, and they that were with him, watching Jesus, saw the earthquake, and those things that were done, they feared greatly, saying, Truly this was the Son of God. ₅₅And many women were there beholding afar off, which followed Jesus from Galilee, ministering unto him: ₅₆Among which was Mary Magdalene, and Mary the mother of ʰJames and ⁱJoses, and the mother of Zebedee's children. ₄₈And all the people that came together to that sight, beholding the things which were done, smote their breasts, and returned.

- f Ps. 31:5
- 15 JST Matt. 27:54
- g GR: died
- 16 Matt. 27:54-56
- h GR: Jacob
- i GR: Joseph

HE WAS DEAD ALREADY — John 19:31-37

₃₁The Jews therefore, because it was the preparation, that the bodies should not remain upon the cross on the sabbath day, (for that sabbath day was an high day,) besought Pilate that their legs might be broken, and *that* they might be taken away. ₃₂Then came the soldiers, and brake the legs of the first, and of the other which was crucified with him. ₃₃But when they came to Jesus, and saw that he was dead already, they brake not his legs: ₃₄But one of the soldiers with a spear pierced his side, and forthwith came there out blood and water. ₃₅And he that saw *it* bare record, and his record is true: and he knoweth that he saith true, that ye might believe.

₃₆For these things were done, that the scripture should be fulfilled, ᵃA BONE OF HIM SHALL NOT BE BROKEN. ₃₇And again another scripture saith, ᵇTHEY SHALL LOOK ON HIM WHOM THEY PIERCED.

- a Exod. 12:46; Num. 9:12 referring to the Passover lamb; see Ps. 34:20, a prophecy applying the symbolism to Christ
- b Zech. 12:10

ENTOMBED — Luke 23:50-56

¹And after this ²there came a rich man of Arimathaea, ₅₁a city of the Jews: ³an honourable counsellor, ²named Joseph, ₅₀and he was a good man, and a just: ₅₁(The same had not consented to the counsel and deed of them;) who also himself waited for the kingdom of God, ¹being a disciple of Jesus, but secretly for fear of the Jews, besought Pilate that he might take away the body of Jesus: ⁴₄₄And Pilate marveled if he were already dead: and calling *unto him* the centurion, he asked him whether he had been any while dead. ₄₅And when he knew *it* of the centurion, he gave ¹*him* leave. He came therefore, and took ₅₃down the body of Jesus. ⁵And there came also Nicodemus, which at the first came to Jesus by night, and brought a mixture of myrrh and aloes, about an hundred

- 1 John 19:38
- 2 Matt. 27:57
- 3 Mark 15:43
- 4 Mark 15:44-45
- 5 John 19:39

130

* SATURDAY	THE WEEK OF THE ATONING SACRIFICE	
ENTOMBED (cont.)		Luke 23:50-56

pound *weight*. ^{6}And he bought fine linen, and took him down, and wrapped him in the linen $^7{}_{40}$with the spices, as the manner of the Jews is to bury.

$_{41}$Now in the place where he was crucified there was a garden; and in the garden a new sepulchre, ^{8}which was hewn out of a rock, $^9{}_{41}$wherein was never man yet laid. $_{42}$There laid they Jesus therefore because of the Jews' preparation *day*; for the sepulchre was nigh at hand: $^{10}{}_{60}$and he rolled a great stone to the door of the sepulchre, and departed.

$_{61}$And there was Mary Magdalene, and the other Mary, sitting over against the sepulchre, $_{55}$and beheld the sepulchre, and how his body was laid. $_{56}$And they returned, and prepared spices and ointments; and rested the sabbath day according to the commandment.

6 Mark 15:46
7 John 19:40-41
8 Mark 15:46
9 John 19:41-42
10 Matt. 27:60-61

* **SEALING THE STONE, SETTING A WATCH**	Matt. 27:62-66

$_{62}$Now the next day, that followed the day of the preparation, the chief priests and Pharisees came together unto Pilate, $_{63}$Saying, Sir, we remember that that deceiver said, while he was yet alive, After three days I will rise again. $_{64}$Command therefore that the sepulchre be made sure until the third day, lest his disciples come by night, and steal him away, and say unto the people, He is risen from the dead: so the last ^{a}error shall be worse than the first.

$_{65}$Pilate said unto them, Ye have a watch: go your way, make *it* as sure as ye can.

$_{66}$So they went, and made the sepulchre sure, sealing the stone, and setting a watch.

a GR: deception

MISSION TO THE SPIRIT PRISON	1 Pet. 3:18-20

$_{18}$But quickened by the Spirit: $_{19}$By which also he went and preached unto the spirits in prison; $_{20}{}^1$Some of whom were disobedient, when once the longsuffering of God waited in the days of Noah, while the ark was a preparing, wherein few, that is, eight souls were saved by water.

^{2} $_{18}$While this vast multitude waited and conversed, rejoicing in the hour of their deliverance from the chains of death, the Son of God appeared, declaring liberty to the captives who had been faithful; $_{19}$And there he preached to them the everlasting gospel, the doctrine of the resurrection and the redemption of mankind from the fall, and from individual sins on conditions of repentance.

$_{20}$But unto the wicked he did not go, and among the ungodly and the unrepentant who had defiled themselves while in the flesh, his voice was not raised; $_{21}$Neither did the rebellious who rejected the testimonies and the warnings of the ancient prophets behold his presence, nor look upon his face.

1 JST 1 Pet. 3:20
2 D&C 138:18-24

MISSION TO THE SPIRIT PRISON (cont.)   1 Pet. 3:18-20

$_{22}$Where these were, darkness reigned, but among the righteous there was peace; $_{23}$And the saints rejoiced in their redemption, and bowed the knee and acknowledged the Son of God as their Redeemer and Deliverer from death and the chains of hell. $_{24}$Their countenances shone, and the radiance from the presence of the Lord rested upon them, and they sang praises unto his holy name.

THE GLORIFIED PALESTINIAN MINISTRY

HE IS RISEN   **Mark 16:1-8**

¹₂And, behold, there was a great earthquake: for ²two angels of the Lord descended from heaven, and came and rolled back the stone from the door, and sat upon it. ³And their ₃countenance was like lightning, and ³their raiment white as snow: ₄And for fear of him the keepers did shake, and became as dead *men*.

₁And when the sabbath was past, Mary Magdalene, and Mary the *mother* of ᵃJames, and Salome, had bought sweet spices, that they might come and anoint him. ₂And very early in the morning, **⁴when it was yet dark,** the first *day* of the week, they came unto the sepulchre at the rising of the sun.

₃And they said among themselves, Who shall roll us away the stone from the door of the sepulchre? ₄And when they looked, they saw that the stone was rolled away: for it was very great. **⁵₃And they entered in, and found not the body of the Lord Jesus.**

₄And it came to pass, as they were much perplexed thereabout, behold, two men stood by them, ₅clothed in long white **shining garments:** ₅And as they were afraid, and bowed down *their* faces to the earth, they said unto them, ⁶Fear not ⁷we: for I know that ye seek Jesus, which was crucified. ⁸Why seek ye the living among the dead? he is risen; he is not here: behold the place where they laid him: ⁹₆remember how he spake unto you when he was yet in Galilee, ₇Saying, The Son of man must be delivered into the hands of sinful men, and be crucified, and the third day rise again.

₈And they remembered his words.

₇But go your way, tell his disciples and Peter that he goeth before you into Galilee: there shall ye see him, as he said unto you.

¹⁰And they departed quickly from the sepulchre with fear and great joy; and did run ¹¹₉and told all these things unto the eleven, and to all the rest. ₁₀It was Mary Magdalene, and Joanna, and Mary *the mother* of James, and other *women that were* with them, which told these things unto the apostles. ₁₁And their words seemed to them as idle tales, and they believed them not.

¹²₃Peter therefore went forth, and that other disciple, and came to the sepulchre. ₄So they ran both together: and the other disciple did outrun Peter, and came first to the sepulchre. ₅And he stooping down, *and looking in,* saw the linen clothes lying; yet went he not in.

₆Then cometh Simon Peter following him, and went into the sepulchre, and seeth the linen clothes lie, ₇And the napkin, that was about his head, not lying with the linen clothes, but wrapped together in a place by itself. ₈Then went in also that other disciple, which came first to the sepulchre, and he saw, and believed. ₉For

---

1 Matt. 28:2-4

2 JST Matt. 28:2; KJV: the angel

3 JST Matt. 28:3; KJV: His

a GR: Jacob

4 John 20:1

5 Luke 24:3-5

6 Matt. 28:5

7 JST Matt. 28:4; KJV: ye

8 Luke 24:5

9 Luke 24:6-8

10 Matt. 28:8

11 Luke 24:9-11

12 John 20:3-10

133

THE GLORIFIED PALESTINIAN MINISTRY

HE IS RISEN (cont.)   **Mark 16:1-8**

as yet they knew not the scripture, that he must rise again from the dead. ₁₀Then the disciples went away again unto their own home.

JESUS APPEARS TO MARY   John 20:11-18

₁₁But Mary ¹**Magdalene, out of whom he had cast seven devils,** stood without at the sepulchre weeping: and as she wept, she stooped down, *and looked* into the sepulchre, ₁₂And seeth two angels in white sitting, the one at the head, and the other at the feet, where the body of Jesus had lain. ₁₃And they say unto her, Woman, why weepest thou?

She saith unto them, Because they have taken away my Lord, and I know not where they have laid him. ₁₄And when she had thus said, she turned herself back, and saw Jesus standing, and knew not that it was Jesus.

₁₅Jesus saith unto her, Woman, why weepest thou? whom seekest thou?

She, supposing him to be the gardener, saith unto him, Sir, if thou have borne him hence, tell me where thou hast laid him, and I will take him away.

₁₆Jesus saith unto her, Mary. She turned herself, and saith unto him, Rabboni; which is to say, Master.

₁₇Jesus saith unto her, ²Hold me not; for I am not yet ascended to my Father: but go to my brethren, and say unto them, I ascend unto my Father, and your Father; and *to* my God, and your God.

₁₈Mary Magdalene came and told the disciples ³**as they mourned and wept** that she had seen the Lord, and *that* he had spoken these things unto her. ⁴**And they, when they had heard that he was alive, and had been seen of her, believed not.**

1 Mark 16:9

2 JST John 20:17; KJV: Touch (GR: grasp, handle, cling to)

3 Mark 16:10

4 Mark 16:11

RESURRECTION OF THE SAINTS   Matt. 27:52-53

₅₂And the graves were opened; and many bodies of the saints which slept arose, ₅₃And came out of the graves after his resurrection, and went into the holy city, and appeared unto many.

THE REPORT OF THE WATCH   Matt. 28:11-15

₁₁Now when they were going, behold, some of the ᵃwatch came into the city, and ᵇshewed unto the chief priests all the things that were done. ₁₂And when they were assembled with the elders, and had taken counsel, they gave ᶜlarge money unto the soldiers, ₁₃Saying, Say ye, His disciples came by night, and stole him *away* while we slept. ₁₄And if this come to the governor's ears, we will persuade him, and ᵈsecure you. ₁₅So they took the money, and did as they were taught: and this saying is commonly reported among the Jews until this day.

a GR: guard

b GR: reported

c GR: much

d GR: keep you out of trouble

THE GLORIFIED PALESTINIAN MINISTRY

THE WAY TO EMMAUS   Luke 24:13-35

₁₃And, behold, two of them went that same day to a village called Emmaus, which was from Jerusalem about ᵃthreescore furlongs. ₁₄And they talked together of all these things which had happened. ₁₅And it came to pass, that, while they communed *together* and reasoned, Jesus himself drew near, and went with them. ₁₆But their eyes were ᵇholden that they should not know him. ₁₇And he said unto them, What manner of communications *are* these that ye have one to another, as ye walk, and are sad?

₁₈And the one of them, whose name was Cleopas, answering said unto him, Art thou only a stranger in Jerusalem, and hast not known the things which are come to pass there in these days?

₁₉And he said unto them, What things?

And they said unto him, Concerning Jesus of Nazareth, which was a prophet mighty in deed and word before God and all the people: ₂₀And how the chief priests and our rulers delivered him to be condemned to death, and have crucified him. ₂₁But we trusted that it had been he which should have redeemed Israel: and beside all this, to day is the third day since these things were done. ₂₂Yea, and certain women also of our company made us astonished, which were early at the sepulchre; ₂₃And when they found not his body, they came, saying, that they had also seen a vision of angels, which said that he was alive. ₂₄And certain of them which were with us went to the sepulchre, and found *it* even so as the women had said: but him they saw not.

₂₅Then he said unto them, O ᶜfools, and slow of heart to believe all that the prophets have spoken: ₂₆Ought not Christ to have suffered these things, and to enter into his glory? ₂₇And beginning at Moses and all the prophets, he expounded unto them in all the scriptures the things concerning himself.

₂₈And they drew nigh unto the village, whither they went: and he made as though he would have gone further. ₂₉But they constrained him, saying, Abide with us: for it is toward evening, and the day is far spent. And he went in to tarry with them.

₃₀And it came to pass, as he sat at meat with them, he took bread, and blessed *it*, and brake, and gave to them. ₃₁And their eyes were opened, and they knew him; and he vanished out of their sight. ₃₂And they said one to another, Did not our heart burn within us, while he talked with us by the way, and while he opened to us the scriptures?

₃₃And they rose up the same hour, and returned to Jerusalem, and found the eleven gathered together, and them that were with them, ₃₄Saying, The Lord is risen indeed, and hath appeared to Simon. ₃₅And they told what things *were done* in the way, and how he was known of them in breaking of bread.

a a distance of about 7.5 miles or 12 km.

b GR: restrained

c GR: unwise

THE GLORIFIED PALESTINIAN MINISTRY

JESUS APPEARS TO HIS DISCIPLES   Luke 24:36-49

1Then the same day at evening, being the first *day* of the week, when the doors were shut where the disciples were assembled for fear of the Jews, 36Jesus himself stood in the midst of them, and saith unto them, Peace *be* unto you. 37But they were terrified and affrighted, and supposed that they had seen a spirit.

38And he said unto them, Why are ye troubled? and why do thoughts arise in your hearts? 39Behold my hands and my feet, that it is I myself: handle me, and see; for a spirit hath not flesh and bones, as ye see me have. 40And when he had thus spoken, he shewed them *his* hands and *his* feet.

41And while they yet believed not for joy, and wondered, he said unto them, Have ye here any ªmeat?

42And they gave him a piece of a broiled fish, and of an honeycomb. 43And he took *it*, and did eat before them. 44And he said unto them, These *are* the words which I spake unto you, while I was yet with you, that all things must be fulfilled, which were written in the law of Moses, and *in* the prophets, and *in* the psalms, concerning me.

45Then opened he their understanding, that they might understand the scriptures, 46And said unto them, Thus it is written, and thus it behoved Christ to suffer, and to rise from the dead the third day: 47And that repentance and remission of sins should be preached in his name among all nations, beginning at Jerusalem. 48And ye are witnesses of these things.

49And, behold, I send the promise of my Father upon you: but tarry ye in the city of Jerusalem, until ye be ᵇendued with power from on high.

221Then said Jesus to them again, Peace *be* unto you: as *my* Father hath sent me, even so send I you. 22And when he had said this, he breathed on *them*, and saith unto them, Receive ye the Holy Ghost: 23Whose soever sins ye remit, they are remitted unto them; *and* whose soever *sins* ye retain, they are retained.

1 John 20:19

a GR: food

b IE: endowed (GR: clothed)

2 John 20:21-23

EXCEPT I SHALL SEE, I WILL NOT BELIEVE   John 20:24-31

24But Thomas, one of the twelve, called Didymus, was not with them when Jesus came. 25The other disciples therefore said unto him, We have seen the Lord.

But he said unto them, Except I shall see in his hands the print of the nails, and put my finger into the print of the nails, and thrust my hand into his side, I will not believe.

26And after eight days again his disciples were within, and Thomas with them: *then* came Jesus, the doors being shut, and stood in the midst, and said, Peace *be* unto you. 27Then saith he to Thomas, Reach hither thy finger, and behold my hands; and reach hither thy hand, and thrust *it* into my side: and be not faithless, but believing.

136

THE GLORIFIED PALESTINIAN MINISTRY

EXCEPT I SHALL SEE, I WILL NOT BELIEVE (cont.) — John 20:24-31

₂₈And Thomas answered and said unto him, My Lord and my God. ₂₉Jesus saith unto him, Thomas, because thou hast seen me, thou hast believed: blessed *are* they that have not seen, and *yet* have believed.

₃₀And many other signs truly did Jesus in the presence of his disciples, which are not written in this book: ₃₁But these are written, that ye might believe that Jesus is the Christ, the Son of God; and that believing ye might have life through his name.

APPEARANCE AT THE SEA OF TIBERIAS — John 21:1-14

₁After these things Jesus shewed himself again to the disciples at the sea of Tiberias; and on this wise shewed he *himself*.

₂There were together Simon Peter, and Thomas called Didymus, and Nathanael of Cana in Galilee, and the *sons* of Zebedee, and two other of his disciples. ₃Simon Peter saith unto them, I go a fishing.

They say unto him, We also go with thee. They went forth, and entered into a ship immediately; and that night they caught nothing. ₄But when the morning was now come, Jesus stood on the shore: but the disciples knew not that it was Jesus.

₅Then Jesus saith unto them, Children, have ye any meat?

They answered him, No.

₆And he said unto them, Cast the net on the right side of the ship, and ye shall find. They cast therefore, and now they were not able to draw it for the multitude of fishes.

₇Therefore that disciple whom Jesus loved saith unto Peter, It is the Lord. Now when Simon Peter heard that it was the Lord, he girt *his* fisher's coat *unto him*, (for he was naked,) and did cast himself into the sea. ₈And the other disciples came in a little ship; (for they were not far from land, but as it were two hundred cubits,) dragging the net with fishes. ₉As soon then as they were come to land, they saw a fire of coals there, and fish laid thereon, and bread.

₁₀Jesus saith unto them, Bring of the fish which ye have now caught. ₁₁Simon Peter went up, and drew the net to land full of great fishes, an hundred and fifty and three: and for all there were so many, yet was not the net broken.

₁₂Jesus saith unto them, Come *and* dine. And none of the disciples durst ask him, Who art thou? knowing that it was the Lord. ₁₃Jesus then cometh, and taketh bread, and giveth them, and fish likewise. ₁₄This is now the third time that Jesus shewed himself to his disciples, after that he was risen from the dead.

THE GLORIFIED PALESTINIAN MINISTRY

FEED MY SHEEP — John 21:15-19

₁₅So when they had dined, Jesus saith to Simon Peter, Simon, *son* of Jonas, lovest thou me more than these? He saith unto him, Yea, Lord; thou knowest that I love thee. He saith unto him, Feed my lambs. ₁₆He saith to him again the second time, Simon, *son* of Jonas, lovest thou me? He saith unto him, Yea, Lord; thou knowest that I love thee. He saith unto him, Feed my sheep. ₁₇He saith unto him the third time, Simon, *son* of Jonas, lovest thou me? Peter was grieved because he said unto him the third time, Lovest thou me? And he said unto him, Lord, thou knowest all things; thou knowest that I love thee.

Jesus saith unto him, Feed my sheep. ₁₈Verily, verily, I say unto thee, When thou wast young, thou girdedst thyself, and walkedst whither thou wouldest: but when thou shalt be old, thou shalt stretch forth thy hands, and another shall gird thee, and carry [thee] whither thou wouldest not. ₁₉This spake he, signifying by what death he should glorify God.

And when he had spoken this, he saith unto him, Follow me.

THOU SHALT TARRY — John 21:20-24 — 1 D&C 7:1-8

₂₀Then Peter, turning about, seeth the disciple whom Jesus loved following; which also leaned on his breast at supper, and said, Lord, which is he that betrayeth thee? ₂₁Peter seeing him saith to Jesus, Lord, and what *shall* this man *do*? ₂₂Jesus saith unto him, If I will that he tarry till I come, what *is that* to thee? follow thou me. ₂₃Then went this saying abroad among the brethren, that that disciple should not die: yet Jesus said not unto him, He shall not die; but, If I will that he tarry till I come, what *is that* to thee? ₂₄This is the disciple which testifieth of these things, and wrote these things: and we know that his testimony is true.

¹₁And the Lord said unto me: John, my beloved, what desirest thou? For if you shall ask what you will, it shall be granted unto you.

₂And I said unto him: Lord, give unto me power over death, that I may live and bring souls unto thee.

₃And the Lord said unto me: Verily, verily, I say unto thee, because thou desirest this thou shalt tarry until I come in my glory, and shalt prophesy before nations, kindreds, tongues and people.

₄And for this cause the Lord said unto Peter: If I will that he tarry till I come, what is that to thee? For he desired of me that he might bring souls unto me, but thou desiredst that thou mightest speedily come unto me in my kingdom. ₅I say unto thee, Peter, this was a good desire; but my beloved has desired that he might do

THE GLORIFIED PALESTINIAN MINISTRY

THOU SHALT TARRY (cont.)   John 21:20-24

more, or a greater work yet among men than what he has before done. ₆Yea, he has undertaken a greater work; therefore I will make him as flaming fire and a ministering angel; he shall minister for those who shall be heirs of salvation who dwell on the earth. ₇And I will make thee to minister for him and for thy brother James; and unto you three I will give this power and the keys of this ministry until I come. ₈Verily I say unto you, ye shall both have according to your desires, for ye both joy in that which ye have desired.

THE GREAT COMMISSION   Matt. 28:16-20

   ₁₆Then the eleven disciples went away into Galilee, into a mountain where Jesus had appointed them.

   ₁₇And when they saw him, they worshipped him: but some doubted. ₁₈And Jesus came and spake unto them, saying, All power is given unto me in heaven and in earth. ₁₉Go ye therefore, and ᵃteach all nations, baptizing them in the name of the Father, and of the Son, and of the Holy Ghost: ¹₁₅Go ye into all the world, and preach the gospel to every creature. ₁₆He that believeth and is baptized shall be saved; but he that believeth not shall be damned.

   ₁₇And these signs shall follow them that believe; In my name shall they cast out devils; they shall speak with new tongues; ₁₈They shall take up serpents; and if they drink any deadly thing, it shall not hurt them; they shall lay hands on the sick, and they shall recover. ₂₀Teaching them to observe all things whatsoever I have commanded you: and, lo, I am with you alway, *even* unto the end of the world. Amen.

a GR: make disciples of

1 Mark 16:15-18

THE PROMISE OF THE HOLY GHOST   Acts 1:2-5

   ₂Until the day in which he was taken up, after that he through the Holy Ghost had given commandments unto the apostles whom he had chosen: ₃To whom also he shewed himself alive after his ¹passion by many infallible proofs, being seen of them forty days, and speaking of the things pertaining to the kingdom of God:

   ₄And, being assembled together with *them,* commanded them that they should not depart from Jerusalem, but wait for the promise of the Father, which, *saith he,* ye have heard of me. ₅For John truly baptized with water; but ye shall be baptized with the Holy Ghost not many days hence.

1 GR: suffering

THE GLORIFIED PALESTINIAN MINISTRY

THE ASCENSION — Acts 1:6-11

₆When they therefore were come together, they asked of him, saying, Lord, wilt thou at this time restore again the kingdom to Israel? ₇And he said unto them, It is not for you to know the times or the seasons, which the Father hath put in his own power. ₈But ye shall receive power, after that the Holy Ghost is come upon you: and ye shall be witnesses unto me both in Jerusalem, and in all Judaea, and in Samaria, and unto the uttermost part of the earth.

₉And when he had spoken these things, while they beheld, he was taken up; ¹**and sat on the right hand of God,** and a cloud received him out of their sight.ᵃ

₁₀And while they looked stedfastly toward heaven as he went up, behold, two men stood by them in white apparel; ₁₁Which also said, Ye men of Galilee, why stand ye gazing up into heaven? this same Jesus, which is taken up from you into heaven, shall so come in like manner as ye have seen him go into heaven. ₁₂Then returned they unto Jerusalem from the mount called ᵇOlivet, which is from Jerusalem ᶜa sabbath day's journey.

1 Mark 16:19

a See again Ps. 110:1 and Dan. 7:13 (as in Matt. 26:64)

b See Zech. 14:4

c 2000 cubits

140

APPENDIX	HARMONIZED PASSAGES	

This Appendix summarizes the passages used in this harmony. In some cases, the primary text has not been supplemented in any way. This may be because it is the sole description of the event in the New Testament, or it may be because the accounts in the other Gospels do not vary from the account given. It could also be because the primary text provides the most complete account of the event in the sacred record and requires no supplementation. Whatever the reason, this Appendix does not cite alternative accounts, only the primary text and any text used to supplement the primary text.

EVENTS	PRIMARY	SUPPLEMENT
THE PRE-MORTAL MISSIONS		
THE PROLOGUE	John 1:1-14	JST John 1:1, 4-5, 7-8, 10, 12-14
THE BIRTHS		
THE ANNOUNCEMENT OF JOHN'S BIRTH	Luke 1:5-25	JST Luke 1:8
THE ANNOUNCEMENT OF JESUS' BIRTH	Luke 1:26-38	
MARY VISITS ELISABETH	Luke 1:39-56	
JOSEPH'S DREAM	Matt. 1:18-25	JST Matt. 2:1
THE BIRTH OF JOHN THE BAPTIST	Luke 1:57-80	
THE BIRTH OF JESUS CHRIST	Luke 2:1-7	JST Luke 2:1, 7
THE ANGELS AND THE SHEPHERDS	Luke 2:8-20	
THE PRESENTATION OF JESUS AT THE TEMPLE	Luke 2:21-38	
THE WISE MEN VISIT	Matt. 2:1-12	JST Matt. 3:2, 4-6
HAROD SLAYS THE CHILDREN OF BETHLEHEM	Matt. 2:13-23	
CHRIST'S YOUTH	Luke 2:40-52	JST Matt. 3:24-26
		JST Luke 2:46
JOHN'S MINISTRY AND JESUS' PREPARATIONS		
THE PREACHINGS OF JOHN THE BAPTIST	Luke 3:1-17	Matt. 3:2, 4-7, 11-12
		JST Matt. 3:34, 36, 38-39
		JST Luke 3:4-10, 13, 19-20
		John 1:15-25
		JST John 1:16-19, 21-22, 26
THE BAPTISM OF JESUS	Matt. 3:13-17	JST Matt. 3:43-46
JOHN'S TESTIMONY OF JESUS	John 1:29-34	Luke 3:18-20
		JST John 1:29-32
THE TEMPTATIONS OF JESUS	Luke 4:1-13	Luke 3:23
		JST Luke 4:9, 25
THE FIRST DISCIPLES	John 1:35-51	JST John 1:42
THE WEDDING AT CANA	John 2:1-12	JST John 2:1, 4
FIRST YEAR: THE EARLY JUDEAN MINISTRY		
JESUS CLEANSES THE TEMPLE	John 2:13-25	JST John 2:24
JESUS AND NICODEMUS	John 3:1-21	JST John 3:18
THE LAST TESTIMONY OF JOHN THE BAPTIST	John 3:22-36	JST John 3:27, 34, 36
FIRST YEAR: THE GALILEAN MINISTRY		
JESUS AND THE SAMARIAN WOMAN	John 4:1-42	JST John 4:2-4, 26, 40
THE HEALING OF A NOBLEMAN'S SON	John 4:43-54	Mark 1:14-15
JESUS IN NAZARETH	Luke 4:16-30	
A DEVIL IN CAPERNAUM	Mark 1:22-28	Luke 4:31-33
FISHERS OF MEN	Matt. 4:18-24	JST Matt. 4:18, 22
		Mark 1:35-38
A GREAT MULTITUDE OF FISHES	Luke 5:1-12	
JESUS HEALS A LEPER	Mark 1:41-45	Luke 5:12
THE CALLING OF THE TWELVE APOSTLES	Mark 3:14-19	Matt. 10:1
		Luke 6:12-13
INSTRUCTING AND SENDING THE TWELVE	Matt. 10:5-42	JST Matt.10:34

141

APPENDIX — HARMONIZED PASSAGES

EVENTS	PRIMARY	SUPPLEMENT
JESUS HEALS A MULTITUDE	Luke 6:17-19	Matt. 11:1
THE SERMON ON THE MOUNT	Matt. 4:25; 5 – 7	JST Matt. 5:3-5, 8, 12, 18, 21, 34, 50; 6:1, 14, 22, 25-27, 34, 38; 7:1-2, 4-12, 14-17, 31, 36-37 Luke 6:20
THE CENTURION'S SERVANT	Luke 7:1-10	
THE WIDOW'S SON	Luke 7:11-17	
PETER'S MOTHER-IN-LAW	Matt. 8:14-15	
HE TOOK OUR INFIRMITIES	Matt. 8:16-17	
DISCIPLES TESTED	Matt. 8:18-22	Luke 9:60-62
JESUS CALMS THE TEMPEST	Mark 4:35-41	
A LEGION OF DEMONS CAST OUT	Mark 5:1-20	Matt. 8:28
A PARALYTIC MAN HEALED	Mark 2:1-12	
THE CALLING OF LEVI (MATTHEW)	Luke 5:27-31	Mark 2:13-14, 16-17
A CONFLICT OVER FASTING	Luke 5:33-35	
PARABLE OF THE CLOTH AND THE WINESKINS	Luke 5:36-39	
HEALING THE WOMAN ON THE WAY WITH JAIRUS	Mark 5:21-34	
THE DAUGHTER OF JAIRUS	Mark 5:35-43	Matt. 9:26
TWO BLIND MEN AND A MUTE	Matt. 9:27-34	
MESSENGERS FROM JOHN THE BAPTIST	Matt. 11:2-19	JST Matt. 11:13-15
JESUS FEET WASHED; THE TWO DEBTORS	Luke 7:36-50	
SECOND YEAR: THE GALILEAN MINISTRY		
THE INVALID OF BETHESDA	John 5:1-13	
IDENTITY, MISSION AND WITNESSES OF CHRIST	John 5:14-47	JST John 5:35, 37
THE HARVEST IS PLENTEOUS	Matt. 9:35-38	
MARY CALLED MAGDALENE	Luke 8:1-3	
THE SABBATH MADE FOR MAN	Mark 2:23-28	JST Mark 2:26-27
THE MAN WITH THE WITHERED HAND	Luke 6:6-11	Matt. 12:11-14
A MULTITUDE ON THE SEA SHORE	Mark 3:7-12	Matt. 12:17-21
BLASPHEMY AGAINST THE HOLY GHOST	Matt. 12:22-37	JST Matt. 12:23, 26
WE WOULD SEE A SIGN FROM THEE	Matt. 12:38-42	
WHEN THE UNCLEAN SPIRIT IS GONE OUT	Matt. 12:43-45	JST Matt. 12:37-39
BROTHER, AND SISTER, AND MOTHER	Matt. 12:46-50	
PARABLE OF THE SOWER	Mark 4:1-20	Matt. 13:12-23 JST Matt. 13:10-11 JST Mark 4:9
PARABLE OF THE CANDLE	Mark 4:21-25	JST Mark 4:20
PARABLE OF WHEAT AND TARES	Matt. 13:24-30	JST Matt. 13:29
PARABLE OF THE MUSTARD SEED	Matt. 13:31-32	
PARABLE OF THE LEAVEN	Matt. 13:33	
WITHOUT A PARABLE SPAKE HE NOT	Matt. 13:34-35	
PARABLE OF WHEAT AND TARES EXPLAINED	Matt. 13:36-43	JST Matt. 13:39-44 D&C 86:1-7
THE KINGDOM OF HEAVEN IS LIKE UNTO . . .	Matt. 13:44-53	JST Matt. 13:50-51
JESUS IN NAZARETH AGAIN	Mark 6:1-6	
THE DEATH OF JOHN THE BAPTIST	Mark 6:14-29	JST Mark 6:21
THIRD YEAR: THE GALILEAN MINISTRY		
FEEDING THE FIVE THOUSAND	John 6:1-15	Matt. 14:14-16 Mark 6:30-36 JST Mark 6:32-33, 36
WALKING UPON THE SEA	Mark 6:45-52	Matt. 14:28-33

APPENDIX — HARMONIZED PASSAGES

EVENTS	PRIMARY	SUPPLEMENT
HEALING AT GENNESARET	Mark 6:53-56	
THE BREAD OF LIFE	John 6:22-59	JST John 7:26, 40, 44, 54
DISCIPLES TESTED BY JESUS' TEACHINGS	John 6:60-71	JST John 6:65
WHAT DEFILES A MAN	Mark 7:1-23	JST Mark 7:10-12, 15
THIRD YEAR: THE NORTH GALILEAN MINISTRY		
THE WOMAN OF CANAAN	Matt. 15:21-28	Mark 7:24-25
		JST Mark 7:22-23
		John 7:1
A HEALING; FEEDING THE FOUR THOUSAND	Matt. 15:29-39	Mark 7:32-37
A SIGN FROM HEAVEN	Matt. 16:1-4	
BEWARE THE LEAVEN OF THE PHARISEES	Matt. 16:5-12	
THE BLIND MAN IN BETHSAIDA	Mark 8:22-26	
UPON THIS ROCK	Matt. 16:13-20	
CHRIST REVEALS HIS DEATH	Matt. 16:21-28	JST Matt. 16:26-29
THE TRANSFIGURATION	Matt. 17:1-13	JST Matt. 17:10-11, 13-14
THOU DUMB AND DEAF SPIRIT	Mark 9:14-29	Matt. 17:20-21
TAXES PAID WITH MONEY FROM A FISH	Matt. 17:24-27	
WHO IS THE GREATEST	Matt. 18:1-6	Mark 9:33-37
		JST Mark 9:34-35
		Luke 9:46-47
PARABLE OF THE LOST SHEEP	Matt. 18:10-14	JST Matt. 18:11
		Luke 15:1-7
HE THAT IS NOT AGAINST US	Mark 9:38-41	
IF THY RIGHT HAND OFFEND THEE	Mark 9:43-50	Matt. 18:7
		JST Mark 9:40-42, 44-46, 48
		Luke 18:3-4
UNTIL SEVENTY TIMES SEVEN	Matt. 18:15-22	
PARABLE OF THE TWO DEBTORS	Matt. 18:23-35	
PARABLE OF THE LOST COIN	Luke 15:8-10	
PARABLE OF THE PRODIGAL SON	Luke 15:11-32	
THE WORLD HATETH ME	John 7:2-9	
THIRD YEAR: THE LATER JUDEAN MINISTRY		
AN EXAMPLE OF NON-VIOLENCE	Luke 9:51-56	
THE MISSION OF THE SEVENTY	Luke 10:1-12	
CHRIST UPBRAIDS CERTAIN CITIES	Matt. 11:20-24	Luke 10:16
		JST Luke 10:17
THE SEVENTY RETURN	Luke 10:17-20	
JESUS REJOICES	Luke 10:21-24	Matt. 11:28-30
		JST Luke 10:22-23
PARABLE OF THE GOOD SAMARITAN	Luke 10:25-37	
A VISIT WITH MARTHA AND MARY	Luke 10:38-42	
INSTRUCTION ABOUT PRAYER	Luke 11:1-13	JST Luke 11:4-5, 14
BLESSINGS	Luke 11:27-28	
PARABLE OF THE FOOLISH RICH MAN	Luke 12:13-21	
EXCEPT YE REPENT	Luke 13:1-5	
A WOMAN HEALED ON THE SABBATH	Luke 13:10-17	
O JERUSALEM, JERUSALEM	Luke 13:31-35	JST Luke 13:34, 36
HEALING A MAN WITH DROPSY	Luke 14:1-6	
PARABLE OF THE CHIEF WEDDING ROOMS	Luke 14:7-14	
PARABLE OF THE GREAT SUPPER	Luke 14:15-24	
THE COST OF FOLLOWING JESUS	Luke 14:25-33	JST Luke 14:26, 28, 31
SALT WHICH IS GOOD	Luke 14:34-35	JST Luke 14:35-38

APPENDIX — HARMONIZED PASSAGES

EVENTS	PRIMARY	SUPPLEMENT
PARABLE OF THE UNJUST STEWARD	Luke 16:1-15	
THE LAW AND THE PROPHETS	Luke 16:16-23	JST Luke 16:16-18, 20-23
PARABLE OF THE RICH MAN AND LAZARUS	Luke 16:19-31	JST Luke 16:23
TEN LEPERS ARE CLEANSED	Luke 17:11-19	
PARABLE OF THE UNJUST JUDGE	Luke 18:1-8	JST Luke 18:7-8
PARABLE OF THE PHARISEE AND THE PUBLICAN	Luke 18:9-14	
JESUS AT THE FEAST OF TABERNACLES	John 7:10-24	Matt. 19:2 Mark 10:1 JST John 7:24
I AM NOT COME OF MYSELF	John 7:25-31	
YE SHALL SEEK ME, AND NOT FIND ME	John 7:32-36	
RIVERS OF LIVING WATER	John 7:37-39	JST John 7:39
A DIVISION AMONG THE PEOPLE	John 7:40-44	
NEVER MAN SPAKE LIKE THIS MAN	John 7:45-53	
THE ADULTEROUS WOMAN	John 8:1-11	
THE LIGHT OF THE WORLD	John 8:12-20	
WHITHER I GO, YE CANNOT COME	John 8:21-30	
THE TRUTH SHALL MAKE YOU FREE	John 8:31-38	
YE ARE OF YOUR FATHER THE DEVIL	John 8:39-47	JST John 8:43, 47
BEFORE ABRAHAM WAS I AM	John 8:48-59	
SABBATH HEALING OF A MAN BORN BLIND	John 9:1-12	JST John 9:4
WHEREAS I WAS BLIND, NOW I SEE	John 9:13-34	JST John 9:32
THE BLINDNESS OF THE PHARISEES	John 9:35-41	
PARABLE OF THE SHEEPFOLD	John 10:1-6	
THE GOOD SHEPHERD	John 10:7-21	JST John 10:8
ABOUT MARRIAGE AND DIVORCE	Matt. 19:3-12	Mark 10:10
BLESSING THE LITTLE CHILDREN	Mark 10:13-16	
THE RICH YOUNG MAN	Mark 10:17-31	Matt. 19:17-20, 27-30 JST Matt. 19:28
PARABLE OF THE LABORERS IN THE VINEYARD	Matt. 20:1-16	
DECLARATION AT THE FEAST OF THE DEDICATION	John 10:22-42	

THIRD YEAR: THE PEREAN MINISTRY

EVENTS	PRIMARY	SUPPLEMENT
THE DEATH OF LAZARUS	John 11:1-16	JST John 11:16
JESUS' COMING DEATH AND RESURRECTION	Mark 10:32-34	Luke 18:31, 34
THE PETITION OF THE SONS OF ZEBEDEE	Matt. 20:20-28	Mark 10:35-37
HE THAT IS GREATEST AMONG YOU	Luke 22:24-30	Matt. 20:27-28
THE HEALING OF BARTIMAEUS	Mark 10:46-52	Luke 18:36-37, 39-41, 43
THE HOUSE OF ZACCHAEUS	Luke 19:1-10	
PARABLE OF THE POUNDS	Luke 19:11-28	JST Luke 19:25
I AM THE RESURRECTION, AND THE LIFE	John 11:17-27	JST John 11:17
JESUS WEEPS	John 11:28-37	
LAZARUS, COME FORTH	John 11:38-44	
PLOTTING TO KILL JESUS	John 11:45-57	
ANOINTING JESUS' FEET	John 12:1-8	JST John 12:7
A PLOT AGAINST LAZARUS	John 12:9-12	

THE WEEK OF THE ATONING SACRIFICE: SUNDAY

EVENTS	PRIMARY	SUPPLEMENT
THY KING COMETH	Mark 11:1-11	Matt. 21:8-9 JST Mark 11:11 Luke 19:37, 39-44 John 12:12-15
HE THAT LOVETH HIS LIFE SHALL LOSE IT	John 12:20-26	
A VOICE FROM HEAVEN	John 12:27-36	

APPENDIX: HARMONIZED PASSAGES

EVENTS	PRIMARY	SUPPLEMENT
BLINDED THEIR EYES, HARDENED THEIR HEART	John 12:37-43	
HE THAT SEETH ME SEETH HIM THAT SENT ME	John 12:44-50	
THE WEEK OF THE ATONING SACRIFICE: MONDAY		
CURSING THE FIG TREE	Mark 11:12-14	
DEN OF THIEVES	Mark 11:15-19	Matt. 21:14-17
		JST Matt. 21:13
THE WEEK OF THE ATONING SACRIFICE: TUESDAY		
FAITH TO MOVE MOUNTAINS	Mark 11:20-26	
PARABLE OF THE BARREN FIG TREE	Luke 13:6-9	
BY WHAT AUTHORITY?	Mark 11:27-33	Luke 20:6-8
PARABLE OF THE TWO SONS	Matt. 21:28-32	JST Matt. 21:32-34
PARABLE OF THE WICKED HUSBANDMEN	Matt. 21:33-46	JST Matt. 21:34, 48, 50-56
PARABLE OF THE MARRIAGE FEAST	Matt. 22:1-14	JST Matt. 22:14
THE QUESTION OF TRIBUTE	Matt. 22:15-22	
THE SADDUCEES' QUESTION	Luke 20:27-40	Matt. 22:23, 29, 31, 33
		JST Luke 20:35
THE GREAT COMMANDMENT	Mark 12:28-34	Matt. 22:34-36, 38-39
WHOSE SON IS HE?	Matt. 22:41-46	Mark 12:35, 37
THE WIDOW'S OFFERING	Mark 12:41-44	
WOE UNTO YOU PHARISEES	Matt. 23:1-36	JST Matt. 23:6-7, 12, 21, 34-35
JESUS LAMENTS OVER JERUSALEM	Matt. 23:37-39	JS-M. 1:1
NOT ONE STONE UPON ANOTHER	Matt. 24:1-2	JS-M. 1:2-3
WHAT IS THE SIGN OF THY COMING?	Matt. 24:3-6, 9-13, 15-28	JS-M. 1:4, 11-12, 14, 17-23, 26-27
THE SECOND COMING OF THE SON OF MAN	Matt. 24:7, 12-14, 29-51	JS-M. 1:28-32, 34-42, 44, 46-47, 55
PARABLE OF THE TEN VIRGINS	Matt. 25:1-13	JST Matt. 25:1
PARABLE OF THE TALENTS	Matt. 25:14-30	JST Matt. 25:29-30
PARABLE OF THE SHEEP AND THE GOATS	Matt. 25:31-46	
BETRAYAL BY CRAFT	Matt. 26:1-5	Mark 14:1
ANOINTING JESUS' HEAD	Mark 14: 3-9	Matt. 26:10
		JST Mark 14:8
SATAN INFLUENCES JUDAS	Luke 22:1-6	Matt. 26:15-16
THE WEEK OF THE ATONING SACRIFICE: THURSDAY		
THE UPPER ROOM—THE SACRAMENT	Luke 22:7-25	Matt. 26:17-18, 26, 28-29
		JST Matt. 26:22, 24-26
		Mark 14:13-25
		JST Mark 14:21, 23-25
		JST Luke 22:16
THE UPPER ROOM—WASHING THE FEET	John 13:2-20	JST John 13:8, 10, 19
THE UPPER ROOM—JUDAS REVEALED, DEPARTS	John 13:21-30	Matt. 26:21-22, 25
		Mark 14:19, 21
THE UPPER ROOM—A NEW COMMANDMENT	John 13:31-35	
THE UPPER ROOM—THE WAY, THE TRUTH, THE LIFE	John 14:1-14	
THE UPPER ROOM—THE COMFORTER	John 14:15-31	JST John 14:30
THE UPPER ROOM—I AM THE TRUE VINE	John 15:1-17	
THE UPPER ROOM—NOT OF THE WORLD	John 15:18-16:4	
THE UPPER ROOM—A GUIDE TO ALL TRUTH	John 16:4-15	
THE UPPER ROOM—SORROW SHALL TURN TO JOY	John 16:16-24	JST John 16:23
THE UPPER ROOM—I HAVE OVERCOME THE WORLD	John 16:25-33	

APPENDIX	HARMONIZED PASSAGES	
EVENTS	**PRIMARY**	**SUPPLEMENT**
THE UPPER ROOM—THE GREAT INTERCESSORY PRAYER	John 17:1-26	
THE UPPER ROOM—PURSE AND SCRIPT	Luke 22:35-38	Matt. 26:30
		Luke 22:39
		John 14:31
PETER TO DENY CHRIST	Luke 22:31-34	Matt. 26:31-33
		Mark 14:31
		John 13:36-38
THE GARDEN OF GETHSEMANE	Matt. 26:36-46	Mark 14:32-34, 36, 40
		JST Mark 14:36-38
		Luke 22:40-45
		JST Luke 22:44
		John 18:1
WHOMSOEVER I SHALL KISS IS HE	John 18:2-11	Matt. 26:48-50, 52-54, 56
		Luke 22:51-53
THE WEEK OF THE ATONING SACRIFICE: FRIDAY		
TAKEN BEFORE ANNAS, THE HIGH PRIEST	John 18:12-14	Mark 14:51-52
		JST Mark 14:57
QUESTIONED BY ANNAS	John 18:19-24	Matt. 26:57
BEFORE THE COUNSEL	Matt. 26:58-67	Mark 14:58-59
		Luke 22:55, 64-65
BEFORE THE COCK CREW	Mark 14:66-72	Matt. 26:70, 72-73, 75
		Luke 22:56-59
		John 18:26
THE TRIAL BEFORE PILATE	John 18:28-38	Matt. 27:2
		Mark 15:1
		Luke 23:2, 5-7
BEFORE HAROD	Luke 23:8-12	
THE SENTENCING	John 18:38-19:16	Matt. 27:15-16,19-20, 23-25, 31
		Mark 15:7, 10, 12, 16-19
		Luke 23:13-16,18, 20, 22-23
THE DEATH OF JUDAS	Matt. 27:3-9	JST Matt. 27:5-6
THE CRUCIFIXION	Luke 23:26-49	Matt. 27:33-34, 37, 46-49, 51, 54-56
		JST Matt. 27:35, 54
		Mark 15:25, 27-32
		JST Luke 23:32
		John 19:19-29
HE WAS DEAD ALREADY	John 19:31-37	
ENTOMBED	Luke 23:50-56	Matt. 27:57, 60-61
		Mark 15:43-46
		John 19:38-42
THE WEEK OF THE ATONING SACRIFICE: SATURDAY		
SEALING THE STONE, SETTING A WATCH	Matt. 27:62-66	
MINISTRY TO THE SPIRIT WORLD	1 Pet. 3:18-20	D&C 138:18-24
THE GLORIFIED PALESTINIAN MINISTRY		
HE IS RISEN	Mark 16:1-8	Matt. 28:2-5, 8
		JST Matt. 28:2-4
		Luke 24:3-11
		John 20:1, 3-10

APPENDIX — HARMONIZED PASSAGES

EVENTS	PRIMARY	SUPPLEMENT
JESUS APPEARS TO MARY	John 20:11-18	Mark 16:9-11
		JST John 20:17
RESURRECTION OF THE SAINTS	Matt. 27:52-53	
REPORT OF THE WATCH	Matt. 28:11-15	
THE WAY TO EMMAUS	Luke 24:13-35	
JESUS APPEARS TO HIS DISCIPLES	Luke 24:36-49	John 20:19, 21-23
EXCEPT I SHALL SEE, I WILL NOT BELIEVE	John 20:24-31	
APPEARANCE AT THE SEA OF TIBERIAS	John 21:1-14	
FEED MY SHEEP	John 21:15-19	
THOU SHALT TARRY	John 21:20-24	D&C 7:1-8
THE GREAT COMMISSION	Matt. 28:16-20	Mark 16:15-18
THE PROMISE OF THE HOLY GHOST	Acts 1:2-5	
THE ASCENSION	Acts 1:6-11	Mark 16:19